RUNNING OUT OF TEARS

ESTHER RANTZEN

RUNNING OUT OF TEARS

THE MOVING PERSONAL STORIES OF CHILDLINE'S CHILDREN OVER TWENTY-FIVE YEARS

The Robson Press

...alone and afraid. I know you'll help.
Tell others to speak out as soon as they can
to anyone. It saves a lot of mental and
physical pain.
I can't say anymore. I hear them coming in.
Please help.

Tiana (age 14)

Tiana isn't my real name. Sorry to lie, but...
...understand?

Esther...
...for you sir?
...about
...don't mention my
...say a
...'Big fat...

Dear Esther,
        When I was 10, I f.. ..
had a normal family. I thought ..
..be spoken to, just shouted at. I ..
..to be scared to go home. I ..
I should never be ..
..before ..
..Childline and ..
..to do to ..
..lost ..

..problem ..
..are we ..
..know ..
..know ..
..things ..
..not to ..
..unhappy ..
..the good ..
..need you ..
..and

Dear Esther Rantzen,
        The reason why ..
..ing to you Personally is be..
..ink you are a Great Lady..
..Up Childline. here's a ..
..to c.. a 16 year old wors..
..more s.. .. n the ..
..ppened.

Dear
Esther..
.. I watch
..t was
..

Dear Esther Rantzen,

Dear Esther,

Dear Esther,

I am

Dear Esther,

... wanting to ...
... some time) ... of abuse
... ou. from ...
... it ... wi ...
have is ...
fin (I'm ...
a ...

... didn't have a very rosey chi...
... my life I have faced poverty
... use, sexual abuse, domestic viole...
... I could go on! I rang child line
... t was younger and they were a
... sure of comfort to me t...

Dear Esther,

Everytime I try to phone ...
I always have to put the phone ...
... w will hear or that someon...
... also why I don't ...

... to ...
... Child line. ... t ...

... Child line.

... y Child ... bath ...
... because marg. 'ster...
!!, the other end of the line ... be...
... akes.

... thanks for everything
... worked him for...

First published in Great Britain in 2011 by
The Robson Press
An imprint of Biteback Publishing Ltd
Westminster Tower
3 Albert Embankment
London
SE1 7SP
Copyright © Esther Rantzen 2011

ISBN 978-1-84954-162-6

10 9 8 7 6 5 4 3 2 1

A CIP catalogue record for this book is available from the British Library.

Cover design by Namkwan Cho
Set in Chronicle and Bryant by Namkwan Cho

Printed and bound in Great Britain by CPI Group (UK) Ltd, Croydon, CR0 4YY

**This book is dedicated to
ChildLine's children**

*"Although the world is full of suffering,
it is full also of the overcoming of it."*
Helen Keller

ACKNOWLEDGEMENTS

Firstly, I must express my gratitude and admiration to the survivors who have contributed to this book. Without exception they did so in the hope that they would, in telling their stories, help to protect other children and also because they wanted to thank the staff and volunteers of ChildLine who had made such a profound positive difference to their lives.

Over the first twenty-five years of ChildLine's life, hundreds of people have dedicated their time and skill to protecting vulnerable children, firstly as part of the ChildLine team, and then when we joined forces, working for the NSPCC. It is impossible for me to name them all, but I must pay tribute in particular to the generous and devoted ChildLine trustees, to the BBC who enabled us to reach out to the nation's children, to the trustees and staff of the NSPCC, who made it possible for us to expand our service in tough times and to the art student Kate Hall, who twenty-five years ago donated ChildLine's smiling telephone logo and whom I have not been able to trace to thank.

My agent, Luigi Bonomi, and my publisher, Jeremy Robson and his team, have been unfailingly supportive and encouraging during the writing of this book. John Spencer, Professor of Law at Selwyn College Cambridge, advised me on ways our legal system could and should protect children more effectively. And my assistant Ashley McGoldrick has been patient and resourceful as we arranged the interviews on which this book is based.

Finally, my love and thanks go to my late husband Desmond Wilcox, who throughout our life together gave me the immeasurable support of his strength and commitment to children's welfare. To my sister Priscilla, and my friend and mentor Bryher Scudamore, whose wisdom and judgement guided me. And to my three children, who have been incredibly tolerant and patient, even in the most stressful times, because, as Emily once told me, 'The children need you.'

CONTENTS

AUTHOR'S NOTE

ChildLine is twenty-five years old, a crucial milestone in the life of any organisation. It's time now to ask the question, in a quarter of a century, what has been achieved? Looking back over ChildLine's history, it would be possible to tell so many different stories: how attitudes have changed since 1986, how the organisation itself has grown and developed since then or the struggles involved in setting up a brand-new charity. And perhaps those books will be written one day.

But ChildLine has constantly been guided by the principle that we must always listen to the children themselves and I have stuck by that principle in writing this book. The stories you will read are based on interviews with people who told me how, when they were children, their lives were changed by ChildLine. I have spoken to others who, as adults, have also been affected by ChildLine's work.

The book concentrates on fourteen very different lives, a tiny fraction of the 2,700,000 children ChildLine has helped since its launch. All my interviewees are adult now, and although for legal reasons I have changed some of the names and places, as well as a few identifying details, the events themselves remain unchanged as they were described to me. In focusing on each personal story, I have found that each one carried its own message: of victory over despair, of hope, of transformation.

So although you may find these stories painful, as I did, I hope you will find they are also inspirational for these are just a handful of the many, many brave children who have taken the decision to ring ChildLine's number 0800 1111, or to contact the online counsellors on www.childline.org.uk.

And without the children's courage, without their trust, ChildLine would not exist today.

INTRODUCTION

The child's voice on the phone was matter of fact as she told her story. Her father had died; her mother's new partner hated her. She felt she had now lost everything: her father, her place in the family, her mother's love. She had rung ChildLine, as many children do, because there was no other way to pour out the pain in her heart.

The ChildLine counsellor listened thoughtfully. Then he said, 'Suppose you found a moment to talk to your mum, could you tell her how you feel?' The child considered his suggestion. 'I think we'd just have another row and I'd run upstairs in tears. Although I think I'm running out of tears.'

Running out of tears. That phrase is so piercingly true of many children who have rung ChildLine over the last twenty-five years. Children who have been so deeply unhappy for such a long time that they have indeed run out of tears, but not quite of hope. That spark of hope is what inspires them to take the first difficult courageous step out of misery, to get in touch with ChildLine by phone, by letter or online.

So why is a ChildLine counsellor, a complete stranger, their only salvation? Because they have nowhere else to turn for help. Social services or the police are out of reach for these children, who believe that way lies disaster: that they will be taken away from the family they still love, or that this will bring catastrophe upon them. They may have been threatened into silence by an abuser, told that nobody will believe them, or worse, someone they love will die, or a beloved puppy will be killed, or Dad will go to prison. Shame may silence them because they feel they must have done something terribly bad to deserve abuse or neglect. Whatever the reason, they reach out to ChildLine because they dare not to speak to anyone else.

I have worked as a trained volunteer counsellor for ChildLine. Many of the children I listen to sound matter of fact about their unhappiness. They have become accustomed to it, it has become a way of life for them. But there have been others who were choked with sobs when they made their first call to ChildLine. Still others cannot find any words, and after long minutes of silence, put the phone down. What they all have in common is that on their own, they were unable to find a way out.

ChildLine's job is to give them options, to empower them, to give them fresh hope, and that can achieve wonderful results. The stories in this book are based upon conversations I have had with individuals who are all adult now, but their lives have been transformed by their contact with ChildLine. Each one is different, because of course every child who contacts ChildLine is different. What unites them is their courage. Without enormous courage and determination, and if they hadn't trusted ChildLine to work in partnership with them, those children would have been out of anyone's reach. As you read these stories, imagine how isolated they must have felt. Indeed, before ChildLine was launched, how isolated abused children were.

CHAPTER ONE

JO'S STORY

I have no memory of ever being cuddled. Was I? Surely I must have been, isn't every child? Perhaps if I had a picture of me, a baby in Mum's arms, I could tell myself yes, there you are, they did love me really. But I have nothing. No picture. No doll, no teddy bear. Nothing at all. And there is nothing in my heart, no certain memory that tells me I was ever loved. Just a kind of bleakness. An emptiness.

The neighbours never knew. I wasn't like the children you see in the charity ads, the ones with broken bones and dirty faces. My parents would never have allowed that to happen: they made sure I was clean, neat, properly turned out, a credit to them. They spent money on me, made sure I had clean, shiny shoes, decent clothes. But they couldn't love me.

I remember – it's my earliest memory – that when I was three my grandad found me in the middle of the road, just sitting there, playing with my toys. He took me home and he was furious: he went mental with my mum because she'd let me wander out of the house. She had no idea where I was.

But then I suppose she didn't care. Not long ago I overheard my grandad telling my nan that it would have been better if my parents had never had kids. So maybe my grandparents always knew. When I look back on the day-to-day life I had as a child, I feel nothing. I suppose every baby is born expecting love, but if that hunger goes unsatisfied, you learn to live without it; something inside goes numb. I got used to being unhappy.

They were respectable people, my mum and dad. Hardworking, too. Dad repaired TV sets, Mum was a bookkeeper. They saved enough to get a mortgage on a small house in a housing estate on the edge of our village in Derbyshire. I remember how tidy it was: I always had to put my things away, no mess. I drew Mum a picture for her birthday once and she said she liked it, but she didn't put it up on the wall, like they did at school, she just threw it in the bin. Mum had a still-born son before I was born. Maybe that death had killed something in her. Maybe she decided she would never care too much again. Or maybe I just couldn't replace the baby boy they lost. Why try and explain it? All my childhood I just assumed it was my fault, that they didn't love me because I was unloveable.

When I was about eight, we were walking to the shop, the three of us. I took Mum's hand. Dad slapped me, took my hand away, and he held Mum's hand instead. They made me walk by myself behind them. That stands out in my memory because that's the way it always was: they were together, I was in the way. I wasn't really part of their lives.

Their friend Eric lived in a bungalow two streets away from us. Short, fat, balding, he used to wear bow ties and fancied himself the moral guardian of the village. He used to grumble for hours about 'litter louts' and spend the whole of Sunday afternoon polishing his car. He and Brenda, his wife, were good friends of my parents. When Mum and Dad went out together in the evening, Eric would babysit me. It was sometimes at his bungalow: Dad would take me there and then pick me up on the way home. Sometimes Eric would babysit me in our house. When that happened, Brenda would never come too. Looking back, that seems strange. Why did she stay at home, alone? Why did he come over by himself to look after me? But at the time, everyone seemed to think it was fine.

It wasn't fine. Not for me. I can remember him one evening in our lounge, pulling up my nightie and touching me, when I was about seven. Though maybe it had started before, and I just can't remember it. I didn't know it was wrong. It was confusing, bewildering. But I hated it. He never gave me treats or presents, like I know some paedophiles do. There was no relationship – I don't think he even liked me. It was just gratification for him. And although I hated him, with his bulging stomach, his rough hands, I got used to it. Just like everything else in my life, I got used to it.

Who knows if he was ever frightened of being found out? I can't enter his mind. God knows, I don't want to. But looking back now, it seems he became increasingly confident that he was safe to do what he liked with me. I have one school picture of myself just before it started. I can see I was a pretty child, with big dark eyes and a sweet smile. I didn't look mischievous or difficult: abusers always pick out the quiet, good children and I'd been trained by my parents all my life to expect little and behave well.

Maybe that's why from the time I was nine, Eric did more and more things to me. In the end he was having full sex with me; he even did it once in his son's bedroom, while his son was out. He used to make me masturbate him. That was his favourite. He'd do it when we were round at his house, when his wife Brenda was out to work. Brenda was a hairdresser, who used to go round to people's houses to wash and cut their hair, so she often worked evenings. Afterwards, even though Eric knew he'd hurt me, he would say it was all my own fault.

He'd say to me: 'Don't try and tell anyone. Everyone knows you're trouble. Your parents know you're trouble. You'll be taken away.' That really scared me.

Because from the time he started to abuse me, I changed. From then on, I was trouble. I spilt a glass of cherryade once, I suppose I was about eight, and Dad hit me for it and told me I was trouble. He'd hit me hard and leave bruises. Sometimes I took photos of the bruises, I don't know why – I never showed them to anyone. To me it was just proof to myself of something. Mum used to tell me I was naughty and hit me with her slippers. I remember creeping into their bedroom and hiding her slippers to try and make it stop, but she found them, of course. More trouble.

At school it was the same: they thought I was a trouble-maker, the teachers used to tell me so. But I don't remember anyone ever asking me why. I used to bully other kids at primary school, pinching their arms, pulling their hair. Maybe I was trying to alert them, asking for help. If so, they never heard me. Mum was called up to the school to talk about it. My teacher said because of the bullying I needed to see someone, that I was 'emotionally disturbed'.

I had to go and see someone in the Children's Services. My mum dropped me there and then went shopping in Sainsbury's and told me to find her there afterwards. You'd think she might have stayed with me, waited outside, asked me how it went. Not that it mattered. The lady in the Children's Services hardly spent any time with me. If she'd taken longer, asked me more questions, would I have told her about Eric? About the anger, the rage he had created in me, that was all locked inside and made me so spiteful to the other kids, who all seemed so much happier than me? No. Even if she'd asked, I don't think I could have told her. I thought it was my fault this was happening – because I was trouble. I thought if they found out they'd take me away, and I didn't want that.

Because one part of my life was different. Once a week I

went to dance classes. My mum paid for the lessons – I think the next-door neighbours had kids who went and Mum had this thing about keeping up with them. She wanted their respect. That was the bit of her I came to despise: appearances were everything to her. In the end that was what killed our relationship, but at the time it was brilliant because it meant I had the chance to dance, and those moments were so precious. They are the only happy memories I have of my childhood. I must have been quite good, though I don't think my parents were ever proud of me. I used to win loads of medals – I think they're in my nan's loft now.

It was the music that stopped me thinking, or being frightened, or feeling lonely. It would take me somewhere else – into a world where I could dance in the spotlight, show everyone what I could do – and the rhythm and the melody would lift me, fill the emptiness in my soul. Dancing turned me into someone else and gave me courage. I could wear spangles on my leotards when I danced and show my body on the stage. The body Eric made me loathe, made me feel so ashamed of. Music and dance allowed me to forget him, to forget being hit and ignored at home. When I danced, I felt as if I had wings and I could fly away. So I couldn't tell anyone about him. If they took me away, I'd lose that magic gift of flight – I'd come crashing down again, with nowhere to escape to.

By the time I was eleven or twelve, I knew what Eric was doing was really wrong, because he kept on telling me, 'This is our secret. If you tell, you'll be taken away.' He knew that would silence me. I didn't even know the facts of life then, so anything could have happened. But then, in 1986, when I was thirteen, the *Childwatch* programme came on the television and my life changed.

We watched it together, my parents and me. I was with them in the lounge; I was sitting alone, as usual, by the door and they were together, as always, on the sofa. It was a long programme and I was holding onto myself, trying hard not

5

to show how it affected me, not to *let* it affect me. Esther Rantzen was talking about me and Eric. Not really us, of course, but the things he did to me. She was saying other children were going through the same horrible things. They said on the programme that it wasn't our fault. And they said they were starting a special phone line for children, ChildLine. I remember the advert they made, with a little girl in a red phone box, and the number 0800 1111. We had a red phone box in our village and the windows were small, so I remember thinking if people were passing they wouldn't be able to tell who was inside it. And they gave an address to write to ChildLine, a free address so you didn't need a stamp.

All this was so hard to take in while the programme was happening, it kept echoing around inside my head. So much information to store, my brain was churning. It was like an explosion that utterly changed the world I thought I knew – the world of secret pain, where I was a prisoner, in isolation. Suddenly hope arrived, like a rainbow, like a peal of bells. The message rang out loud and clear. That it wasn't my fault; that there was a way to reach out for help; and that I wasn't alone any more. I sat very still, not daring to reveal the explosion that had shattered the chains, all those rules and taboos that had imprisoned me all my life. I dared not let my parents guess the way I felt because all the time I could hear Eric's voice in my head – 'It's our secret, you'll be taken away.' He was still in charge of my life.

My parents were just sitting there all this time, watching as they did any other programme. I looked down and saw my hands were shaking so I hid them in my lap. But why on earth did I think they'd notice, or ask me what was wrong? They never noticed anything, unless it was something they could say was naughty and hit me for.

For the next couple of weeks – it must have been the beginning of November – Eric left me alone. Not for any reason connected with the programme, I think it was just luck that he was busy and I had that time to let my brain settle down and stop churning. And it did slow down enough to keep reminding me, over and over again, that I wasn't the only one. That other children had suffered, like me. That there was help out there. That I wasn't evil; it wasn't my fault. So I told my best friend, Sian.

I hope Sian and her family know how important they have been to me. I used to go round there after school and they always made me welcome. Her mum was a dinner lady and her dad was a school inspector, so I guess they just liked and understood children. So even though by this time I was a sulky, troubled teenager they still made me feel better about myself. But I couldn't even tell them about Eric. Adults, I knew instinctively, would have to do something. And that something was to take me away. No, I couldn't tell them, so instead I told Sian. Not in detail – that was too shameful and disgusting – but just in general terms. I was crying. She could tell how upset I was, so she didn't ask any questions or argue with me when I said I wanted to write to ChildLine.

We worded the letter together. I remember I wrote it in biro, on a page of lined paper torn out of a spiral notebook. And I used Sian's address. I said what Eric had been doing and that I knew now that it was wrong, and I asked for advice. ChildLine replied really quickly, in less than a week. Sian told me the letter had come, and I went round to open it with her – I was too scared to read it by myself. After all, I'd disobeyed, I told someone when I'd been instructed not to. Would they send someone round? Would they send the police round? What had I done?

But when I read ChildLine's reply, I knew I'd been right, after all. It said the things Eric was doing were wrong and asked if I had any adults that I could talk to about it. And it said I could ring that freephone number 0800 1111 any time if I wanted to talk to ChildLine. It was signed Julie C. What should I do? There wasn't an adult in my life I felt safe to talk to. I was scared, but not too scared to agree with Sian when she read it and said that I should ring ChildLine, and maybe that would help.

Two days later, Sian came round to my home after school. We sat together on the bottom of the stairs and I dialled ChildLine's number. When they answered, I could hardly speak, I was crying too much. So Sian took the phone and talked to them. She told them about my letter, and their reply. They said we could ring back, and they gave us a day and a time to ring, when Julie C would be there. Then I got Sian to hang up quickly. I was still terrified. Eric had his own key to our house: he used to call round and let himself in whenever he wanted, whenever he thought I'd be there alone. What if he walked in now? But after we'd put the phone down I remember hugging Sian, knowing that from now on everything would be different, and perhaps better.

So when the day came I rang, as they had said I could, and for the first time I talked to Julie C, the counsellor who had written to me. Her voice was very distinctive: gentle and low, with a slightly husky edge to it. She didn't tell me I was evil or a trouble-maker. She didn't push me to tell her more than I wanted to. And she didn't ask me where I was calling from, though she was always concerned to know if I was safe. And sometimes I wasn't. Once when I was on the phone to her I saw Eric's car coming down the road towards the house and I hid behind the sofa so he couldn't see I was at home, alone. Julie told me to lock the front door against him. She calmed me down. Although she was so worried, I knew she wouldn't do anything to try and find me, not without my saying that would be alright. After the first time I rang it got easier and easier to talk to ChildLine: they'd told me they wouldn't tell anyone else, and it was true, so I felt I could trust them.

I spoke to Julie maybe eight or ten times while she was suggesting different ways of stopping Eric doing anything more to me. It was difficult at first for me to believe that I was worth helping, but she was so determined that I had done nothing wrong, that he was entirely responsible and to blame, that in the end I began to believe her. She said he was a dangerous man; that what he was doing to me he might also be doing to other children. And gradually she gave me the confidence to think about telling somebody else. So when she said she would tell the NSPCC for me and they would help me, I agreed.

By a horrible coincidence, the first NSPCC person they suggested I could meet was another man called Eric! I freaked out, I couldn't believe it. I said to Julie it had to be a woman, and she understood. I think ChildLine always believes that children need to be taken seriously, not stifled or contradicted. Looking back, I feel as if I had always been stifled until I contacted ChildLine, unable to breathe freely until they gave me the opportunity to tell the truth about my life. Anyway, they found an NSPCC woman instead, who came to meet me and talked to me in her car. But it frightened me. I didn't feel comfortable. Especially when she told me she knew which school I went to.

So I got out of her car and ran home in the dark. I was really frightened. I felt completely out of control of my own life. What would happen next? Was it true she knew my school and if so, would she tell them? I began to panic. School already had me down as trouble. Would they accuse me of making it all up? Would it go to court? Would I be sent to prison? When I got home, the light was on in the kitchen. I opened the door. Dad was getting a bottle of milk out of the fridge. He had his back to me, somehow that made it easier. So I just blurted it out. 'Dad, I've been sexually abused. Eric, he's been abusing me.' Dad turned round. I half expected him to hit me, but instead he held out his arms. He hugged me, and I clung to him. 'Don't worry, Jo,' he said, over and over again. 'It'll be alright.' And being held in his arms for the first time feeling safe, I believed him. 'Don't worry, Jo, it'll be alright.'

But it wasn't alright. I was crying with relief when I went to bed that night, but Dad still had to tell Mum. And when I came down the next morning dressed for school she was already there, waiting for me, sitting on the floor beside the fire in our lounge. She was a heavy woman – her dark hair was tangled around her shoulders, her eyes were puffy and her whole face was in a grimace of rage, not at Eric, at me. 'You little liar!' she screamed at me. 'You little liar! What have you been saying? It's nothing but a pack of lies! You always were a troublemaker. How dare you make up such wicked lies!'

I tried to explain. I tried to say what had happened, how I felt, why I needed her, but of course I hadn't a chance. For years she'd shut me out of her life and now she had no intention of letting me wreck it. 'You're never ringing ChildLine again!' she screamed. 'Your dad and I are locking the phone. We won't have it! You're a dirty little liar and I'm ashamed of you.' By now the tears were pouring down my face. I turned and ran out of the room, sobbing.

When I got to school, the first teacher I met was Mrs G, who taught me English. We'd always got on well. She saw the state I was in and quickly took me into a quiet office. There I told her, sobbing and not really making much sense, what had happened. But she heard enough to realise it was serious, took me to the sick room to give me a chance to recover and went straight to the headmaster. I learned later that they had rung my mother to ask if they could consult the NSPCC and arrange another meeting with them and me, but she had flatly refused permission.

The next thing that happened to me was a visit from a social worker, Mrs A, who also lived in our village. She insisted on talking to me on my own and somehow she wheedled the whole story out of me, including Eric's name and address. My nan told me later that the social worker had boasted how she'd tricked it out of me. I honestly don't remember, I think by that time I was so exhausted and frightened I had no defences left.

My parents were as good as their word and put a padlock on the dial of the old-fashioned phone downstairs. I was past caring: the next day I went down with chicken pox and was really ill with it. The police rang and asked to interview me, but my parents told them it was impossible because I was too ill. After a week, when my parents were out, I crept upstairs and used the push-button phone in their bedroom to ring ChildLine. I asked them to let Julie C know what had happened, and that I was OK. The next day the police rang again for an interview; they said they knew I'd rung ChildLine, but I'm quite sure nobody at ChildLine would have told them. This time they got their way.

I had to go to a police station to be interviewed, a nice little house in a nearby village. It was only used part-time as a police station, and I was interviewed in the kitchen, sitting at a pine kitchen table. Two police officers interviewed me, a man and a woman. I was driven there by my parents, but they stayed outside in their car. Instead, they sent their solicitor in with me, a man I'd never met before. Just before I got out of the car, my mum turned round to me and said, 'Don't you dare say you've ever seen Eric's penis. Don't you dare.' All those years of anger and intimidation paid off: I was too scared to disobey.

So the interview was a farce, a stupid, painful, unforgettable farce. With my parents' solicitor sitting next to me, standing guard over everything I said, what could I do? The police's first question was, 'Why have you got a solicitor with you?' All I could say was, 'Ask my parents.' So then they started to ask questions about Eric. The solicitor was making notes all the way through. I couldn't admit anything. And when they asked 'Did you ever see Eric's penis?', I said 'No.'

So that was that. The interview finished, I went back to the car, my parents got out and talked to their solicitor, beside his car. Then they came back, got in and said nothing to me. Not one word. Not how are you feeling, are you alright? Nothing. They never did say anything about it to me, ever.

I know the police did go round and speak to Eric, and somehow the story was cooked up that I must have misinterpreted a hug in some way. But the strange thing is that a week later Eric came to our house and, in front of my parents, apologised to me. When I say apologised, he just said, 'Jo, I'm sorry.' But he didn't admit to anything: he certainly didn't apologise for abusing me all those years.

Whatever the apology meant, and whoever had persuaded him to do it, it didn't stop him continuing to try and get me alone, to carry on where he'd left off. My parents made me go to parties and events even though often they knew he'd be there too, and he'd always get me to dance with him. I used to try and avoid him – I hated any contact with him – but because I had to try and act normally, I couldn't make a scene. So he would grab me and whisper in my ear, 'This is nice, isn't it,' and I'd want to scream, 'Get away, you bastard, you evil bastard!' But I had to be good, be respectable and not let my parents down.

There is no question in my mind. My parents protected Eric and his wife, not me. I came nowhere. Only ChildLine and Julie put me first. Even though my parents continued to forbid me to ring, I managed to speak to Julie regularly over the next months. She was very concerned to make sure I was safe and to try and help me to understand why my mother wouldn't believe me, or wouldn't admit to believing me. But my relationship with my parents, never good, was now even worse. We hardly spoke to each other at all.

Then for two years I tried to get on with life, to try and forget the past and concentrate on my school work. I kept myself right away from my parents, going straight up to my bedroom and working there. I got seven GCSEs and was doing quite well. Then my mother was diagnosed with cancer. It was the first year of my A levels. She had to have an operation, the cancer was in her liver. When I heard the news and realised what it meant, I found it terribly difficult to cope. I hated what she'd done to me, but now she was so gravely ill, I couldn't bring myself to hate her. I needed to speak to someone who could understand and help, so once again I turned to ChildLine.

I rang the number 0800 1111 and a ChildLine switchboard operator answered, 'You're through to ChildLine, can we help you?' as they always did – welcoming, accessible. But I recognised the voice, the husky edge to it, and I couldn't believe it. Out of literally hundreds of volunteer counsellors, Julie was working a shift on the switchboard and she had answered. My heart leapt. 'Is that Julie C? This is Jo.' She remembered, even though it had been two years since I'd last spoken to her. She asked someone else to take over the switchboard and she talked to me. Once again, I was not alone.

My mum died five days before my eighteenth birthday. The last month of her life was terrible. She was at home, wasting away while I watched her, and I had to nurse her – wash her, feed her, everything. I was caring for the woman who had never cared for me. The day before she died the vicar came round to bless her and she was hysterical, kept asking for her daughter. So I said, 'Mum, I'm here,' and she said, 'You're not my daughter.' Maybe she was remembering her baby daughter, that's what the vicar said, but to me this was just another rejection.

In that last week Mum actually told Eric's wife that they both must look after me after she'd gone. To do that, after everything that had happened – she must have had such an amazing capacity for denial, to lie to herself. When she died, my grandad told me I was responsible for her cancer because of all the stress I'd put her through. I remember crying hysterically when he said that. After a month of me nursing her. Even now the cruelty of it stings.

So then I went right off the rails. I did no work: I went to school for the registration at the start of the day, but then I came straight home again. I used to cry my eyes out, day after day. Funnily enough, during this period I got on well with Dad for the first time. I cooked for him, did his washing and ironing, and we'd both go to our beds and cry ourselves to sleep – I'd hear him from my bedroom. I had terrible dreams. All this time I was ringing ChildLine, speaking to Julie. I wrote a diary for her, telling her how I was feeling. She sent me stuff about bereavement and also ways of calming down, relaxing. Nothing worked. I just didn't know how to cope with hating Mum one moment, and the next crying my eyes out because she wasn't there any more.

The school called me in. They told me I was going to fail all my A levels. By now I wasn't eating. My friends tried to force-feed me, but I couldn't bear to eat anything. When I took the exams, I said to myself, I'll prove everyone wrong. But I did fail Human Biology, which was my favourite subject. I passed Geography, though. It took me half a day to open my results: I actually opened the letter standing by my mum's grave.

I thought about it all, then talked to Julie. And she had such faith in me, she was so sure I could pass, that I decided to re-sit my Human Biology and take a one-year accelerated Psychology course. But I was still totally messed up. I would run round the house crying and I used to lie on Mum's side of her bed. It's bizarre when you think how I hated her because she hadn't protected me.

The constant dream I had was that I was a tiny person inside Mum's head, trying to shoot the cancer cells. Every Mother's Day really upset me and on Christmas Eve I'd cry my eyes out. But all this time I was talking to Julie. Even though by now I was over eighteen, they didn't say I couldn't carry on ringing ChildLine. Julie knew I needed it. She was the only one who had heard the whole story, could see the whole picture and how one thing affected another. She talked me through the bereavement process and explained that the way I was feeling was normal, the loss, the anger. But I was stuck at rock bottom. I can't remember if it was Julie who made me see it was the abuse that stopped me moving on, but now I realise it was.

Then, in 2005, ChildLine put out an appeal. They said that they were so short of money that year they might have to close down their night service. I panicked. For the children. What would have happened, one of those times I had crept out of our house – like on Christmas morning, really early, when there was hard frost on the ground – suppose there had been nobody there to answer the phones? There's always going to be children like me, who have nobody else to turn to. So I got in touch with my local paper to tell them my story, to raise money for ChildLine and increase awareness of the work, so maybe they could get more volunteer counsellors and children would know where to turn when they were desperate. They printed an article. When I saw it, it was scary: people you know are going to read it. I was nervous about my nan seeing it. At first it was hard for her, she said, because I was criticising her own daughter, but I think she understands now. My mum had never spoken to her about the abuse.

Then, amazingly, I met Julie. It's really rare for a ChildLine counsellor to meet a child they've helped, but a reporter brought us together. And while I was being interviewed, I blurted out that I'd helped Mum, but she hadn't helped me. Julie heard me say that. She wasn't looking at me, she was sitting at the back of the room looking down at her lap, but she knew my voice so well she could tell I'd said far more than I'd intended. She could hear the pain. And that made me see it too: I realised for the first time how angry I was. Up until then I hadn't been able to admit how I felt, even to myself.

Then I went back to my mum's grave by myself. It was winter, very cold. It's a big churchyard. There was no one around. There's a piece of flat, sunken Welsh slate where her ashes are buried. Horrible – the cheapest Dad could buy. I stood there next to it and I said, loudly, 'Why didn't you look after me? I looked after you. Why didn't you look after me?'

That is still the big question for me. I think it was just she couldn't face the shame, the scandal, everyone knowing. That she had let him come into the house whenever he wanted, babysit me with no questions asked, and never protected me from the terrible things he was doing all those years. I don't think she could admit all that, even to herself. I certainly don't think she could have lived with herself if anyone else had known. If there had been a trial, if Eric had been charged, the whole village would have known. So she sacrificed me for the sake of her reputation.

And maybe she sacrificed other children, put them in danger too, by never letting me report to the police what really happened. Because now I come to think of it, Eric's wife had a niece younger than me and they used to see her all the time. Maybe he hurt her too.

Thanks to Julie, I survived. I must have had hundreds of conversations with her, but without them I know I wouldn't be alive now. I would have killed myself.

Sexual abuse leaves so many scars. I've been on antidepressants; I saw bereavement counsellors at university – Julie helped me get in touch with them. I couldn't have done it without her help. It's so much easier with the anonymity you get when you ring ChildLine. I found it much more difficult to talk to counsellors face to face: it puts a lot more pressure on, makes it far harder if they can look into your eyes, watch your body language. But Julie supported me throughout.

So yes, her faith in me was justified. I did get my A levels and I did win a place at university, where I studied Psychology and got my BA Honours degree. At that point Dad kicked me out of our home. He'd got a new girlfriend, and he wanted to sell the house and move in with her. He gave me £5,000 from the sale and my mum's china cabinet; that's all I've got from my childhood. In it there's a 'Happy Mother's Day' plate I gave her and presents from my twenty-first birthday, which I had to arrange myself. My friends sometimes look at all the stuff and say, what are you doing with all that rubbish? But it's all I've got.

Since Dad kicked me out, he's dead to me. He never showed me any love, I never meant anything to him. The man who slapped me for holding my mum's hand, who punished me all my childhood, who said he'd look after me when I first told him about Eric and then totally abandoned me. And then, when I'd done things he could have been proud of – got a good degree and now a very good job – he just turned his back on me. Fine. He's dead to me now.

But ChildLine really cared about me all through my childhood, and I will always care about them. Now I try and raise money for them, to help them whenever I can, for the sake of children who are desperate, like I was. I was once invited to a ChildLine Ball, and I told the guests how much help I'd had over the years, that they'd saved my life. I only said two sentences and we raised £33,000! I didn't even have a ball gown – I wore a full-length black skirt. It was the only smart thing I had.

And I got married. It was a very small wedding. I invited Julie, I wanted her to be there. She'd often told me how proud she was of me, that I'd managed in spite of everything to grow up, get married, hold down a good job in medical research. And I'm so proud of Julie: her commitment, she's achieved such a lot, helped so many children, helped me so much. So she came to my wedding, wearing a sparkly pink top, and I gave her my bouquet as a way of saying thank you. She was very touched by that.

I **KNOW** from meeting hundreds of ChildLine counsellors over the years that Julie C is not unique. ChildLine has nearly fifteen hundred counsellors around the UK, listening to children and answering them online. The vast majority are volunteers, donating their time to help children. It's a tough job, but they are very carefully trained. And many of them, like Julie C, have worked with children in different roles. Some are paediatric nurses, some are teachers. There has even been a consultant paediatrician who spent years as a ChildLine counsellor and once told me the work she does for ChildLine is some of the most valuable work she has done. But volunteer counsellors also come from widely varied backgrounds. Lawyers, actors, accountants, unemployed people, students... what they have in common is a dedication to protecting children and an empathy that enables them to identify a child's needs. Julie C, who eventually became the Head of ChildLine's centres in Wales, supported Jo for years. This is her story.

CHAPTER TWO

JULIE'S STORY

When I first spoke to Jo, listening to her, it struck me forcibly that her loneliness, her fear and isolation were so different from my own childhood. I was very lucky, I know that now. I grew up in Anglesey, the beautiful island in North Wales. We had a big, noisy family. I was one of five children, all of us growing up together in the countryside. We were privileged.

Not that we were rich: our home was a little old three-bedroomed house built in traditional Welsh grey stone, on the side of a farm. I remember I had to walk through the fields to get to school and I loved the way they changed, all the bright colours of spring flowers, then getting burnt gold in the summer and white with snow in winter. I can't remember ever feeling the cold. Looking back, I had an idyllic upbringing. We spent from April to September in the sea, on those wonderful beaches around Amlwch, in and out of the water, paddling in the rock pools – hours of freedom, all us children playing together.

I suppose that closeness, that happiness made me who I am today. Maybe that's what's given me a driving commitment to other children, to try and offer lonely, isolated young people the kind of support and strength I got from my own family.

We were brought up Catholic. My father worked as a structural engineer; my mum was a stay-at-home mum, but she was always busy. She used to help with the church and the local youth club, which was a bit of a pain when we were teenagers because whenever we went down there she was always there, too. I was very happy at school, did lots of sports, and I'm still in touch with the friends I made. My first ambition was to become a psychologist: I did Psychology A level and a degree in Social Psychology in Loughborough. I wanted somehow to get a real understanding not just about myself, but also effective ways of helping others.

I graduated in 1982 and my first job was in an NHS adolescent unit. It was a twenty-bedded unit; the young people stayed during the week and went home at weekends. It was tough work, a steep learning curve for me. The young people were very disturbed: we had some young girls who were anorexic and other young people who were themselves sex offenders. We never labelled any of the young people. The work was in its day quite innovative: we gave them group therapy and family therapy as well. Did it work? It cost the same as Eton and we had some successes, but in the end they pulled the plug on it.

But it was very useful for me because I could learn from the other professionals. It was a multi-disciplinary team and it gave me really valuable experience of working with young people. I stayed for three years, then I went on to work with male drug users in Esher. That was difficult, especially when some of them discovered they were HIV-positive. One of them went to Piccadilly, then overdosed and died. At twenty-six, I found that very difficult, so I resigned.

Suddenly I was out of a job. By then it was 1987. At the end of my last week in Esher I remember going to an agency on a Friday afternoon, just to find a temporary post while I was working out where to go next. They told me about a brand-new telephone counselling service for children. But I wasn't impressed – I remember thinking, well, what help can you give a child over the telephone? But it would pay the mortgage and I needed to find work somewhere, so I agreed. It was short term, after all. Who knew whether this new line for children would last more than a few months? That was nearly twenty-five years ago and ChildLine is still here.

So one Monday in early May, I went into ChildLine for my first morning there, feeling quite cynical. It wasn't at all grand, or glossy. I remember a shabby, overcrowded little office on a narrow street in the shadow of St Paul's Cathedral in the City of London. There were a dozen desks, with telephones on them, and I remember children's drawings pinned up on the walls. The whole service was fitted in two small rooms with a separate little briefing area. It was so close to St Paul's that once when the window was open and the bells started to peal a child caller said to me, 'Are you in a church?' There were ten desks for counsellors; when a child was very upset, sometimes a counsellor had to sit under the desk to hear them. You could tell from the counsellor's body-language how distressing the call was. Sometimes they would curl up on the floor. And there were a lot of those calls.

That first day a supervisor showed me my desk and said: 'There's your list of resources.' This was a list of places to refer children to, but there were precious little of them. It amazes me still that there is no network of refuges in our big cities for children who run away; people just seem to think it solves every problem to find them and take them home again. But sometimes they have every reason to try and escape. Then the supervisor gave me the forms we used for details of the calls we took. The vast majority of the children themselves were anonymous, so we just wrote down their first names and their ages, the general area they lived in and the reason why they had rung, so that we could find their stories again if they rang back. We didn't want them to have to start from scratch all over again.

In those very early days there'd been a lot of suspicion from the social work profession about ChildLine. They were quite sceptical, just as I had been. Some of them were concerned that we wouldn't protect children adequately, which was another reason we kept a record of the calls, making notes of what the children told us and the advice we gave them. The professionals took a good many years to understand that we could help children even though they were anonymous. They were extremely suspicious because we referred very few children to social services or the police, even young people who told us about abuse. Firstly, we couldn't. After all, there was no way we could trace their calls so we didn't know who or where they were. Because it was way before mobile phones became common, many of the children rang from phone boxes. It was the only way they could be safe and not overheard. Secondly, it would not have been in the children's best interests. Most of them weren't ringing because they wanted anyone else brought in, they just desperately needed to talk safely to someone, as we said on our first posters: 'speak to someone who cares.' So many of the children believed nobody cared about them until ChildLine was launched.

So there I was, sitting at my desk next to my phone on that first day, with no idea what to expect. With all my training and the work I'd done, there was no guidance about helping abused children who try to take control of their own lives and ring a helpline for assistance. Obviously, there had never been a helpline like ChildLine before. As bad luck would have it, the first call I got was an adult abuser, wanting to talk in detail about the abuse a child in his street was suffering. He was clearly enjoying himself. We still get those calls. I don't know whether they are 'mad or bad' as the tabloids would say, but for whatever reason they ring ChildLine for their own gratification. They don't care how many children they prevent from getting through to us, or maybe that's part of their fun. Perhaps if I'd had a few of those, I would have given up and tried to find other work, but I was hooked that first week. Twenty-five years later, I still am, and I remember the call that did it.

It was from a young girl. Maybe about nine years old, she only had time to make a very short call from a phone box next to her bus stop. She was on the way to school, she said, but she rang because she couldn't stand her life any more. She was being sexually abused at home. For the next three days she rang again, always at the same time, 7.30 in the morning. They were very short calls, but each time I used them to try and build her feelings of self-worth. At first she thought she must be bad for this to happen to her – worthless and dirty. So I had to work as hard and as fast as I could to convince her that she was not to blame at all; that what was happening was not her fault. And somehow I managed to find enough time to talk about her family, about who she felt close to, who she could tell. And on the third day when she rang, she said she had told her grandma. Grandma agreed to talk to her mother and she trusted them both to protect her. They hadn't blamed her: they had listened and understood. I never heard from her again, but that last call was the moment when I became hooked on our work.

With four short phone calls ChildLine had made such a difference to this little girl. We had given her hope and the confidence to find a way out of her suffering. And when she had built up her courage and her confidence, her grandma had believed her.

It was such a contrast to the work I'd done before. When I'd worked in the therapeutic unit, I remember a child who was there for six months. We all suspected she was being abused.

There were so many clues from her behaviour, the way she drew pictures, the way certain things distressed her, but even though she came to trust us, she never had the strength to tell us in words. I can only imagine the sort of threats, maybe even the violence that her abuser had employed to silence her.

ChildLine discovered a totally new way of liberating children from this kind of prison. The telephone gave them the safety of anonymity. An abuser need never know the call had been made. It wouldn't cost anything, there would be no record of it on a phone bill. And it was confidential, so that meant a child's world was not going to fall apart if they talked to us and told us the truth. So many abused children fear that if they ask for help, they will be responsible for bringing catastrophe into their family's life. And many just long for the abuse to stop so that they can live normal lives, like their friends. I remember one little girl told me: 'I love my dad, but not my night-time dad.' And at ChildLine, although of course we wanted to protect the children, we knew we had to hang onto their trust or we would lose them. If we let them down, they would hang up and never ring again; they would just give up trying to find any way out. So we had to work at their pace, not try and force them to let us intervene before they were ready.

I remember I'd had my fingers burned very early on when we moved a child too fast and she had retracted. Diane was fourteen when she rang us because she was being sexually abused by her stepfather. He was brutal and violent. We were worried about her, so I persuaded her to let me get a social worker involved, but that made the bad so much worse. Because when the social worker went home with her and told her mother, the woman lunged at her daughter's throat and half-strangled her, shouting at her that she was a horrible little liar. Under that barrage of physical and emotional violence, Diane changed her story, broke down and said she'd made the whole thing up. The worst thing was that when she claimed that she had lied, the social worker decided that she must be disturbed to make such horrible things up and had her put into an adolescent psychiatric unit.

But when Diane was eighteen she rang ChildLine again and asked for me. She told me it had all been true. I said I'd never doubted it for a moment. She told me she was back home and it was as bad as ever, but she gave me the name of her GP and I got him to work with me to find her safe accommodation.

A year or so later I was visiting a drop-in centre we used to refer children to and this young woman standing next to me heard me say something, turned to me and said, 'I recognise your voice. You're Julie. I'm Diane.' My heart stopped for a second: it was so wonderful to meet her, after everything she'd been through. My instinct was to give her a cuddle. She looked like a stranger, but when she spoke to me I knew her so well. I told her how bad I felt about the way things had turned out. Obviously we couldn't have a long conversation together, but she wrote to me to tell me what she was doing and that made me realise how crucial ChildLine had been in her life. Now she's doing a social work degree.

But that experience with Diane taught me how crucial it was not to try and persuade children to let us intervene too early or too suddenly in their lives. We must let them gain confidence first. We must be sure we aren't just making things worse for them.

By the time Jo wrote to ChildLine I was still working in our tiny first office in Addle Hill in London, but I had become a supervisor. It was about three months after we opened, so it was still early days; we were still putting structures in place and working out the best ways to help children. I remember that morning I wasn't on the phone – I had a pile of letters from children I was working through. They used to mount up if we weren't careful and the letters could be just as urgent as the phone calls, so we had to answer them systematically. Children can still write to ChildLine Freepost 1111. They don't need money for a stamp. And of course this was years before we started the online counselling service we have now. So there I was, dealing with all these letters and well aware that we had to be very careful how we replied, because we never knew who would open the letter. We used plain envelopes and plain paper, not to give anything away. And we had to hold onto our own emotions, otherwise we ran the risk of putting a child in even greater danger.

It's not easy. Whether it's on the phone or you're reading their letters, it's never easy. It's shocking to get a letter like Jo's – so brave, so ashamed. She described what was happening to her in general terms, but clearly enough for me to understand that she was being sexually abused by a man her parents liked and trusted. What a horrifying situation for any child. But I sent back a very bland letter not revealing how distressed I was: 'Dear Jo, Thank you for writing to ChildLine. We'd really like to talk to you, we hope to hear from you soon, I'll be on duty two till ten.' So, if the wrong person did open my letter and confront Jo, she could always say she'd just written to offer support. Or invent some other reason.

It was Jo's friend who rang. In the earliest days, when a child said she was ringing 'for a friend' we used to suspect they were really talking about themselves, which is sometimes the way adults protect themselves when they are unsure what response they will get. But ChildLine's children very often do ring on behalf of a friend, and usually have that friend standing next to them and hand the phone over to them. It's one of the really impressive things about children: the way they offer each other support when they most need it. Anyway, Jo's friend rang and said she had Jo with her. It was nice for her to have someone there.

So then, with her friend next to her, Jo summoned up the strength to talk to me. I remember her voice, very strained, a very scared voice. And I remember so clearly the picture in my mind of this frightened young girl, talking about a man who was a friend of the family and used regularly to babysit and abuse her. From then on we talked to each other regularly. That's how ChildLine works with some of our children, having regular 'booked' calls with named counsellors. It builds the trusting relationship. I knew Jo really wanted the abuse she was suffering to stop and I hoped that as soon as her parents realised what had been going on, they would protect her. It took about six or seven calls before Jo could agree she wanted help. I looked through our list of resources, and found a local NSPCC project. As bad luck would have it, first they offered a man called Eric, the same name as her abuser, which made Jo extremely upset – I could hear her shuddering at the idea.

It would have been totally wrong to try and persuade her, so instead I told her I could quite understand and that I would find a woman. We did indeed find someone, but the result was very, very disappointing. Her mother's furious reaction hurt Jo badly: she felt the whole thing was being brushed under the carpet. The police interview with her parents' lawyer present was a real disaster. Jo was instructed to say she had never seen Eric's penis, when she had many times. Indeed, he had forced her to have full sex with him. She told me that her mum and dad hadn't gone in with her; that she had to deny what had happened. That she was made to feel like the bad one. It was a second trauma, an ordeal almost as bad as the original abuse, not being believed by the very people who should have cared the most. She felt utterly betrayed by her parents.

And the devastating blow was that far from protecting her, even after the interview her parents still allowed the man Eric into her house. My heart went out to her. Jo was a young person who was always eager to please, and to be made by her own parents to deny the truth was really frightening. They put locks on the phone and told her she couldn't ring ChildLine, although she managed to continue to talk to us from a call box. But they left her completely vulnerable to this man. During one call she said, 'I can see Eric's car coming along the street towards the house.'

I could hear the panic in her voice when she told me that her parents were out. 'Jo, go and bolt the front door,' I said. Normally, she told me, he just let himself in, but this time she went away, then came back and sat on the floor out of sight of the window and carried on whispering to me. In the background of the call I heard the doorbell ring, over and over again. I was so concerned that she was still in danger and it was desperately unfair that after all she had done to try and protect herself, she felt so badly about herself. The abuse, and the reaction of her parents profoundly damaged her self-esteem.

Then for a year or so Jo stopped ringing ChildLine. In 1990, she rang back, and by chance I was on the switchboard, answering calls and putting them through to counsellors. She recognised my voice, she said 'Julie, it's Jo' and I remembered her instantly. So I asked someone else to take over the switchboard while I talked to Jo.

This time she told me that her mum had just been diagnosed with cancer. The woman who had abandoned her now needed her help. So we started once again to have regular conversations, until her mum died. Understandably it was a very complicated time for Jo – the grief, the anger, the things unsaid between them, alongside all the intimate nursing she was doing. At that time she had to take her A levels. I was so proud. She opened her results when she was on the phone to me. I remember saying, 'Don't worry, you've done your best – you've been through so much.' In the end she got high enough grades to go to university and once again I was so proud: she not only survived, she got herself to university. She had wanted to open the envelope containing her results with somebody safe, and that was ChildLine.

At university, away from home, the loss really hit her. She used to write journals and send them to me. I encouraged her

28

to put down her feelings on paper, as a letter to her mother, to say the things she had never been able to say while her mother was alive. Jo had been so caring and maternal to her mother, who had never cared for or protected her. She thought she should be grieving but she was feeling so many different emotions. And when she could, she would pick up the phone to me at ChildLine. Then her dad sold the family home and told her there was no place for her there. Once again she had been abandoned – there was not even a family home to come back to. She had to stay strong to survive. And she did.

All this time I'd had a picture of Jo in my mind, but never met her. When she decided publicly to talk about ChildLine's work, and how we had been there when she needed us, and had nobody else to turn to, a reporter came to talk to me about ChildLine's work, and they invited me to a hotel, and a tall young woman came towards me. It was Jo. That's what amazed me: on first sight, she was so much taller than me, not at all like the picture in my mind of the child and young person I'd been speaking to all those years. She was very emotional. We hugged each other. It was very special.

We don't usually have endings at ChildLine – we don't see who we help. It was a privilege to meet her. But although when I saw her she was a stranger, when I looked away and just listened to her, I knew her so well. Then I saw the context of it all: I went to her village and to her mother's grave. When we went to the grave, we were linking arms. I could feel her pain. ChildLine had been a witness to her childhood trauma, had been alongside her through it all, and that moment cemented it all for me.

It says so much about Jo that she now wants to be an ambassador for our work, to help ChildLine. When she is asked to speak about her work she still phones up to tell me, does a little practice, or phones up after the event. And I feel protective of her. I do feel maternal, yes. She asked me to her wedding, said to me: 'Will you please be there?' I asked permission first. I phoned the Director of ChildLine, Anne Houston, just to make sure it was not a problem. But she didn't hesitate. She said yes, that's fine. I went alone to the Registry Office. I was so pleased to be there.

I think Jo's story proves that ChildLine is a lifeline. If you need evidence, there she is. She is not the only one, of course. There are many other children who also owe their lives or their happiness to ChildLine. Like little Jenny who got in touch with us because a lodger living with her mum, a lorry-driver, turned out to be a paedophile who groomed her and then abducted her. Very fortunately she managed to text us, so we traced her and the police rescued her. And children like the young boy who rang us after we talked about our work on the children's TV show *Blue Peter*. He said that his parents had parted, dad had left, and he missed his father terribly. He told us about the activities they used to do every weekend, fishing and football. I asked do you think your dad knows how much you miss him? How would your grandmum feel if you told her? A week later, he rang back to say he had talked to them both and he was going to carry on fishing and football at the weekends and have a sleepover with his dad. Then a month or so later, he rang again to say they were all going to spend Christmas together with his mum. Those are the calls that stick in your head and in your heart.

But in Jo's case I have a face to put to the story. Usually we never meet the young people, never know how things turn out. But in her case I have the pleasure of knowing the end of the story, the joy of being able to help her through her life. She has done tremendously well.

PEOPLE often ask me how I got the idea of ChildLine. Now it seems a simple obvious idea, to create a helpline for children in distress or danger, a freephone which was open every hour of every day. But it had never been done before.

By launching ChildLine so that children themselves could ring for help, we were putting children in charge of their own lives. It was up to them to decide to ring, and when. And up to them whether or not to put ChildLine's suggestions into practice. If children rejected ChildLine's ideas, all they had to do was hang up. All this was blasphemy at the time. In fact, a couple of years after the launch the NSPCC (which now runs ChildLine, and of which I am a trustee) honoured me by making me an honorary council member because, in the words of their chief executive, 'ChildLine broke the mould.'

So in a way it may have helped me that I have no professional background in child protection or social work. If I had, I might have thought it was impossible, or inappropriate, to put such crucial decisions into a child's own hands. At a time when all the most important decisions in children's lives were always taken by adults, it was a revolutionary concept. Not that I understood that at the time.

In 1986, I was the mother of three small children, wife of the documentary-maker Desmond Wilcox and was working for the BBC, producing and presenting the consumer programme *That's Life!*

It was a strange, mongrel programme, reaching audiences of up to 20 million with its eccentric combination of talking dogs and cats that could play ping pong and tough reports about conmen and dangerous playgrounds. Although designed to be entertaining, because the programme reached a huge audience it was influential. Government ministers watched us. Heads of industry watched us. Sunday night was a convenient time for MPs to watch us, and as it turned out, a large proportion of the nation too.

31

Our audiences were very responsive. We were one of the first interactive television shows: the viewers wrote and telephoned us in droves because they knew they had a crucial part to play in the programme. It was about them. They could actually take part; for instance, they could come into the studio to demonstrate an unusual talent, like the twins who played tunes by hitting each other's heads with spanners. And they sent us thousands of letters suggesting investigations they wanted us to make.

They also took part in surveys which had become part of the armoury of the programme. Thousands of viewers filled in elaborate questionnaires and the enormous amount of information they gave us was extremely valuable. For instance, we created one survey about tranquillisers which revealed how harmful an addiction to these powerful drugs could become. Another about hard drugs revealed cigarettes were the most common gateway drug and that cannabis can be addictive. And for our third survey, on which the *Childwatch* programme was based, we decided to mount the biggest survey ever undertaken into our viewers' experiences of child abuse.

Childwatch was created because at that time the BBC had appointed an inspiring, creative man to be controller of BBC1. In 1986, Michael Grade (now Lord Grade) had recently come back to Britain from the USA and one of the first programmes he commissioned on his return was about the dangers of drug-taking. It was a landmark programme called *Drugwatch*. He decided it should take up the whole of one Sunday night and it was a great success, inspiring the creation of a national network of support groups for addicts and their families.

The head of the features department, Will Wyatt, was in charge of producing *Drugwatch* and, seeing its impact, wondered whether there was another programme to be made in the same style. Producer Ritchie Cogan came to ask me that question and he caught me at just the right moment. I had been horrified by a recent case of child abuse: the murder of little Heidi Koseda, a toddler who had starved to death locked in her bedroom. Every few years one of these heart-rending deaths of vulnerable little children would occur. Perhaps we could make a programme designed to save these precious lives by finding more effective ways of protecting children at risk? We could call it *Childwatch*.

I took a letter I had received from a survivor of abuse and went to see Michael Grade with this idea. He agreed at once and asked how long the programme should be. I suggested one programme before the nine o'clock watershed that children could watch and one later in the evening, which could be more hard-hitting, for an adult audience. He agreed to this too and decided that Thursday evening would be ideal. So it was scheduled to broadcast on Thursday 30 October 1986.

I have since asked Michael Grade why he had given over the whole of one evening's viewing to a programme about child abuse. He said, 'Clearly it was an issue of huge importance that got little or no coverage on the BBC's main channel. And then it's always an issue of trust. You commission from somebody because you trust that person not to let you down, to make something you're going to be proud of.'

But when the programme was eventually made, it launched ChildLine: a brand-new idea, a helpline for abused children. Wasn't that a huge gamble, to launch a brand-new service for children, a brand new charity, on a television programme? Michael said, 'Why not? What have you got to lose? When you launch it, you'll discover if there is a need for it or not. If you didn't launch it, you'd never know. If it fell flat on its face and no children rang, you'd just have discovered there was no need for it. Either way, what have you got to lose?'

So we were off. We used the method which had proved

so successful with our *Drugwatch* programme. We decided to base our *Childwatch* programme upon the experiences of *That's Life!* viewers, since they had been prepared in the past to take part in confidential surveys.

But of course a great many children watched *That's Life!*, partly for the fun of watching a horse doing arithmetic, but also because of the serious reports contained in each programme. Some of those children might be suffering abuse themselves. So when on the show I introduced the idea of our survey into child abuse, I also said that after the programme we would be opening a special helpline for any child who might be suffering now. The line was only open for forty-eight hours, but in that time it was jammed with calls. One hundred children told us about the abuse they were suffering, much of it sexual abuse.

I will never forget walking into my office the morning after the programme to meet the social workers who had been running the helpline with Richard Johnson, the founder of the Incest Crisis Line. We talked together about the calls they'd taken and the fact that children were ringing to disclose abuse they had never talked about to anyone before. I knew in that moment that working to help protect abused children was far more important to me than any of my previous work. As I heard about these hidden children, all guarding a terrible secret, I passionately wanted to be able to help them. It was the most important cause I had ever worked for.

And in that moment I also realised that if only we could have kept our lines open throughout the year, we might be able to help hundreds, maybe thousands more children.

Meanwhile our viewers had begun to write to us, offering to fill in our survey into abuse. It was a long, detailed questionnaire and what I didn't know was that very process of answering it would in itself change lives, like Christine's.

CHAPTER THREE

CHRISTINE'S STORY

I don't feel I have parents. Only ex-parents. I was born to them, but now they mean nothing to me. But then I never felt any tenderness from them. I thought they put up with me during my childhood, but nothing more.

I was always a plain child, or so they told me, and I believed it myself, with my short, cropped hair like a boy's. I was a good little girl, always well-behaved. It wasn't surprising, given how strict my ex-parents were. I went to school very young – two-and-a-half – and that was strict, too. For instance, we didn't have puddings at home, but at school we had to eat everything up, and I couldn't eat the puddings, custardy sort of things, so they always put me in another room alone to finish them as a punishment.

Some of the children had worms, my ex-mother told me, so I was not supposed to sit on the toilet at school. I thought they'd be huge snake-like things, so I was very frightened of them – I didn't know where they were coming from. And I didn't know how not to sit on the toilet. But I didn't ask my ex-mother: she wasn't that sort of woman, she was distant. She was very good at cooking, keeping the house in order, making sure I had nice clean clothes, but she never played with me. I was a lonely child. Carol, my younger sister, and I lived so separately, our lives didn't meet. And my ex-father Jim was a dictator.

Jim was an intimidating figure. Tall, with a straight nose, broad face, thinning red hair – a handsome man, or at least that's what he thought he was. Until I was nine, he was in the police force, but they threw him out when he drove drunk, hit a motorcyclist and instead of stopping to help him just drove away. The cyclist was terribly injured. Jim tried to tell some kind of story to cover his tracks, but in the end he admitted it. I've seen newspaper stories about it, and the time when he violently attacked another policeman. All the neighbours knew he was violent and unpredictable. I overheard the people who lived next door calling him a menace and they were right: he was frightening.

He had a split personality, two different characters in one. To us at home he was the head of the house, without question; he ruled us with an iron fist. But outside our home people just thought he was larger than life – noisy, hard-drinking, good company. Some people thought he was charming, absolutely charming. If you liked that kind of thing I suppose he was, you'd think he was fun-loving. Because he was so loud and extrovert, he was always the centre of attention, but he was vile with women. He'd just put his hand down the front of someone's dress, indecently assault them. He's had loads and loads of affairs. If you didn't like that sort of thing you'd say he was boorish, an absolute nuisance, to be avoided at all costs.

Interestingly, he was always more in tune with children than with adults. In company he'd always focus on them – do things like a Donald Duck voice, that was his party piece. He seemed to be easy in the company of children, able to engage them.

Up to the age of nine I took life as it came. Looking back, nobody ever said they loved me, or that I was special. But at the time I thought that's just how families behave. I accepted it, that's how life was – I didn't know anything different. I suppose I even thought at the time that I was happy. Although once my sister was born, we were always being compared: she was the good one, the pretty one. I was ugly, I was badly behaved. My ex-parents were always scolding me and asking why I couldn't be more like her. As I saw it, she was far more loved than me. I was wrong.

Maybe my ex-father was consciously making us jealous of each other, keeping us resentful. That way it was divide and rule so that he could do what he liked with us and we would never confide in each other. And it worked.

When I was nine there was a girl in my class who started to talk about periods. So I went home and asked my mum what periods meant. She went and brought a book home a few days later: it was about butterflies and moths and grubs and things. I had no idea what it meant. It was a biology book and she must have thought it would explain the facts of life to me. It didn't, but I didn't question it. I didn't ask her anything about it. It would have been out of the question for her to sit down with me and look at it with me – we never did that sort of thing together. So I just put it away.

But I suppose she must have told him. And he began to think about me, maybe, and fantasise about me. I can't bear to try and enter his mind. Imagine thinking that way about a little girl of nine, a good little, shy little girl. Because that's what I was.

Around that time the family went for a picnic to a beach near Bognor. My ex-mother and my sister were lying next to each other in the sunshine, on their tummies on their towels. I copied them and lay down next to my ex-dad. While I was lying there, he put his hand inside my swimming costume and sexually assaulted me. I didn't know what he was doing,

I didn't have a clue, but it felt horrible and wrong so I moved my body away. When it was time to go, we all went to the car park, but instead of going to our car, my ex-mother took my sister to the toilets. So then I was alone with my ex-dad. He opened up the car, told me to get in and he did it again in the car, instructing me how he wanted me to sit while he did it. Now I was really frightened. And that's the moment when my world changed.

I felt so troubled. I knew it wasn't right, but I was also terrified of him – far too terrified to protest or call for help. He was a very frightening man all his life to adults, let alone a child, a lonely ashamed child. So when my ex-mum and my sister came back from the toilets, I didn't say anything. Nobody said anything.

Then there was a gap of a few months. I tried to put that memory out of my mind, but it kept swimming back into my brain. Fragments, like a nightmare you can't help remembering because the images are so horrific. Then the regular abuse started. He'd never shown any interest in me before. Now he did. He would call me into the bathroom when I was in my bedroom and he'd masturbate in front of me. No words were said to me, just the sound of his breathing as he did it in front of me. I had no idea what it was, except that it wasn't right. At other times he came into my bedroom and he made me do it to him. Or he'd find times when he'd expose himself to me, always when other things were happening around the house.

It became the undercurrent of my whole life. I used to wake up at night and find him standing next to my bed. He got in my bed once, too. He'd even touch me when my ex-mum was in the room. She'd be doing the ironing behind us, we'd be sitting in front of her on the settee. I can't think she didn't know what he was doing – she could see the fly on the wall behind her. If I so much as twirled my hair and she didn't like it, she'd notice and smack my hand away. She used to biff me quite often. There's no way she didn't know.

I hate my ex-mum now, I absolutely loathe her. As a mother she didn't stand up and protect her children. I believe she knew exactly what was going on. When he was in the bath once she told me to go up and wash his back and I said I didn't want to, but she made me. Nothing happened that time – I just scrubbed his back and ran out. They're both perverted: I call them Fred and Rose West, two bad people who brought out the worst in each other. And because of her, because she stood by him and didn't protect me, years later I put my own dear daughter in harm's way. And for that I will never forgive them. Or myself.

My sexual abuse went on for about two years. Then I had my first period, and I remember clearly saying to my ex-mother, 'Tell Dad I've started my period.' Somehow I knew it would put him off. Because he had just abused me in a major way, not penetrating me, but only just.

After that there was no more abuse. But boy, oh boy, did my world change. From then on it was hell. He continued to expose himself to me whenever he got the chance. As I got older, I'd just get up and leave the room. He bad-mouthed me all the time, said I was evil and worthless. No matter where I went in the house, I was never safe from him. If I tried, if I went into a bathroom and locked the door, my ex-mother would go ballistic. There was nowhere in that house for me to escape this drunken, violent, wealthy man.

Because by this time he was rich. He was no fool. When he left the police force he set up a company, selling insurance. It was during the boom when businesses were flying, prices were sky high and he did really well. Both my parents are very clever, good at making money.

I ran away once, just to the end of the road, just to get away. I spent as little time as I could in my home – I wasn't safe in that place. He was absolutely vile to me, paranoid about all my relationships. It was as though if he couldn't have me, nobody else could. Throughout my teens he'd follow me. If I went to a friend's house, he'd ring up and ask the parents what I was doing. He even blocked one of my friendships because they let me go out to a youth club. He made me out to be a bad lot, saying derogatory things to my ex-mother, saying I'd get pregnant, whereas in truth I couldn't cope with anything to do with boys. I didn't feel like other girls: I felt frigid, I wasn't right. But he would just smash my character to my ex-mum in front of me.

And all this, all the unfairness, made me angry all the time. The unfairness, and the terrible secret he made me keep. I was boiling with anger from about the age of twelve. When I could bear it no longer I remember once saying to him, 'I'm going to tell somebody.' He went bright red with rage, came right up to my face and said through his teeth, 'They'll never believe you because you're still a virgin and they'll put you away in a children's home.' Which, looking back, would have been the best thing for me.

And all the time the theme was how wonderful my sister Carol was. So I thought they cared about her. She went to private school and had lovely long hair. And yet the tragic thing was all that time the same thing was happening to her. Now I know my sister was abused by him: he raped and assaulted her. She denied it to me for years.

Not that he was any better to my ex-mother. From the time I was about ten he would be rude and critical to her about the way she looked, dragging her down. He constantly told her nobody would want her, 'Who'd want you, ugly bitch?' He used to come home drunk and insult her. He'd put his hand up her skirt while she was serving the food. I used to feel very sorry for her, very sad for her – she just seemed to accept it, whatever he did to her. When I was older I used to come across her crying quietly by herself because of something he'd said or done to her, something that hurt her physically and mentally. He used to beat her, he'd punch her, he even stamped on her hand once, and the violence got worse once I had left home. He became a brutal drunkard.

All this time I was at a 'good' school, a girls' grammar school. I wasn't interested in work, except when I could I'd be argumentative, like in Religious Education. It was a strict school, with a regime rather like my own home: you couldn't even cough in assembly without getting a grim look from the headmistress. She'd been the head in my mother's time too. It was really old-school, rigid, and of course I couldn't talk to anyone there. I was unloved at home and unliked at school. That was me, I thought, unlovable and unlikeable. There was nowhere I felt comfortable or safe. At the end of the miserable school day I had to go back to this home I hated.

I just about got through O levels; then I knew I had to get away. And I had the chance. I'd met a boy of seventeen who said he loved me. It was all I needed to hear. He was my passport. So I left school, went to college for a year and married at eighteen. I had escaped.

I moved away, far away, to be with my husband's family. Solved, you might think. But no. I had two girls in this marriage and my first daughter was disabled – she was injured at birth. So I had a lot to cope with and the marriage fell apart. All the time I had known it was the wrong reason to get married: I would have married anyone who asked me, just to get away. Somehow it lasted seven years, but all that time while my daughters were growing up, my ex-parents would come and visit every four weeks. Each time they'd tell me they were coming up, not ask me. I didn't want them – I would be on edge from the moment they said they were coming. I couldn't bear his presence around me, couldn't stand being in the same room as him.

My first daughter was so badly disabled she really never got beyond a mental age of three. I cared for her at home as long as I could. But as my second daughter Lucy got older, the ex-parents invited her to stay with them for holidays. My heart told me no, screamed at me that Lucy would not be safe with them, but my brain told me I must be wrong. All my childhood I had thought that what happened to me must have been my own fault. I thought, I'm adult now. I must get this straight in my head – after all, he's fine with my sister. Because of course I never knew the truth about her. So I had that battle constantly in my head, should I let her go to them or not?

Now of course I realise I should just have kicked out all the arguments in their favour, all the clichés about family life right out of my head. I so wanted things to be right, to be normal. But I can't forgive myself for not listening to what my heart was telling me. Maybe I just couldn't bear the truth, the vileness of the man. The last time she stayed with them was when she was about eleven.

That was in 1985, about the time when the BBC programme *That's Life!* sent out questionnaires to adult survivors – they were putting together a survey into child abuse. That changed everything for me. I remember watching the programme, I always did. It started with the bits when Esther would go out on the streets and get people to do daft things. Then Esther began to talk about people who had suffered child abuse. They wanted to find better ways of stopping children suffering; they said maybe from the survey they were asking survivors to take part in, they might find a pattern of abuse and a better way to find children and protect them from abuse. And they were going to use the information in a new programme called *Childwatch*. There was an address to write in to.

My head was churning as I watched. I really had told nobody about what my ex-father had done to me, except my husband. By then I was married to my second husband, John. (We've been married thirty-three years now.) I had told him about the abuse before we got married. It just poured out of me one uncontrollable night when I was a bit drunk. I don't know why I was able to tell him when I hadn't told anyone else – I think it was just that I couldn't contain the secret any longer. When I told him he was completely silent, couldn't say anything to me. So when the programme talked about it, I was still in a simmering stage: I had never faced or dealt with any of my worst memories.

After the programme, we didn't sit round talking about it, but I told John what I wanted to do and I sent off for the survey. When it came, it was very long – I remember how thick it was in the envelope. Loads of questions, and some of them really stirred me up; they made me think more deeply, made me realise how long I'd suffered, what he'd done to me. And it made me wonder about my own children now. It brought everything to the fore.

I remember feeling very disturbed about it all. It wasn't a way of solving things, but it was the first time ever I had written in depth about my experience and I had to face exactly what had happened to me. After I'd sent it off, the BBC producer of *Childwatch*, Sarah Caplin, wrote back, thanking me. She said how sorry they were to read about my painful childhood and she told me that there were a couple of organisations offering help for people like me who were still suffering as a result of childhood abuse. Obviously they'd thought about all that and realised they'd be reminding people of things they might have kept secret for years. Sarah told me a couple of places which could help adult survivors like me. One of them was a helpline: Incest Crisis Line. I rang them. The man who ran it, Richard Johnson, was so helpful that from then on I rang them regularly. And that gave me the strength to confront my ex-father.

So in June 1987 I wrote him the letter with all the things I'd never dared to tell him. I told how his abuse had destroyed my childhood and almost wrecked my life. I said that he dominated my ex-mother so completely that if he had told her the sky was black, she would have believed him. And that my first marriage had failed because of him. And I said he should ring the Incest Crisis Line too because they had a lot to say to him.

When I sent the letter it was as if the sun had suddenly come out. I thought that's it sorted: everything would be fine. It was out in the open. He'd have to take responsibility for what he'd done to me. It was his crime, not mine. I really thought I'd put it all right. How ludicrous was that. As if he was going to take it on board, admit anything. And it was way too late. I should have confronted what he'd done and what kind of brute he was before I had any of my own children. Unlike my ex-mother, I should have been strong. I have blamed my ex-mother for not protecting me, but I'm no better. I let it happen to my own daughter. I can say it now about myself: I let it happen. All I can say in my defence is that I had convinced myself that it wouldn't happen to anyone else, not to my own daughter. But it did.

My letter solved nothing. All he did was write back to me threatening legal action. He blamed me for everything. He said if my object was to destroy him, I would *never* succeed. He said I was wallowing in self-pity and that I was self-destructive; that I had made him a ready-made excuse for all my failings. He ended by saying that he and his solicitor were quite prepared to take legal action against me. I read it and all the old fear welled up inside me.

But I had changed. When I filled out the survey and got the BBC's letter back saying they had read it, I felt so relieved, so validated. At last I'd put it on the record and been believed. The threats from my ex-father, that nobody would ever believe me, evaporated when I read that letter. And the calls to Incest Crisis Line supported and strengthened me. Then, when *Childwatch* happened that autumn and ChildLine was launched, I watched the programme with my family: my two daughters and my husband John. And I thought it was wonderful. I felt so glad that I had in some way helped to get to that point, contributed to the creation of ChildLine. And now for the first time there was something in place for the children of today.

But at the same time, as I watched I felt sad for myself, that I hadn't had anyone safe to talk to all those years of my childhood. Because I would definitely have rung ChildLine, without a doubt. Now as an adult I have experienced the difference talking can make. Because through finding my voice, for the first time, even this late in my life, I can really talk. So after the programme, we made it a deliberate focus in my family, we discussed it. We pointed out to the children that if anything had happened to them, ChildLine was there for them, any time. I think in my mind I was thinking that if anything had happened to Lucy, I really meant if my ex-father had done anything to her, she could ring ChildLine. Now she had a way of finding help that I'd never had.

At the time I had very mixed feelings. I think I was petrified of her saying anything, I dreaded it. But in my heart I think I knew. And very, very soon after ChildLine was launched, at the beginning of November, Lucy came home from school on a Friday, came upstairs and said, 'Mum, Grandad has touched me.' And I turned to her and said, 'I believe you. Because he did that to me.' She said that she had told a teacher and the teacher said she must tell me. So she did. I held her. I said, 'I'm so sorry. It's not your fault, it's my fault.'

My immediate thought was to get straight into my car and run him down. I really meant to do it – I felt so horrified, so revolted, so enraged, and I suppose, so guilty. But John, my husband, stopped me. What would that achieve, except the family would lose me? There must be a better way of punishing him without destroying my family.

So instead I phoned my ex-father and said, 'You fucking bastard. You're not getting away with it this time. I'm telling the police.' 'You sound strong,' he said, almost as if he respected me for the first time. But then he put my ex-mother on and she started shouting at me. I can't remember exactly what she said, only that she accused me of making it all up, that I was mad. This is the woman who, when the hospital had discovered my first baby was brain-damaged and I was heart-broken, I rang, weeping. And her husband rang back and said, 'Do not keep ringing your mother and upsetting her.' They felt nothing for me at that terrible moment when I had just discovered the injury to my first baby. My pain meant nothing to them. My baby's pain meant nothing. If you can't feel that then, you can't ever feel. And they never felt anything for me.

So I went to the police and social services. They took statements from us. I admit I was a mess – I broke down, I was crying a hell of a lot. So my memories of that day are a bit hazy. But our police were great. They sent all the papers to where my ex-dad still lived, the area where he used to work with them himself. And then I heard nothing.

After two months, in January I rang the police station and the policeman I spoke to said, 'I thought your family would all have got together again over Christmas and things would be fine. Do you really want me to go round and see him?' I said I certainly do. So they did, and they rang me back and said, 'Well, he's not very happy.'

And in the end they told me they couldn't do anything, that my case was too old. And they said my daughter would not make a good witness, so they didn't proceed.

I rang my sister Carol. I told her he had abused me and my daughter. And Carol went right up in the air, shouting at me, saying I was mad. Then she put her husband on the phone. He said I was mad. And our relationship broke. The break lasted for years.

But nine years ago I got in touch with Carol again. This time she told me the truth. She said that she had tried to tell her own daughters the truth: that my ex-father had abused her. But her own daughters hadn't believed her. Terrible for her, but it actually started to make things better between us. We had so much in common. Except that she told me I looked like him and that made it difficult. So it all went wrong again. With our history, and our ex-parents setting us against each other, I suppose it's not surprising that our relationship has been so volatile, so up and down.

Then last year my sister wrote to me and said she had started the process of taking our ex-father to court. She has three granddaughters and he has access to them. She was frightened for their safety. It took a year to put the case together and get it to court. We had several hearings, then they dropped it. It had gone a year and a half, but because they had lost the papers relating to my daughter Lucy, even though she wasn't part of this new case, they couldn't proceed. The police department where he had worked had lost all the papers relating to the complaint I had made against him. There's not a trace of it and yet it was only in 1986.

I don't blame the current police working there. Some of his colleagues really wanted him to go down. One told me he was in the top five of the worst men he'd ever met. But all the same I thought it stank. After the case my ex-father got in touch with his sister saying he'd been acquitted (which he wasn't; it never went before a jury and all the charges are still on file). His sister was going to be a witness for me because she had seen the violence at home. She saw my ex-mother returning from the honeymoon beaten around the face, with black eyes. So he said to his sister, now it's goodbye. So she copied all the court documents and sent them around the family. None of them was surprised.

But the family is split now. My aunt, my ex-mother's sister, still stands by them. My godparents don't: my godfather was going to be a witness. He told me that when my ex-mother got pregnant with me, my ex-dad had tried to abort me with a knitting needle. They should never have had children.

After the court case my husband spat at my ex-dad and called him a bastard. And he looked round and smirked at us. He'd won. But at least we know that he had to go through that process. And they both had to move out of their dream home because the whole village knew; they were forced to move. But there are still children who are very vulnerable to him. It makes me feel ill to think about that.

Not my children, not any more. In 1986, after my daughter disclosed, I wrote another letter to my ex-parents. They had sent the family Christmas presents. I returned them. It was a short letter. I said I disowned them. I said we would never see them again. I said, 'We are returning these presents. You will have no contact with us any more and no access to my daughters.'

It was heaven after that.

My daughter Lucy, because she was able to talk about it almost as soon as it happened, has had no lasting problems. She doesn't carry a burden of guilt like mine; there are no lasting scars. But she has told me that she thinks if it hadn't been for the launch of ChildLine she would have been damaged long-term, had as much pain as me. I've had counselling now, I've got a good job and a good marriage, but I know carrying that secret from childhood to adulthood without being able to talk about it damages you permanently.

Oh my God, I don't know where we'd be without *Childwatch* and ChildLine. I think my mind would have gone if I hadn't been able to sort this out. It has taken the whole of ChildLine's life, all twenty-five years, for me to get through it and out the other side. But I've done it.

I became a nurse: I started out as an auxiliary, did that for a year, then began my nurse training and ended up as a nursing sister in the community. I loved it. In fact the work gave me an outlet – I could forget my own background, my own pain, and concentrate on helping other people. A lot of nurses are motivated that same way: they have suffered in the past and remember what it was like. So they like to give, to be needed.

With all the child protection training I've now had as a

community nurse, I would say there were classic signs that could have alerted people to what was happening to me at home. Like my dominant ex-father, us isolated children, the power thing, the way we children were utterly controlled by my ex-dad, never able to speak out. I know now that his own father was a brute, fathered many children by many women, had multiple affairs, beat his wife, my grandmother, emotionally abused her until she ended up in a mental hospital. He worked down the mines. I met my grandfather once. He was cold with a very harsh-looking face and a beautiful wife. She was a beauty once.

I've been married thirty-three years now. I have three daughters and three grandchildren, none of whom have ever, or will ever, see my ex-parents. They are safe. And it's all due to *Childwatch* – the fact that the programme put abuse on the agenda and the survey enabled me to put down my experiences, to help other children. I felt I had somebody who believed me when I sent in my questionnaire and got the letter back. That had a huge impact on me. I was empowered, even though I was still a babbling wreck.

And when I got Incest Crisis Line's strength around me, I felt I had at last started to deal with something that had been bubbling inside all those years. I could take all the steps necessary to protect myself and my family against those vile people. And I knew there was no going back. The launch of ChildLine liberated my daughter, prompted her to talk about her abuse, saved her and countless other children.

One question haunts me still. All my adult life I've had to take responsibility and make tough decisions, so I still don't get why I couldn't say sod off when I first escaped from my ex-parents. When I first got married I should have said now I've gone completely, do not follow me. But I suppose something in me still yearned for a proper family, for caring parents, even though I'd never had them. And I didn't think about the threat to my own children.

Why didn't I speak out as a child? Nobody asked the question. At school if somebody had asked me, I think I would have told them about it, but in those days, when nobody really thought about sexual abuse in so-called 'respectable' families, I would have been made out to be an insane liar. My ex-father said that, and it was true. A policeman's daughter? Who would have believed that?

I think he still has a hold on me because not having a father or a mother is such a terrible loss. When I see other people with their parents I feel that loss. I didn't have a white wedding because I couldn't bear that man to walk me down the aisle. But I've come to terms with it. Now I have no father and no mother, just an ex-father and an ex-mother. My ex-parents. That's all they are to me now, and all they ever will be.

WHEN our survey into child abuse began to come back to us in the post, we were amazed at the number of people who had spent long hours filling out the hefty, detailed questionnaires. More than three thousand *That's Life!* viewers had trusted us with the stories of their lives and as we read their completed questionnaires, the answers revealed so much new information. For instance, that child abuse can happen in any home, anywhere. There had been a popular theory that abuse only happened in very poor homes or was the result of drug abuse or drunkenness, but we discovered it can happen in the most opulent homes, the most respectable households. And that very few of the children dared ask for help, for fear of the consequences.

It was clear from what they told us that their memories were fresh and unhealed, as if the abuse had only happened yesterday. One woman said: 'My father abused me from when I was seven until I was twelve. I was afraid to tell anyone in case the courts took us away from my mother and tried to blame her. I kept my secret. I was screaming on the inside but nothing came out. I was being silenced by fear. I ache when I think that so many children are still suffering as I did. Please do create somewhere that victims can go and be believed, where you will not fear that the courts will hand the child back for more abuse and punishment for telling the secret.'

Often physical abuse, emotional abuse and neglect would be combined. As another survivor told us: 'He used to pull me round by my hair and hit me. When I wet the bed, he took it away and gave me an old coat to sleep on. I was locked in my bedroom every day – I could never understand why I couldn't play outside like other children. I used to feel nobody wanted me. At Christmas, when all the shops had Christmas trees in, I used to look in the windows and my only wish was that I could have a tree and a little doll, but my wish never came true. Instead I used to get a good hitting for being late home. My best time was when I was taken into care and the first things I saw were that Christmas tree and the doll I had seen the year before. At last somebody loved me.'

Even if these children dared ask for help, they were often rebuffed. As one woman said: 'I was abused and, dare I say, tortured for the best part of five years. I have not forgotten, I will never forget the pain, anguish and confusion linked to it. Most vivid is the fact that as a twelve-year-old no one would listen to what I was saying. They didn't want to hear. What you are telling they find as unbearable as the abuse itself.'

Even being in a big family was no protection, as a woman told us: 'The worst moments for me were the nights, four sisters sleeping in one room and all of us wondering who would have to suffer. I used to feel filled with guilt wishing that he wouldn't pick me.'

Another elderly woman wrote: 'It happened to me almost daily. I tried to take an overdose of tablets but it only made me sick. He used to frighten me by saying that my mother would be put in a workhouse and that I would be put in a home if anybody found out.'

Many reported that they had tried or seriously considered suicide. As one wrote: 'I still have nightmares. I have no friends, never had a boyfriend, and wish I had died at fifteen. Please help all the children who are suffering sexual abuse and cruelty, because they will always be left with the mental pain.'

So the pain stayed with them, but not always the memory. Some memories are so agonising, the only way to survive is to block them, as Laura did. Only to find that submerged pain has a way of emerging to frighten and damage, even years later.

CHAPTER FOUR

LAURA'S STORY

My memories of early childhood are patchy – I think I have suppressed the thoughts I found too painful to re-live. But over the years I've pieced things together and filled in some bewildering gaps.

I was born in Birmingham, in 1947. I suppose we were quite a glamorous family – water-skiing in Cannes in the summer, living in a beautiful big house in a leafy suburb. My parents both came from poor backgrounds but by the time I was born, they were on the up and up financially: middle class, comfortably off. My father was a very successful business man. As a little girl I really adored him. He was entertaining, he was powerful, not attractive exactly but charismatic. And my mum was film-star gorgeous, with dark hair that shone auburn in the sun, pale skin, high cheekbones, blue eyes – glamorous in a quietly understated way. Her clothes were glamorous, her hair was immaculate, she was always beautifully made up. Exquisite.

I was an elfin child, very blonde, quite adventurous. In

1949, when my mum was pregnant with my brother, I think she can't have been well because they took on a live-in house-keeper called Irene. Irene could not have been a greater contrast to my mother. She was Irish, short and thick-set, with coarse black hair. She was also overweight and very unattractive. But she and I became extremely close. In our neat, disciplined household, I was only allowed one soft toy on my bed – all the other toys were in a cupboard in Irene's bedroom. So I had to go there to get any toys to play with. Every afternoon she would encourage me to play with her in her room and she was very kind to me. We'd put my toy farm out and she'd help me move all the little animals around. She was very attentive and gave me lots of time. So we became good friends.

While she was encouraging me to trust her and rely on her for affection, Irene would talk to me about the baby my mother was expecting. She'd say it would probably be a baby boy and subtly began to imply that when he was born, he would become my parents' favourite child and from that moment I would be surplus to requirements. I was already missing my mother and worrying about losing the time I used to spend with her, so I think that disquieting thought took root and began to grow in me.

When my baby brother was born I was very torn. Upset because Irene's suggestions were alive in my mind, that he was the most important one in my parents' life, and indeed I saw my mother less and less when he was tiny. But at the same time I loved this little newcomer. I wasn't allowed much time or contact with him at first so I would turn to Irene when I was lonely and when I cried, she was very comforting. But all the time she was still sowing the bitter seeds, the idea that I had been supplanted, that I would never regain my place in my mother's heart.

Irene was very comfortable and comforting to cuddle up to and she would lift me onto her lap while she told me stories. Gradually these cuddles became more inappropriate and intimate. And then she told me something she said was a very important secret: she told me that there had been a mistake at the hospital when I was born, that I was actually her little girl and she had been desperately looking for me. She said that if my parents knew this, they would get rid of her and I'd never see her again. That frightened me because by now I was extremely dependent on her. She said then I would be put in a children's home where a lot worse things might happen to me. There was a children's home next door to our house, which was run by nuns, and even though I was still extremely young, just over two years old, somehow I knew that was what she meant, and those children didn't have mummies and daddies.

At the same time, while she was telling me this 'secret', the abuse was moving from pleasurable stroking to much more painful things. And when that happened, she would turn into someone else. Suddenly her face would change and she became ferocious, like a monster. I was very afraid of her, but at the same time, lonely as I was, I was also addicted to the nice Irene.

She had groomed me and now she imprisoned me. There wasn't anybody in my life to tell. There was the overriding fear that if I tried to tell my parents they would know then that I wasn't really their child and that I'd been doing something bad. I really felt they wouldn't know how to cope and that no one else could help. The abuse went on until I was nearly five, school age. Often it would happen at night when my parents went out and I would scream for them to stay at home with me. Then after she had finished with me I would cry for hours, watching for them from my window.

We had a nanny then, for my brother. One day the nanny took both of us children away for a few days at the seaside. When we came back, as I was going upstairs to my room, I saw that Irene's door was open and through it I could see the room was completely empty, everything was stripped bare. I said nothing, just went straight into my room and closed the door and there I froze, overwhelmed by two emotions. There was the huge relief that the abuse had stopped, but alongside it, the deep grief that this woman who said she loved me and that she was my 'real mum' had vanished without even saying goodbye. Nobody in the family ever mentioned her name again, and I didn't dare because I thought perhaps they knew. I thought that must be why she'd gone. And so at that point, when I was five years old, I buried my memories deep inside me. They were completely repressed and didn't resurface until I was thirty-nine.

My father died in 1964 and I'd been interested in boys before he passed away, but now I went right off the rails. I became promiscuous, had many boyfriends, and the endings of these relationships were always quite sudden and painful. I was always attracted to what they used to call 'bad boys', who wouldn't treat me well. I had an abortion when I was nineteen. But with all this, I had no memories whatsoever of the abuse. When I looked through photo albums, my mum would say that was your first nanny, or that was Irene chasing you around the flowerbed. But I had no memories. Not of the abuse, or anything else. I vaguely knew she'd been in our house for a time. And there were times during the sixties and seventies when I thought I might have been abused, which would have explained my behaviour. But though I went through all the men who'd had contact with me as a child, I knew none of them could have abused me. So I just assumed I must be wrong.

At five, I went to school. I was clever, I could already read. I remember having my face slapped because I was way ahead in my reading book. I constantly sought attention from the children and the teachers, and as a result I was quite unpopular, I think. From primary school, I went to a prestigious ballet school. The fuss my mother made when I passed the audition was fabulous and I enjoyed the glory, but I had no idea it meant that I would have to leave home. Maybe memories were stirred up in my mind of Irene's threats that I would be got rid of one day. And my fears were realised. I was very unhappy at school: being away from my familiar environment was very difficult, not really knowing anyone, a sense of dread of them all, and needing to please everyone, though I adored the four hours of dance a day.

When I was twelve it was clear that I was not going to be built for ballet but the school wanted me to stay on because I was good at modern dance and I had acting ability. But it was ballet or nothing for my mother, so I left. I thought that meant I could stay at home, but she had found another boarding school even further away, and without the dance lessons I loved. So I was even more unhappy but I hid it all the time behind being a joker and a leader. I still didn't know where all my distress and rebellion really came from.

The cleverness I had shown in my primary school never came to fruition. I failed three of my A levels although I got an A for English. So I went for a couple of temporary jobs, the last being as an assistant in a private primary school. I absolutely loved it. So from there I went to a teacher training college, which I also enjoyed. And then I met my first husband. He was good-looking and charismatic, and waiting for a divorce. We got married in 1972 when I was twenty-five. I left teaching, we moved to the country and I ran a book shop, but things started to go badly wrong right away. He would become violent when he'd had a drink, although he was always very apologetic once he sobered up. I can't pretend the faults were all on his side either, but to try and save the marriage we had a baby son in 1975. My husband was serially unfaithful, but in between the bouts of violence he was a charmer. He was all I thought I deserved. But when my son was two, I was so worried he would witness me being beaten up that I ended the marriage.

I had an even shorter second marriage five years later, which showed me that the failure of the first marriage wasn't only down to my partner. This time he wanted to leave, but I still didn't understand why. But when I was thirty-nine, I was up late one night and I put the TV on. I saw the second half of a film, *Sybil*. It was about a very large, plain, unattractive woman abusing a little girl. This was the first time the idea of an abusive woman had crossed my mind. As I watched, I started to shake. I rang a therapist, who said I was her seventeenth phone call that morning, after the film. And from then on I began to have flash-backs. I knew it had happened and I knew who it had been. My abuser wasn't a man: a woman had abused me. It was the kind of abuse you didn't hear about, only rarely hear of even today – the sexual abuse of a little girl, by a woman.

The memories came back, piece by piece, over a number of years. During that time I had therapy, which gradually helped me come to terms with my abuse. Then I went to see the nanny who had come to look after my brother and who was still a great family friend. I told her what I'd started to remember.

She told me that the day she arrived Irene had said to her, 'You're only here for the baby, leave Laura alone. She's my little girl.' And Irene had threatened her, that if she didn't leave me well alone, she would make sure she got the sack. Indeed, she was as good as her word. One day she went to my mother and said that on her evening off she had waited all night at the bus stop, watching the lit windows of our house. The only light on was in my father's room. That proved, she said, that my father and the nanny were having an affair. It was such utter nonsense that my mother sacked Irene immediately for trying to make trouble.

When I told her what Irene had done to me, the nanny was horrified, but also very compassionate and sympathetic. And she believed me at once. She hadn't liked Irene at all. We'd been taken away to the seaside when Irene left because my mother was afraid I'd make a scene, because they all thought I'd become much too attached to her.

As the memories returned I became extremely angry with both my parents for not having noticed anything. When I was suffering the abuse I had constant nightmares, and I was always having enemas because I was so constipated. Nowadays I hope those symptoms would have been picked up. Some years later, I wrote to my mother telling her about Irene's treatment of me and saying how having this terrible secret had been a barrier between us, preventing us from being close to each other, and that was why I wanted her to know now. She wrote back some weeks later and I was surprised because she didn't question the truth of what I'd told her at all. Instead she was devastated and blamed herself for being a bad mother, for allowing such terrible things to happen to me. She begged me never to speak about it with her. Only then did she think she'd be able to cope for the rest of her life.

That really confirmed it for me that I'd been right not to disclose the abuse while it was happening because if she couldn't cope with the thought now, she certainly wouldn't have been able to handle it then. Also there wouldn't have been anywhere for her to turn for help. And as Irene had threatened me, it would have made everything worse.

I used to watch *That's Life!* regularly and I vividly remember the first time they mentioned ChildLine. Watching it, I wept with relief. Until then I hadn't realised that I was carrying the pain of all the children like me, who were living with fear and abuse but hadn't been able to disclose or get any help. It felt as if a huge weight crushing my soul had been lifted.

Now I understand why, when my first marriage was deteriorating, I kept trying to love him more and give him a child to change him. I was desperate for his love, the way I had been desperate for love as a child. My doctor knew I was being beaten up by my husband even though my injuries were always where it wouldn't show, but he was out of his depth and didn't know what to do, so he just gave me prescriptions for Mogadon and Valium. I was being abused and not walking out, but at the time I couldn't see why. Now, with the knowledge of what really happened in my childhood, I can see that I was as addicted to my husband as I had been to Irene. And that I expected pain to be a part of love. I blamed myself for everything, including his affairs with other women. Because I wasn't getting all his attention I thought it must be my fault. Abused children always assume it must be their fault. That's what first made me suspect I might have been abused.

I can see the effects the abuse has had upon me throughout my life. When my son was coming up to two years old, the age when my abuse started, I would sit on the floor in a corner of the room and he would sit in another, and I would just cry and cry and cry. Sometimes I would suddenly lose my temper with him, but then I would immediately feel remorse, pick him up and love him. It must have been terribly confusing for him. But I never hit him. Now that he's an adult I have told him some of the reasons. I have said to him he can ask me any questions he wants.

I've suffered a good deal from depression, which I have been able to hide for a long time, and a deep clinical depression in my first marriage, when I was being beaten up. And it has since returned from time to time.

Above all, it's made me realise how vulnerable all children are. I have met people from the aristocracy who have been abused and others from council estates. Now I realise that when parents themselves are struggling to make their way as mine were, not able to give their children attention, those children are ripe for grooming. Because children will do anything for time and a kind word from an adult.

Things have changed for the better in the last twenty-five years. In my time there were no trained counsellors who knew about abuse. It would have been considered freakish that a woman could sexually abuse a child; it's unlikely I would have been believed. In the fifties the prevailing view was: let's sweep things under the carpet and pretend they never happened. Irene got a good reference from my mother and went to work in another comfortable home. There may be a lot of people out there who, like me, were abused by her.

I've come to a place where sometimes I can understand her. Now I have rediscovered about eighty per cent of the memories, I no longer feel the necessity to go back there and revisit them all. I've reached a good place, now I'm coming up to sixty-five. There have been periods when I wanted to find Irene – I hated her, I wanted to hunt her down and kill her. And there have also been periods when I wanted to know what had happened to her, what had warped her. She must have had a terrible childhood herself. And I think it was thoughtlessly insensitive of my mother to employ her in a beautiful house, working for a beautiful woman married to a wealthy man: Irene's jealousy must have been intense. So perhaps I was a way of getting revenge on the world and my mother; I gave her a sense of power. And perhaps I gave her the nearest thing to love she had ever known. So I understand a bit more.

Abuse creates a horrible chain that has stretched back to the dawn of time, but I think now, since the advent of ChildLine, with all the changes in attitude and other improvements in child protection we may come to a place where that hideous chain is finally broken. And breaking that chain will be the most crucial gift of love towards all children.

CHILDWATCH was broadcast on 30 October 1986 and on that night, ChildLine was born. I will never forget watching the immediate, immense impact on the telephone exchange on the floor above our office. Fifty thousand people, many of them children, were ringing ChildLine's number. Downstairs, an army of forty volunteers were answering as many calls as they could and children were already being helped.

But to get to that point, we had needed a little help from our friends. One of the most significant was BT, who agreed to meet me at their headquarters with their then chairman, Sir George Jefferson. I read to him a quotation from one of the women who had taken part in our survey into child abuse.

'I was never frightened of walking home alone in the dark,' she wrote, 'of being raped, or mugged. I knew what was waiting for me at home was infinitely worse than that.'

I told Sir George that the helpline we had opened after the *That's Life!* programme had proved, as I said to him, 'For the first time the telephone itself can become an instrument of child protection.' I talked to him about my own children's bedrooms – precious, personal and safe, places of refuge for them. But the survey revealed that for many children their bedroom was a torture chamber, the place where they waited in dread for the footsteps coming up the stairs towards them.

Sir George was clearly moved. 'How can we help?' he said. I asked for a phone number so simple that any child could remember it. He gave us their engineering test line: 0800 1111. I asked for premises for our counsellors. He gave us our first office, near St Paul's Cathedral, and when we outgrew that, premises in Islington. BT have supported our work ever since. Their staff are wholeheartedly behind us. For years, their operators have spoken to sobbing children who were unable to get through to ChildLine because all our lines were busy. They know only too well how crucial our work is and how vital it is that we have the resources to take every call.

There were individuals, too, who were invaluable to us right at the beginning. Sarah Caplin, the BBC producer of the *Childwatch* programme, became a creative and influential trustee of the fledgling charity, inventing the name, 'ChildLine'. I also met a wonderful, generous philanthropist, Ian Skipper – I became his most expensive friend because he agreed to underwrite our first year and became one of our trustees. Once we had the money, that meant we could appoint a chief executive – Paul Griffiths, who came to us from the NSPCC – and recruit half a dozen full-time paid staff. We also found forty or so volunteer counsellors, none of whom had ever counselled children on the telephone before. But then, nobody had.

Norman (now Lord) Fowler, the Secretary of State for Health and Social Security, agreed to meet me and when he heard our plans for ChildLine, gave us a grant of £25,000. So did the Variety Club – generous friends for many years.

The then Prime Minister, Mrs Thatcher, gave us a reception very soon after our launch in No. 10 and continued to support us throughout her time in government. On one visit she brought out a personal cheque – quietly, in a corridor of our London centre – from the recesses of her famous handbag. On another she told the assembled press and dignitaries, 'You may call this ChildLine, I call it a lifeline.' And when I met her recently, at a time when she was very frail, I thanked her for her support over the years. She looked intently at me with her famous blue eyes and said: 'Nothing is more important than protecting children from abuse. Nothing.'

And over the years a galaxy of stars has come out to help us. Wet Wet Wet gave us the proceeds from their first number one hit 'With A Little Help From My Friends', equally billed on the double A-side record with another cover, 'She's Leaving Home', recorded by Billy Bragg. It spent eleven weeks in the charts, four of them at number one, paying for ChildLine's first base in Scotland. Tom Jones and Dave

Stewart also made a cover version of another much-loved Beatles' song, 'All You Need Is Love', for ChildLine. Among the many celebrities who have generously supported us were George Michael (who gave us the royalties from 'Jesus to a Child'), Fiona Bruce, Anton du Beke, Charlie Dimmock, Wendi Peters, Anne Diamond, Gloria Hunniford, Lulu, John Hurt, John Cleese, Simon Cowell, Amanda Holden, Ant and Dec, Nicky Cox (editor and creater of the award-winning children's newspaper *First News*), our Patron, the Countess of Wessex, and many, many more. Cherie Booth chaired a conference for us about the law and invited Hillary Clinton to be our keynote speaker. Politicians, from John Major, Kenneth Clarke and David Mellor to Tony Blair, Jack Straw, Shaun Woodward and Gordon Brown, and the present Cabinet supported our work. All of them fully understood that ChildLine could become a lifeline for a child.

The most famous woman of our time was also one of our most empathetic supporters. Diana, Princess of Wales presented us with a personal donation soon after ChildLine opened. She gave a speech at our tenth anniversary celebration, signed a book which we auctioned and visited several of our bases, but what I remember most is the way she spoke to the children she met at ChildLine, children like Charlotte.

CHAPTER FIVE

CHARLOTTE'S STORY

W e never had much money when I was young but my parents both worked hard. My dad had been in the army, working as a groom for the Blues and Royals, and the family was posted to Germany when I was a baby. Then he left the army, came back to Britain and worked in a factory. Mum was a cleaner for a local company, a firm of caterers. She worked in their kitchen as the tea lady, very long hours, which meant she had to work in the evenings. I had two younger sisters and a younger brother. I always got on really well with my brother, but my middle sister and I were cat and dog all the way through. We get on much better now, but when we do have an argument she always says, 'It's all your fault, you wrecked our family.'

I never knew Dad's side of the family. I know they didn't go to the wedding because when Mum invited them, his mum said she didn't want to meet 'his woman'. I have no idea why. Mum was really close to her own mum, my nan. They saw each other each day, except when my parents were posted to Germany, and even then my nan would write to Mum every day.

Mum was brought up to be really religious. They were a farming family and they had to move all the time to follow the work from farm to farm. I think she had a very hard childhood – they all lived in a corrugated-iron air-raid shelter even after the war finished. She was one of seven children and it was only when someone from the welfare came round and saw her brothers had to sleep in a tin bath that they were given a council house.

So my nan was pleased when my mum married my dad, although he was short and fat. He had curly hair and a moustache – he wasn't exactly what you'd call a catch. Not a man you'd ever notice in a group or a crowd, not an ambitious man; he never even learned to drive. But my nan treated him like a son. Which explains, I suppose, why she was so hard on me when it all came out.

He wasn't a very fatherly person. I don't remember Dad ever being a big part of our family life: he would give us some loose change if we wanted it, but apart from that he was very quiet. We children rarely saw him. In the evenings he was either out down the pub with friends or upstairs in bed. He was always the softer of my two parents, never the disciplinarian. That was Mum. She was very strict, like a rod of iron.

I don't know how early the abuse started, it just seems always to have been a part of my life. Maybe Dad groomed me, I really don't remember. I do recall waking up in the middle of the night and he'd be in bed with me. I'd just try to pretend to be asleep. I shared a bedroom with my sisters, they had bunk beds – I don't know how they slept through. It happened every week, at least once a week. At first I thought it was normal – I thought it happened to all my friends. Then I realised it wasn't, and it didn't.

As I got older and I realised what was happening, even though I hated the abuse, I didn't hate Dad. I remember being very protective of him. When he was taken away, when he went to prison, I just remember being mortified that it had gone down that road. That wasn't what I wanted at all; I just thought they'd make him stop. Not that they'd wreck everyone's life, the way they did.

I remember saying to Dad once when he was doing it, and he made me have full sex with him, I said, 'What would you do if I told Mum?' He just said, 'Don't be stupid.'

Then, when I was twelve, we watched the launch of ChildLine on the telly, just Mum and me together. In the programme there was a woman sitting there knitting while her husband was abusing her daughter in the bedroom behind her. And that was the first time I ever saw abuse being talked about. It almost gave me permission to speak to Mum, in a way. So while we were watching, I said to her, 'What would you do if it was happening in this house?' And she said, 'Don't be stupid! It wouldn't happen here, it couldn't happen in my house.' Then the programme finished.

But it stayed in my mind. I remember a film in the programme, of a girl phoning ChildLine from a phone box, and the phone number 0800 1111. There was a special jingle that made it stick in my mind. And they also gave the address; it was free, you didn't need a stamp, Freepost 1111. But there was another film in the programme of an abused girl who sat in the corner silently staring at her mum and that really annoyed me. She was just sitting in the dark, portrayed as a victim, and completely helpless. I had a real issue with that. It was like she had tattooed on her head, 'victim'. Because I wasn't a victim, I wasn't helpless. And yet, in a way I was alone, in the dark, like her, because I couldn't tell anyone either.

Not long after that I had an awkward time with a girl at school who was very clued up about sex. She was the 'school bike' and she collared me because she said I had a hicky on my neck; she gave me real grief about it. I said, 'Don't be silly, no it's not.' Which was awkward because how else would I know about it? Anyway, she was like a dog with a bone. She got all her friends around to have a look. From then on, she called me that dark horse. It didn't seem that significant at the time, but now I think blimey, he left marks on me. But it was so routine, so much a part of my life, that I put up with it.

We had sex education at school. Mum was always quite open about sex, no subject was off limits. But she was very traditional in her morals; she told me you can't have sex before marriage and you can only have one partner for life. And I thought, well, it's too late then.

Then, when I was twelve, a couple of weeks before my thirteenth birthday, my period was so late I thought I was pregnant. It had to be Dad's. I'd never been with anyone else. I considered phoning ChildLine, but then I thought no. The idea of talking to someone about it frightened me too much – I was always better with pen and paper. So I wrote two letters. The first one I ripped up: I couldn't post it, I just couldn't face it, and I destroyed it because I didn't want anyone finding it. But then I decided I must write. There were two reasons. Firstly, the fear that I was pregnant by Dad, but also, my sister was getting older and she was becoming closer to Dad. He was getting her to sit on his lap and he'd give her sweets, so maybe I was scared he might start abusing her. Anyway, I wrote a second letter to ChildLine and I sent it to them.

Even when I'd written the second one I kept walking past the post box, backwards and forwards round the block with the envelope in my hand, really, really unsure whether I should send it or not. I was really scared. So I said to myself, just push it through the slot, do it, and I did. I remember the moment I posted it immediately regretting it, so even after I'd posted it, I thought I might wait until the postman arrived and ask for it back.

It was a detailed letter telling ChildLine exactly what had

happened and saying I was scared I was pregnant by Dad. It was a long letter. I gave my first name and my age; also the school name so they could contact me there. I knew something would happen. I was waiting a few days, it felt like ages. Every time someone came to my classroom I thought that would be it. And then, after what felt like years, ChildLine rang the school and asked to speak to me. They asked for me by name, Charlotte, and they told the school my age. But there were two Charlottes in my year, so the Head of Year had to make sure which one it was. He came to find me first and took me to his office; he said that ChildLine had phoned up and said there was a Charlotte who had written to say there were things going on at home and was it me?

I worried about the other Charlotte: I knew she'd deny it, she knew nothing about it. So I said yes. At that time I remember thinking this was the point of no return.

The rest of that meeting is a bit of a blur now – I know it went on the whole afternoon. The police came in, and I had to tell my story over and over again. Then I went off for a medical examination, where they confirmed that I wasn't pregnant, but I had to tell my story over again. There was medical evidence that I'd been torn. Then I had to give my statement to the local police station – that took forever because they had to write down every word. I was in a void. I didn't know where I was. I didn't know what was happening at home. I didn't know what was happening to Mum. I didn't want to talk to her, that was part of the fear.

I got home at gone midnight. Mrs E, my godmother, was there – she'd been due to take me out that evening for my thirteenth birthday, which was the next day. Mum was there, but I don't remember how she was. My father wasn't there.

It was horrible. There was a blackness, a dread over the whole house. But nobody talked to me, everything was very quiet and uncomfortable. There was just an awkward silence. I went straight up to bed.

The next day it really hit. The huge guilt of what have I done? I just cried and cried, sitting at the top of the stairs. Mum was not good: she didn't want to talk to me, didn't want to know me. I was in the complete depths of despair, I was absolutely alone; I'd never had that feeling before. The abuse had only affected me and my world, but this affected everyone and I just felt that they all hated me.

Turns out that they had arrested Dad around ten at night. At first when they arrested him he denied everything, so I was told I'd have to go to court and give evidence. People made it sound awful for me: I'd be grilled by barristers, who would make out that I was lying. Mum told me that. But my godmother's husband, Major E, Dad's commanding officer in the army, was still a friend of his. He and the Colonel went to see Dad every day; they had both been his commanding officers and he respected them. Every day they saw him, they told him 'No, no, no, you are not pleading "not guilty", you are not putting your daughter through this, you are not making her go to court.' Then he changed his plea.

I remember the court day. I went to my teacher's house, so that I could be out of the way. That was difficult; I still felt major guilt. Because Dad pleaded guilty he got a much lighter sentence. The teacher told me he got three years. But I didn't want him to go to prison at all because of me. I was devastated. I thought it was really unfair, not real – it shouldn't be happening. They should have just told him off, made him promise never to do it again but not sent him to prison. I walked straight out of the house and tried to run away, but the teacher followed me, brought me back and consoled me. He must have told me not to blame myself, that none of it was my fault. I suppose he did, but I didn't believe him.

I wouldn't talk to my social worker. So she said that if I didn't talk to her, I'd turn into an abuser and I'd sexually abuse other children. She said those who are abused, abuse others. I was angry: I couldn't believe she'd think that, let alone say it to me. If you've gone through that terrible experience there's no way you'd put someone else through it.

I will remember her saying that forever. Luckily she left. I had so many more social workers and therapists, each one kept asking 'How do you feel?' I'd sit at meetings quietly. I had no feelings. I was numb. Confused. Not angry. Not vengeful.

Sandy, who was a child psychologist, was much better. He was lovely, easy-going. We'd walk down to the vending machine and get coffee. He never pressurised me; he didn't mind the silences. The others, when we had the whole family group thing, I used to dread that any minute they'd come to me and try and make me talk about it; it was just hideous. I felt that they were out to get me, as if the whole world hated me. I can't stand being the centre of attention anyway and in these group therapy sessions it just felt as if they were grilling me. They wanted me to be angry; they kept trying to make me say I was angry. But I couldn't. Because I didn't feel angry, just totally guilty.

Dad was in the local prison to start off. We used to visit him regularly and go to more therapy sessions there. The first time was really difficult. I hadn't seen him for ages, though he used to write to me regularly. But he never said he was sorry for what he'd done. He did say in one letter I shouldn't feel guilty, that it wasn't my fault. We used to go as a family, in a room with all the prisoners meeting their families. And we also had private sessions, with therapists. I felt really awkward meeting Dad. I still loved him. And I still felt guilty.

And that guilt was made even worse by the rest of the family because of what had happened to them, the impact of it on our whole world. My brother and sisters used to tell me all the time that it was my fault, that I'd ruined their lives. Mum was totally lost at first because everything she'd relied on – our routine, our family life – had been destroyed. We'd lost Dad's income, though the army sorted out paying for our school uniforms, and we started having free school meals. The army gave Mum some money so she could buy shoes for us. My nan told me I was a home-wrecker. She was really nasty to me. 'Look what you've done to your mother,' she used to say. She was really cutting and it hurt me deeply. Even years later, when I was at college near her and I used to pop round at lunchtime, I remember her telling me that I shouldn't have written to ChildLine, it was all my fault. By then I honestly thought that bygones were bygones. I was so upset.

The teacher who had been my head of year stuck by me. He'd look out for me the whole time I was at school – he was a lovely man, very supportive. I took my GCSEs, then went on to a beauty therapy course. But I had to leave. They tried to teach us full body massage. The other girls couldn't wait but I couldn't stand the idea of it. I couldn't possibly strip off – I still can't.

So instead I went to college and got a BTEC in nursery nursing and worked all through. So I got my National Diploma and I was introduced to teaching. I had to do one day a week at the local school and I absolutely loved it. I decided to teach juniors, so I studied and got my Maths GCSE, worked part-time at the chippie and a one-stop convenience store. Then I went to university, got a degree in education and I've been a teacher for eleven years. I still love it.

But I still hate my body. I don't have full-length mirrors at home, only small ones that show my face. Nothing that shows my body. I hate buying clothes. I'm not comfortable with my body at all.

So I don't go to the doctors. And I won't have smear tests, I just can't do it. Not since the internal examination I had, the medical examination. Now every time they try and persuade me it's time to have a smear test I work myself up and put it off. It's the bane of my life. That's still a major, major issue.

I won't ever have a baby. No. If I ever felt maternal, I might adopt a baby, but I would never have my own. I couldn't bear the whole pregnancy, the examinations, the labour. It's not just the pain factor, it's all the people looking at you, all the examinations, no.

The first time I got married it was to Arthur. We had met when I was sixteen (he was eighteen at the time). We were together for twelve years. Then we got married but we divorced after three years. He wanted to start a family, so I thought it would be better for him to find someone else who did want babies. Now my partner Alex and I have been together five years. He doesn't want to have babies either, so that's fine.

I remember when Princess Diana came to ChildLine very soon after it all happened, and I was invited to meet her and give her a bouquet. I remember a teacher at school showing me how to curtsey, and I practised until I got it right, but when the moment came to give her the flowers, I forgot to curtsey. I was thirteen, it was soon after my birthday. I remember her hair, it was perfect.

The Princess looked at me and said, 'Are you glad you contacted ChildLine?' I'm sure everyone expected me to say yes, that I had been saved from being abused. But I was honest. I said, 'No, it was my job to suffer.'

I had to tell her the truth, that was how I felt. If I'd put up with it, suffered in silence, the family would have stayed together. As it is, Mum and I have had to rebuild our relationship. I have talked to my mum now that it's almost twenty-five years since it happened. I understand how she feels.

She told me: 'I loved your dad, he was my husband. I did my very best to be a good wife to him. That included having sex with him every night, that was what a good wife does. So why would he want you, Charlotte? Did I not give him what he wanted? Was that my fault, too?

'I had no idea what he was doing to you. I have no memory at all of him ever leaving my bed. But then I worked cleaning every evening; I got home from work at eleven at night, shattered, and then I had to be up again at half past five, minding children for a friend. Then I'd spend all day looking after the home and the family, then out at work all evening again. So I was working really hard.

'Also, I suppose I was naïve. I am religious, I'd had a very sheltered life, very old-fashioned. I believe in doing the right things, those vows I took when I got married, until death us do part, I believe in them. And no sex before marriage. I knew nothing about contraception until after you was born.

'Your dad didn't take much interest in the family. He was out a lot with friends, but he never came home drunk. Nobody in my family drinks, I don't drink either. He was out when the *Childwatch* programme came on. I remember a film of this woman sitting on a chair with the bedroom behind her. I remember you asking me that question, Charlotte, saying what would I do if that happened in our house? I suppose that was you trying to tell me, but it never occurred to me.

'You see, I was adamant that it couldn't happen to us, we were a good, strong family. I made sure we had a proper routine, that everything was properly organised. We lived a routine. I always had a dinner waiting for your dad when he came home and a pudding on the table for him dead on half past twelve. And the house was always clean, you children were always clothed. It was impossible that anything like that could happen in our home, it was outside my comprehension of what life was supposed to be like. But then life doesn't always work out like that.

'My whole life was blown away at four in the afternoon with a phone call from your headmaster. I couldn't really take it in; I was in a state of shock. Then the phone rang again and somebody told me you would be late home because you'd been taken somewhere or other. They didn't tell me where, or why, or what was happening to you. Then my sister-in-law came round, my brother's wife. She came in and I had to tell her; I was in tears. The conversation was a blur. Then he came in. I said straight out, "What the hell have you been doing?"

He said nothing – he just turned round and went out again. I don't know where. He came back at half past nine at night. The police came at ten and took him away.

'Then everything was like a whirlpool. You came back very late, with two women – a police officer, I think, and a social worker. And one of the women said to me, "You've got to choose between your husband and your children." Because if I had said I choose my husband, they were ready to get all the children out of their beds and take them away. So I said, "Of course my children always come first – they always have."

'But the way I was given that ultimatum, when I'd only just found out, and my husband had just been arrested and taken away an hour before. I didn't talk to you because I couldn't – I just couldn't take in what had happened.

'The next day they rang and said I had to come down to the police station and bring what he needed: a small case with underwear and so on. I'd never even been in a police station before. But I went, and I spoke to him, this man I'd been with for sixteen years, but they wouldn't let me talk to him alone. To ask him why he had been doing this.

'They never let me see the statement you made to the police. They kept saying, "If you knew what was in her statement..." and I kept saying, "Show me it, then," but they said they weren't allowed to. So I never really knew what had happened. I think it was my right to see it.

'All I could think was that I wasn't somehow satisfying him, that he needed to go to you because I wasn't good enough. The trouble is you assume that when you're married to a man, you never think for a moment that he's going to choose your daughter over you. And there you were, waiting in your bedroom for him, and there was he, like an insect, creeping out of my bed. They're sly, secretive, these child abusers – like insects coming out of a crevice in the wall.

'Then he was all over the front page. I've kept it. But he was not named in the paper and I only told one person. She was so shocked that I hadn't known what was going on, that it made me feel even more guilty. So I didn't tell anybody else. I can't help blaming myself. I must have missed something or done something wrong for my own daughter not to be able to come and tell me; also to miss the signs when you tried to tell me that time, that was unforgivable. For a mother to miss something that was almost spelt out to me. But I was so ignorant, I totally missed what was going on.

'A woman psychiatrist as good as told me it was my fault because I was such a strong, clear-headed good manager who knew how to work and organise and manage money, the home and family etc., so he thought of me as his mother. And you, Charlotte, as his wife. His own daughter.

'When he pleaded guilty, I went to the trial. His sentences were all concurrent: there were about eleven charges. He got four years. Looking at him standing in the dock was really strange, he wasn't the man I thought he was. He was like an intruder in our life. Then he went to prison and everything went all completely haywire. Money was a real problem: our income was terrible because it turns out he left me lots of debt that I had to pay off. I'm a very organised person so I had to pay off the £800 debt he left me, somehow. I felt that was my whole function.

'My mother, your grandmother, had very strong opinions and the trouble was she liked your dad. She couldn't believe it had really happened. That's why she was against you, Charlotte. She was old-fashioned. She doted on him, really. And he was a good bloke in some respects. If only I'd known about it, I could have stopped him. Though he wasn't a good, fatherly man.

'If there hadn't been two Charlottes in your year, I suppose you could have talked to ChildLine on the phone, instead of the school calling the police. And maybe they could have got you to tell me. I don't know what I would have done. They say they always work at the child's pace, so maybe you would have said you could tell your godmother. Maybe that would have been easier for you because you knew that it would just blow me away. And maybe we could have managed things so that he would stop what he was doing. Then you'd still have your dad, and I would still have my husband, and none of this horrible guilt – I don't know. As it was the whole thing was taken out of my hands.

'It came between us, Charlotte, that I know. I used to look at you and think, why didn't you tell me? I looked at you and thought you just dropped a nuclear bomb. And the hard thing is you can't talk to anybody. It would have been much easier if he'd died. Then you can go to the funeral, everyone will talk to you and they'll all support you. But as it was I felt so ashamed, so I couldn't tell anyone else.

'The visits to prison were strange. I don't know how you felt when you saw him again. I felt such a conflict, you can't just switch off love. But my children always come first, that's what I told the police and the social workers, and it's true. So I tried to divorce him, but when he came out of prison I couldn't find him. I was only able to divorce him in 2000, and then only because he found me; that was when he was with his new lady, who had children. He'd lied to her, of course. Otherwise she'd never have let him near them.

'And you and I get on alright now, Charlotte. But still the trouble with you is that even when you're with me and in company, it's as if you're behind a glass window. You just sit there, I never know your opinion: you're mute.'

When she told me all that, I understood how Mum feels. But I know she still doesn't really understand me and I infuriate her because I can't talk easily to her about my feelings. She calls me mute. Maybe I'm mute now because that's how Dad's left me. Maybe I had to keep that secret so long, I had to push my real feelings down so deep that now I can't let them out. I don't know.

When Dad came out of prison and went away, we had no

idea where he'd gone. Only when he asked my mum for the divorce and my sister traced him, did she find out that he was living with a woman with children. He'd told his girlfriend that he was sent to prison for burglary, but my sister enlightened her; said, no it wasn't, he was a dirty old man. So I hope that put paid to that relationship and her children were safe. I hope so.

Dad is dead now. My sister visited him twice before he died – she said he was really ill. I think she felt she'd sorted things because she'd spoken to his new girlfriend. She said that would make up for what he did to me. Maybe.

BY THE TIME Charlotte wrote her letter to ChildLine, the tiny new charity had begun to learn crucial lessons. In July 1987 our second chief executive, Valerie Howarth (now Baroness Howarth), joined us: an extraordinary woman who combined insight into children with tremendous skill as a manager. And she needed it. The huge numbers of anonymous children ringing for help (fifty thousand calls that first night, a level of demand that continued for many weeks) were unprecedented anywhere in the world, so ChildLine had to create a brand-new style of counselling and discover effective ways to support our volunteer counsellors. Julie C in chapter two described the stress of taking the calls. Not surprisingly, our full-time staff quickly burned out in the earliest days from the strain of listening to suffering children all day and every day, with no means of rescuing or protecting them, so they learned that volunteer counsellors were better placed to take the strain. Volunteers, after all, spend most of their lives in the outside world, where children are loved and protected, and only spend one shift per week in ChildLine. Even so, the staff had to support and debrief them after every shift, talking to them about their most painful calls so that they did not take the memories of those anonymous children away to haunt them when they left. Otherwise the work would become too painful and they would be forced, for their own sanity, to give up.

And I had learned crucial lessons. When *That's Life!* opened the helpline which had inspired me to think about creating ChildLine, I believed we must take action to prevent any abuse we discovered. If abused children were reluctant to tell us who and where they were, we should persuade them. When I was briefing the people we had recruited to answer the helpline, one of the social workers looked at me gravely. 'Esther,' she said, 'when children ring to say they are being abused, you feel horrified and want to rescue them straightaway. But remember, that is *your* crisis. You have only just learned about it. That child has been living with it for months, perhaps years. Distressed as you are, you must tread carefully. If you go in with hobnail boots, you may do more harm than good.' I was not convinced.

So when a little girl rang to say her father was sexually abusing her, the counsellor managed to persuade her to give them her name and address, and they contacted the police.

When I went into my office on the Monday after our programme, the social worker told me what had happened as a result. A policeman had turned up at the child's home and rang the doorbell. The front door was opened by the child's father, with his arm around her. When the policeman explained why he was there, the father smiled affectionately down at her. 'She's always up to something, this one,' he said. 'Tell the policeman it was just a joke and say you're sorry for wasting his time.' The child obeyed, the door shut and the policeman left. But if it had not been a joke – and all of us believed it had been a desperate, genuine call – the child was in graver danger now than ever. Because now the abuser knew she had disclosed once, and might disclose again, and would be more determined than ever to shut her mouth.

Lesson learned. So ChildLine has developed our 'trusted adult' route to protect children, one we still use. Unless a child's life is at imminent risk, we keep what they tell us confidential. We don't pass it on to police or social workers, if the child asks us not to. The most dangerous thing we can do is break a child's trust in us, so that they don't ring back any more. So instead, we use a different, more effective way to protect our children.

When children ring, we talk to them about their lives. Our aim in every conversation is to build children's confidence to the point when they can talk to someone they know, who they believe loves and cares about them. And most of them do, with our support. The tragedy is that some children are so utterly alone, that, like Jo in chapter one, they don't believe anyone cares enough to stop the abuse. For them, ChildLine becomes their only friend and supporter. But many children are protected by mothers, aunts, friends' parents, caring neighbours or grandmothers, like Mary.

Mary was a cleaning lady who worked in one of our bases. On one visit I made there, she beckoned me aside. She told me that her granddaughter Deirdre had rung ChildLine because her parents were neglecting her and were violent to each other, and to her. The home was chaotic. Deirdre had begun to miss school because she was so ashamed. Unknown to the rest of the family, her parents were both drug and alcohol addicts.

Deirdre told ChildLine's counsellor that she believed her grandmother might help her. Mary described to me her horror when a counsellor contacted her, at the child's request. But she responded well and her granddaughter told her everything. 'She's living with me now, Esther, and doing very well. I don't think she would be with us any more if she hadn't rung ChildLine.'

Another lesson I learned very early on was that in spite of the generally held belief that they must be aware, very often wives and mothers had absolutely no knowledge of the abuse going on in their own homes.

Soon after we had launched ChildLine, I received a letter from Julie. She told me that she had been sexually abused by her stepfather for eleven years from the age of six, had been made pregnant by him, lost her baby and had then been persuaded by a friend to ring ChildLine. Her letter said:

'I am writing to thank you for having set up ChildLine. I know you must be busy helping other children and haven't really got time for my letter so I'll try and make it short.'

She told me that she had rung ChildLine several times and written to them once. She went on:

'Although I didn't say much, the fact that someone cared

was enough to make me realise something had to be done. It was about three months later that I finally told my mum. She believed me and when she asked my stepdad, he admitted it and said he was sorry and it would never happen again, and it hasn't yet. We still live together but although things seem to be going all right, I'm still an unhappy person. I have been out with a few boys and managed to sleep with one but it was awful and I don't want to go through with it ever again.

'So unless I find a man who can go the rest of his life without sex, which I know I never will, I'm going to be lonely for the rest of my life. I've always been alone and so I suppose I should be used to it by now, but I'm not. I think it's because I love kids and I'll probably never have my own.

'I know you're thinking I'll find someone to love but I won't. If I meet a boy and he wants to take me out again, I feel as though I've got to give him something and I've nothing left to give. I don't feel as though I deserve anyone who'll love me. I suppose happiness is an emotion I will never know – I think I was born to be hurt.

'It doesn't matter what I try and do, I still feel the same. I guess he's totally ruined my life: he's taken away my pride, my dignity, self-respect, self-confidence and I still feel dirty and humiliated. I'm just one of the unlucky ones. Some people have it all, others have nothing, but that's life.

'I probably sound ungrateful to you, but that's the way I feel. At least I'm not being raped three or four times a week in my own home anymore and when I think of that, it always puts a smile on my face and that smile is keeping me alive.

'Thanks for taking the time and trouble to read this and I hope a lot of young children use your ChildLine because that kind, caring voice on the other end of the line is all it takes.

'Thanks for everything.

'All my love.'

When I received it, with Julie's permission, I read her letter out on our programme, *That's Life!* Among the viewers were Wet Wet Wet and the morning after the programme broadcast, their press team came into our office. Tommy, their drummer, had been so moved by Julie's letter that he had come up with an idea. The band offered to make a single of their version of 'With A Little Help From My Friends', together with Billy Bragg's version of 'She's Leaving Home' as a double A-side, all their royalties to go to ChildLine. As I have said, the record went straight to number one and stayed at the top of the charts for four weeks, paying for our ChildLine base in Scotland.

Soon after it was released I received another letter, which I have also treasured ever since. It says:

'Dear Esther, I have been meaning to write to you for some time now, thanking you from the bottom of my heart. Why, you may ask?

'My two sons, aged nine and eleven, were victims of serious sexual abuse by a neighbour. To cut a long story short, my eleven-year-old twice tried to kill himself, cutting his wrists and taking an overdose. I knew something was wrong, but didn't know what. We sought doctors, psychiatrists, anyone I thought might help.

'Then things got slightly better. One night in July 1991, my sons came to me and told me everything. I immediately phoned the police and this man was arrested. He admitted everything and was charged with twenty charges of gross indecency and buggery. He is to be sentenced on 22 February.

'But the thing is from January, after the first suicide attempt, Steven, the eleven-year-old, had been phoning ChildLine. It took a while but they persuaded him not to attempt suicide and to try and tell us as soon as possible. I still encourage Steven to talk to ChildLine if he can't tell us something or if he can't talk to his social worker. I am convinced if Steven and John hadn't contacted ChildLine, I would only have one son today. God bless you in all your efforts. My husband lost his job, we can't contribute at the moment to your fund but we will be buying the record, along with most of our family and friends. Thanks again for setting up this very essential helpline, children need it. Yours sincerely...'

I have met that brave mother and when I met Steven, I hugged him. He told me he must have rung ChildLine fifty times before he mustered up the courage to tell his mother what the neighbour had done to him. I took him to ChildLine and he met our counsellors there. It's not often they have the opportunity of meeting the children whose lives they save, day in, day out. It was a very moving meeting.

I have often wondered how those children's lives – Julie, John and Steven – turned out in the end and how far they were able to recover from the terrible damage inflicted upon them.

If only children ring us in time, ChildLine can help them and some survive triumphantly. Like Maria.

CHAPTER SIX

MARIA'S STORY

I was born homeless. My father Charles and my mother Sheila were twenty and nineteen in 1970, when I was born. Dad had met my mum in a phone box in Brighton. Mum was in the phone box. She had long blonde hair. He must have fancied her and realised she was having difficulty making a phone call, so he opened the door and showed her how to get a free phone call. That's how they started. He had black hair, blue eyes, eyebrows that met in the middle. My mother says he was a looker and he did have women throw themselves at him. He was only back from America a few months: they'd deported him as an undesirable alien. Allegedly he'd stolen a car and driven it over state lines.

Mum wasn't pregnant when they married, but soon after wards she was. Their first baby was stillborn. I was their second and on my birth certificate it says Dad was an electrician, but I wouldn't have hired him. He once wired our house up and set it on fire. The kitchen was pretty well unusable after that, but we couldn't complain to the council because they would have made us pay for the damage.

His father, my grandad, was an electrician too, and a horse trainer. Their family were Italian circus folk – they worked for a variety of circuses, there were quite a few around at that time. My grandmother was a trapeze artist. I've seen her in an old newsreel online. She was beautiful. She smoked for England, but even when she was in her seventies she could kick her legs as high as the door frame and do the splits. She died at seventy-two. All her children spoke to her disrespectfully, extremely disrespectfully. I don't know anything about the way my grandparents brought up their kids, except that I heard that my aunt, my dad's sister, was done for child abuse in America. I'm told one of my cousins was tied to a chair and beaten.

Mum's family were so different. Robert, my mother's dad, was a lovely man. He died on the eve of the Millennium and that broke my heart. That man had the kindest bones any man could ever have. His wife, Mary, was Spanish. Mamma Nanny, my great grandmother, couldn't read or write, but she was hilarious. She couldn't speak English, but she used to read comics and sit there smiling at us. She would give us fondant fancies – gorgeous, just pure sugar. And my mum's a lovely lady, too. She's sixty-two this year. But my early memories of her were not good at all. I thought she knew what was happening and approved of it. Now I know she didn't know a thing, until I told her.

I was in nappies when my father started to abuse me. He used to tuck us up in bed at night and he would spend a little bit longer every time. I would turn round and pretend not to be there. You get numb: in my head I wasn't there, I was in another place so I couldn't see anything, I couldn't sense anything. I never told anyone what he did. He used to threaten to kill the cat if I did, or the dog; he said no one will believe you anyway. Once at home he suddenly came out with, 'If you ever tell anyone what I do to you, I'll kill you and cut you up in little pieces and no one will ever find you.'

And I believed it. God, he was such a horrible bloke, you know, capable of anything. My brother Dave is three years younger than me and my father physically abused him. I remember once Dave dropped a bottle of ketchup on the floor and it smashed. He was only five. My father picked him up by the neck, shouted at him 'Get Out!' and threw him across the kitchen. He was badly hurt. We got taken to hospital several times, my brother and me. Once it was because Dave was concussed. Another time Dad stabbed me with a fountain pen when I leaned over him while he was doing a crossword and that left an indelible scar. He was a right bastard, I can tell you.

Dad had loads of different jobs, mostly dodgy. He organised a van once a week to sell broken biscuits he'd stolen from the factory. When he worked for a big bakery he used to overcharge the corner shops and pocket the difference. Always dodgy.

He did drugs, I think it was acid. He'd smoke marijuana. And he was violent. He beat up on my mother. There was one episode I specially remember. I was five years old, my brother was two. I can see my father now, dragging my mother by her long blonde hair through two rooms. Then he kicked her in the chin and banged her head over and over again on the kitchen floor. By this time she was unconscious. She is a diabetic and he thought she was hypo. My brother and I were screaming: we wanted to protect her, to stop him, but we were so young we didn't know what to do. We were frozen, we didn't run; it was as if we were paralysed with fear and confusion. When Dad realised she was unconscious, there was a packet of sugar on the table and he poured it in some milk and tried to feed it to her. He didn't realise she was out of it because he had concussed her, he thought she was in a diabetic coma.

The row was because she had just found out he was having an affair with her best friend. He had even an affair with our babysitter, having sex in the marital bed. I walked in and saw them. I once worked out he'd had affairs with twelve women; I'll bet there were even more.

And all the time he was sexually abusing me. When I was five I remember hiding in the wardrobe when he was coming into the bedroom to tuck us in at night. I used to try and hide behind the door. I would pray, 'Please let Mum come in and tuck us in.' Because by now he was handling me. There was no penetration until I was seven. Then he raped me.

It happened in our house in Gloucester. Fred West lived near us, the man who killed and raped so many kids. They knew each other, Fred and my dad. Dad had taken disgusting photos of me, really disgusting ones – I believe he got them developed by a friend. I imagine they're in paedophile-land now, being exchanged. I was naked, seven years old. It was very painful so I escaped in my head, I got out of myself. I went numb, I didn't exist, at that point I was dead.

It happened in my bedroom. Mum was downstairs: she must have thought he was a good dad, taking care of his children. I thought of calling out to her, but it sticks in your throat. Fear does some strange things to you: it freezes you. I used to wet the bed a lot when he came in. I would defecate everywhere because sometimes the smell made him stay away. Sometimes.

Dad used to get his pornography from Fred West; he used to take us there in the car. He had a huge collection of porn that he kept in a box under the sofa. We had to wait in the car, or go into West's house in Cromwell Street. They've pulled it down now, now they've found the bodies under the floor. Now everyone knows the terrible things Fred and Rosemary West did.

I knew them both. I remember Fred West standing in that kitchen, pouring Corona into a glass. He smelt of BO. He had massive huge side-burns and green teeth, and he had a broad Gloucester accent. He hadn't washed for years. I was very frightened of him because of what my father was doing to me.

I was frightened of all men. When I saw on television what the police had found in that house, I was terrified. Then I had a breakdown, one of many. I had a psychiatric nurse – I was seeing her maybe once a week – so I talked to her about Fred West and I told her how like my dad he was.

It makes me horrified when I think how close I got to the Wests. When I was an adult and working on the local paper, Fred West used to ring classified ads. I'd recognise his gruff Gloucester voice. He'd say, 'Put the ad in the paper, room to rent.' At one time I thought of renting it myself because it was cheap and so close, but because they were so awful on the phone, I didn't, thank God. Nobody was safe in that house.

I got to know Rosemary West quite well, too. She was arrogant, she was foul-mouthed – she was a dirty cow. Awful. She had four children hanging around her. I thought she was looking after them, I didn't realise they were hers. Anne Marie, her daughter, told me that Rose had sex with black men, lots of them, when she was a prostitute. Anne Marie was always unhappy. Their son Stephen West always smelt of wee.

When I was seven I ran away from Fred West. It happened one day in July, when Dad was somewhere upstairs in the house. Heaven only knows what he was doing, so I was alone with Fred. He was talking to me, when there was a wave of fear that came up from my chest. I don't know what he was saying to me, I just remember that panic breaking over me, so I ran outside to the car. I found my brother Dave there and waited for Dad. I remember my father came out rather rushed, harassed, and he shouted at us to get in the car and we drove away.

Not that I was safe at home. Sometimes Dad's sexual abuse would happen every night for a week. Other times it wouldn't happen for a month. It never happened at Christmas. Mum always made Christmas good. One year she was in hospital with her diabetes, but she signed herself out for Christmas Eve and went out, bought us a tree, bought presents, wrapped them and got the food; she made Christmas.

But I have no happy memories of being with father. None. I hate him. I like to hate him. If I gave him any compassion now it would let him back into my life. He's in Brighton now. He is regarded as being in the highest risk category of sex abuser. If he ever came after me, I would kill him, if it took my last breath. I wouldn't let him do it again to me. Or to anyone else.

He brought me up by saying, 'You're shit. You're thick and you're bloody stupid. How can you be my kid, come from my loins?' And I thought he must be right. All the time I was going to school, I was smelly, I was withdrawn. My teacher pointed out something was wrong to my mother, but she didn't click. When I was eight my mum was called up to school – by this time he was raping me big time. My dad said, 'You take her, she's your kid.' So she did, but still I didn't dare tell them what was happening. Not that they asked.

My secondary school was good, though. They taught me a lot and when I was there, I didn't feel like the 'shit' Dad said I was. I was very good at sport: I adored hockey and played for Gloucester; I won loads of certificates for running. And I loved drawing pictures and reading. I was the comic at school, that was my way of dealing with it.

But all the time my father tried to control me, to silence me. He was always threatening to kill me, to stab me, to take my pets away. He said, 'I'll kill Buster the dog and Mush the cat, and if you tell anyone, they'll take you into care. You're a lying little shit. You disgust me.' So I knew I could never tell anyone.

One day when I was eight my friend at school said, 'Have you seen the dead dog at the gates?' So I went over to the fence to look and it was our dog Buster. So that made me believe Dad's threats, it compounded the idea he'd pounded into me, that he could do anything. In fact Buster had been run over.

When my friends came home, they never came into the house because they knew my father was weird. He abused one of my friends. I can see it now. I thought poor cow, because when I walked in, he had Katie sat on his lap on the rocking chair and he was messing with her. When he saw me, he threw her off. She never talked to me about it. But another friend said she didn't want to go in my house. I remember him putting his hand on one of my friends' shoulder. She flinched away at once and said she had to go.

When I was eleven I used to think 'Would I get married? Could I get married?' Because I felt so unclean, so dirty that I thought nobody would want me. He used to rape me vaginally, and bugger me, it was a power thing. I hate Thorpe Park because once when my father raped me, the next day he took me to Thorpe Park. A boy patted me on the bum and my father turned round and shouted at him to stop. As if I was his property. And yet my father was there with a girlfriend of his. I thought she knew, I thought everybody knew, but she could see I felt sick and she said, 'Are you alright?', very concerned. I hate Thorpe Park, I haven't been back since.

Around that time my parents separated. I felt great. Outside I'm pretending to be sad. Mum said, 'I'm so sorry, children.' I said, 'It's alright, Mum.' Inside I'm shouting 'Yes!' By this time I was developing an interest in boys. I remember Graham, he was lovely, but we didn't kiss or even hold hands. He said nice things to me, said he liked my new haircut. I never associated having a boyfriend with what my dad was doing to me.

I didn't even know it was rape until I read the word in a Shakespeare play when I was fourteen. I didn't understand it, so I thought I'd better look it up. I found a thesaurus, I saw 'buggery' and the definition, and I thought, oh my God that's what's happened to me. I saw the other words and I realised for the first time that what was happening to me had words, so maybe it was happening to other people. It wasn't just me, it wasn't that I was the only one, that I was weird.

After Dad left, my mother met another man. Within a week of her new boyfriend moving in, he punched me. Mum did nothing. That really pisses me off; it underlines how little she really cares about me. It's always been like that. I know now she has left everything to her grandson in her will. Yes, that's her decision. I just wish she had left me something, just a keepsake. But she hasn't. She says 'You'll be alright, Maria.' Yes, I'll be alright: I've had to be. I took myself to the police station, all by myself. She didn't want me to go.

When I was fifteen, sixteen, I rang ChildLine. I still thought I was shit, like Dad said. I was a mess. I had long brown hair, I was unkempt; I never took any pride in my appearance. I only had my uniform to wear. My mother would only buy me clothes on my birthday. I remember once she bought me a pair of white trousers and a green shirt – I wore them forever – and a fluorescent green belt. It looked really cool but then you washed it a few times and it faded and didn't look cool then.

I didn't fit in because I was living on a council estate. I had some friends, but of course I never told them. I told nobody, he frightened me too much. I thought he'd kill me. I hated him so much it made me furious inside. I think other girls at school were frightened of me because I had a temper.

My mum knew we had a bad relationship, Dad and me, but even after they parted, she used to make me visit him. When I was with him I felt weird, I felt like a freak. I wanted to hit him because he'd hurt me so much, physically and emotionally; I had this intense hatred that was eating me up. And yet I had to pretend to like seeing him. Living up to what other people expected of me.

I hated him more and more. He didn't know or care. Once my brother and I had gone up on the coach to see him. My brother had hit me on the breast for no reason and it really hurt. He laughed and my father laughed too. I hit my brother back. Then my father sat down next to me, his face close to mine, and he said to me: 'You're evil, you are.' I just stared at him, saying nothing, but I believe he saw at that moment how much I hated him and he flinched away. He was frightened and for the first time, that gave me power.

Which may be why in the end I rang ChildLine. It was a struggle for me. I couldn't bring myself to tell anyone until I had knocked down the wall he'd built first, telling me over and over again that no one would ever believe me. And him threatening me that he'd know if I ever did speak. But I saw Esther on TV saying that you can phone in safety and that your number wouldn't be recorded anywhere. So I rang.

The phone number had been on the programme I had watched with my dad. He said, 'It's disgusting what some people do to their kids.' I said nothing – I was a kid, you never answered my dad. When I saw the ChildLine number I was so pleased. No, pleased isn't the word, excited isn't the word either: it meant I had some place to go. I could speak to some-one and nobody would know. Once on the school notice-board somebody put up the ChildLine number, I thought, too bloody late to stop what he's done to me, mate.

But still, I needed to talk to somebody, so I rang one day when I was at school. When I heard the number ring the first time, I hung up straightaway. Then the next time I'd get the engaged tone. And the next. I would sigh with relief when I didn't get through. But then I'd try again. And again. But each time I'd ring off before they answered. When they finally answered the first time, I didn't say a word.

I'd got used to hearing it just ring and ring and ring. But one day somebody picked up and said, 'Hello, you're through to ChildLine.' The tears come even now when I remember that, still. At the time I just stood there. Everything blocked my throat, as if someone had punched me in the throat. I couldn't say the words, I couldn't speak. I rang them four or five times before I managed to speak. My first word was 'Hello'. When somebody said, 'Hello, it's OK, you can talk to me.' I said my dad had raped me. They said nothing. I cried. I bawled.

I asked the question he'd put in my head all this time, all

these years. 'Do you believe me?' They didn't say, 'No, you're a dirty lying bastard.' He'd told me nobody would believe me, they'd say I was a liar – he'd screw with your head, say things continually until you broke down. But ChildLine said, 'Yes.'

It gave me a good feeling inside. I was able to breathe out. I was breaking down the brick walls he had put inside my head. So each time I told them a bit more. I told them about the rape and the sodomy, and the punch on the jaw and the punch in the stomach.

I just wish ChildLine had come a bit earlier. After that first time when I spoke to them, I rang ChildLine two or three times a week. I didn't always get through. When I rang them, I spoke to men sometimes and women. Each time someone different. They did ask me if I wanted a regular counsellor to talk to face to face, but I didn't: I just wanted to talk to them.

One of the ChildLine counsellors gave me the details of a survivors' group. There were twelve women there, all like me – every colour, every age, every shape. There were rich women, beautifully groomed women. I was a Pikey from a council estate. They all helped me. I sat there for two hours before I could join in. It started at ten, finished at two. I said, 'Did it hurt when you first had sex with somebody else?' They all said yes. It turned out I had vaginismus, but these ladies were able to tell me to relax, it will happen when it will happen. And it did, with someone I was with for twelve years.

ChildLine made such a difference. It was so powerful to talk to someone, not know them, not to see them, not to have them see me – you could just shut your eyes and speak, it was beautiful. And when I did ask a question, I got a good answer. There was no judgement. For instance, I said, 'Should I tell my aunt Madge?' They didn't just say yes or no. They said, 'Do you think she would want to know?' I said yes. So they said, 'Well, then you should.' And I did.

I rang her at two o'clock in the morning reversing the charges after I'd spoken to ChildLine. She was the first person in my family I told and I swore her to secrecy. Madge couldn't stand my dad – my mum went off on her for her attitude to him – but still my aunt said nothing.

I talked to ChildLine about whether I should tell my mum. By then I'd left home: I was eighteen, it was two months after I'd told Madge. I explained that I couldn't find the words to tell my mum, but I said I would try. So I went to see her and sat there on the sofa, still working out what to do, still screwed up in my head, nothing was in order. But then my father phoned the house. When I realised it was him, I made a face, looked disgusted. Mum said, 'Have you had an argument?' I shook my head, I couldn't speak. Then she asked, 'Has he hit you?' But I still couldn't tell her. In the end she said: 'Has he touched you?' I nodded. She said, 'Oh my God, *when*?' I just stretched out my arms and said: 'All my life.'

Then we talked and talked and talked for hours – until two, three in the morning – and she realised all those strange times, when she had gone up to school to talk about what was wrong with me, all the time it was him to blame, not her. After I told her, I walked back home to where I was staying. And that walk was good; that was when I realised that she was shocked. She believed me, she really hadn't known.

Then, when I was still eighteen, I confronted my father. I was in the pub where I was working. I rang him up and asked him to come down from London. He came down with my brother. He left my brother in the van, because he knew what I was going to say. I took him out into the garden. I said: 'I hate you, you're scum. I can't have sex with my boyfriend because of what you've done to me. I don't ever want to see you again. To me you're dead.' He just sat there, shaking his head. Then he got back into the van and drove away. My brother said: 'I'd been hoping for a drink.' He had known what was happening; he witnessed it.

Without ChildLine I'd be six foot under and nobody would realise why. When I was sixteen I was terrified Dad had given me an STD. That was the first time I was able to go to a doctor. ChildLine had told me I was old enough so the doctor wouldn't tell anyone else. He gave me the clap test, the AIDS test, and while I was waiting for the results I tried to slit my wrists. But I couldn't: I shaved them instead! I didn't tell anyone.

ChildLine didn't try to control me, they didn't say do this, do that. It was my idea to go to the police. I had asked them when I first started to ring them, can I prosecute? But it wasn't important at that time. It took me two years to decide. I had depression, I had very little happiness in my life; I had to stop it destroying me. I had two options: I had to kill him or I had to make him spend a long time in prison.

I'd been off work with the depression and I found a video: it was the film *Buster* about the Great Train Robbers. I listened to the song at the end, 'Going Loco Down In Acapulco', I was singing along. Then the screen went all snowy and I saw what I'd taped over, which was a documentary about the Moors Murders: it said Ian Brady and Myra Hindley would spend the rest of their lives in prison. That decided me, to make my dad go to prison for the rest of his life.

By now I was in my early twenties. I was under psychiatric care, depressed, trying to come to terms with it all. The news was full of the Fred West case at that time. I saw Heather West on the TV. I knew her, she was the same age as me; I used to think how pretty she was. I mentioned to my nurse that I'd like to prosecute my dad. She said, 'Would you like me to find out who to contact?' She told me the name of the police officer, Miriam, and the phone number – I remember it still. I made an appointment.

I told my boyfriend, but he wouldn't come with me. I've never felt more alone; no one I asked would support me. That hurt me so much. I went to my mother and told her I was going to prosecute. She begged me not to do it, she screamed, she banged the floor. 'Think of Dave, think of your brother,' she said. 'I'm doing it for me,' I told her. People thought I was mental, now I wanted them to believe me. I think she was worried about our name getting in the paper.

When I told my brother he cried and said he didn't want me to do it. Then he said I had to do what I had to do. I was twenty-five when I went to the police. I made the statement in a room about five by twelve foot, with one brown wooden door with a glass pane with metal in it. The walls were yellow and chipped, the table was brown, the ashtray was black. Miriam, the police officer taking my statement, reminded me of Laura Ashley – beautiful clothes, her dress was long and flowery, blue and violet. She had a bobbed hairdo, the room was dark. That day I smoked eighty cigarettes. Poor Miriam.

She asked me very difficult questions, to pick three or four episodes: the dates, the places. She took my details. Then I told her how to get hold of my mum and I walked out of that station. I felt as if a big shadow had been sucked out of me. Outside was a tree, a lovely tree. It was like a big oak, big, green, healing, beautiful. The courthouse was opposite it and I thought, that's where the bastard is going. It was liberating. I got into my car. There was this song I was listening to, 'Promised You A Miracle', with the windows wide open. Next day I went into work and told them everything. The people I worked with were protective of me, they kept it to themselves. Even when the case hit the court, they didn't say anything.

So now I was gearing up for the trial. I knew it was going to be tough, reliving all that pain, talking about the things he did to me, being cross-examined, all in open court. I decided I didn't care: he was going to spend the rest of his life in prison.

They issued an arrest warrant: they traced him because I knew from my brother where he was working. And I gave the police the name of a pub he used to go to. I was told that the police went into the pub and said, 'Is Charlie here?' His friends pushed him under the pool table to hide him, so the police didn't find him. When I heard that I was so angry.

I rang the company he worked for and told them everything. They believed me. I heard later my father got beaten
up there. Miriam arrested him there and brought him back to
Gloucester. He denied everything. I had a sleepless night but
in the morning Miriam rang and said: 'He's admitted it.' He
not only admitted to the two incidents I'd told them about, he
told them about another one: when he'd raped me in the back
of a car, when I was wearing my mum's red coat.

Then Dad got properly lawyered up. He was charged with
two specimen counts of gross indecency and two specimen
counts of lewd and libidinous conduct, and one rape, when I
was seven. All that should have got him a minimum of fourteen years. His lawyer was the same one who represented
Fred and Rosemary West. My father copped a plea. He admitted everything except the rape (he was advised to because
that meant he'd get a much lighter sentence). The rape had
been the most serious charge.

So he pleaded guilty, which meant they didn't need me to
give evidence. All the same I went to the trial, of course: I
wanted to have my day in court. I really wanted to tell the
jury everything he'd done over the years. If they heard it from
my mouth, even if there had been the most evil people in the
jury, I knew I'd get a guilty verdict. But I couldn't. Sitting
silently there in court, watching, like everyone had warned
me, it was hard. By now my father was forty-five, living in
bedsit-land. A total loser. I looked at him in the dock. He had
a broken leg. He was balding. He looked pervy. No friends
or family were there, except my brother, Dave. He was very
much for him. When I asked him why, he said he needed
my father. But Dave didn't blame me, he just tried to sit on
the fence; I resented that. During the trial I just wanted it
over. When I got the conviction it was *Yes!* Now nobody can
disbelieve me.

Pleading guilty, my father thought he'd get let out, but the
judge said no, I'm sentencing you now. He was sentenced to

a total of twenty-one and a half years, but it was all concurrent, so all he actually served was three years, four months. I could see it was a shock for him to go straight down, from the dock straight to jail. Summing up, the judge said I would never recover. And I know there are scars: I get depression, there are times I'm suicidal. But when the judge said that I thought to myself, no, you're wrong; I won't let that happen. I refuse to let my dad go on wrecking my life. And I haven't. I've got a degree now and a place at an excellent college to study for an MBA.

My dad's first night was in Gloucester prison. A lot of the people I had been to school with were in that prison. Somehow they got to him. He was so badly beaten up that his lips were split, his leg was put in plaster and he couldn't open his eyes for two weeks – they were like blue mushrooms.

I know who did it and some time later I shook his hand. By then I was running a bin-cleaning business; it was the first time I made my own money. Doing my rounds I knocked on a man's door and when he opened it, he looked at me and said: 'I knew your father.' I said: 'He was a nonce and he went to prison.' He said: 'Yes, and he got beaten up, didn't he? I might know something about that.' 'Can I shake your hand?' I said. He was covered in tattoos, he had a big belly. All the same I felt like giving him a big cuddle, but I didn't.

My father's name is on the Sex Offenders' Register now. I don't know what he's doing, and I don't want to. My mum's retired. She's blind. We're not in touch now. When she let her new man hit me and did nothing, I ran away. I was really hurt, with everything. I went to stay with my aunt Madge for seven or eight months. I got to know my cousins and I'm very close to them now. When I was seventeen I got my own place and from then on, it was great. I was going out, I was meeting people – we had fun. By day I was working in a supermarket, and by night in a club until three in the morning, and I had a third job, shift work as a commis chef at a big hotel.

I'd left school at seventeen, but now I wanted to go to university. I'd sorted my life, and I felt I'd missed out. So when I was twenty-eight I went to London with £200, a suitcase and a suit. My first job was working in a pub for three months and I had a wonderful time. From there I got an office job – I hated it, but it gave me money – and I rented a bedsit and met some good people. Then I saw adverts for IT people. So I applied and I got a job in IT recruitment. From there I got a job in the City, then another, and then in the end a job which paid me almost £100,000. Finally, I decided to take a degree.

My ambition now is to help people like me to make changes happen so they have a fabulous life, because they deserve it. I deserve it, and I'm making it happen. When I leave this life, I want to be able to say I had a shitty start, but the middle and the end were pretty fabulous.

I still keep my eye on ChildLine: I've donated loads of money to them over the years. I was very concerned when they had financial problems. Ten per cent of what I earn goes to ChildLine because that makes me feel good. This year I want to raise enough money to pay for a counsellor. It's so important to give back; it's an investment.

I'm really pleased that ChildLine is going into primary schools these days to talk to children there. When I was very young, my teacher, Mrs Chapman, spoke to my mother: she said I was drawing death, my pictures were all black, there were weird things in my story-telling. There were clues there, but nobody picked them up and I myself didn't understand what was going on: I thought I was weird. ChildLine only got to me when I was fifteen or sixteen. I was brought up to be seen and not heard; that's damaging.

Paedophiles say children like it. They don't; it's assault, it's violence. It's not loving, like the sex I've had many times since, or fun, as I've had many more times. I think every nonce should be inside for life, I don't think they'll ever be cured.

My father is still a danger – there is no way on this planet he will ever change.

He is an abuser, at his core; it is what he is. I don't know what I am at my core. When I said that to Esther, she told me: 'Maria, you are a survivor.'

ONE of the great tragedies is the number of children ChildLine cannot reach. Not just because our resources are limited, although that is a constant challenge, but because some children and young people feel so helpless that even an anonymous phone line is out of reach. Maria has described how horrifically close she was to Fred and Rose West, the serial killers. I met their son Steven and he told me of a meeting all the West children had together when they discovered that Fred was abusing the oldest daughter, Heather. They desperately tried to think of a way of saving her. ChildLine existed and they discussed telephoning, but they decided against it. They only had each other – their murderous abusive parents had isolated them from any other friends or family. And they thought if anyone intervened to save Heather, they would all be split up and taken into care. Then they would lose the only security they had: each other.

Andrew was a child who was also totally isolated. He rang ChildLine too late, when he had already decided that death was the only solution for him. But miracles do happen. This is what Andrew told me.

CHAPTER SEVEN

ANDREW'S STORY

have no memories at all before I was five, at primary school. I suppose my earliest years just don't exist for me because half has been wiped from my mind, half I never knew.

I know I was born in June 1975, in London; my mother Lily was twenty-seven. She divorced my father Richard a year after I was born. She used to tell me my father was a very bad man. She said he molested me, interfered with me, but I have no memories of that. She told me he was an alcoholic and a gambler. All my life, my father used to come to see us twice a year, June and December, with money. But my mother took out an injunction against him so that he couldn't come anywhere near me when he arrived. Mummy used to send me into the bedroom when he came. I always knew it was because he was a bad man and he wasn't allowed to come near me.

I loved my mother, but I resented her at the same time. She'd always molly-coddled me. I used to share her bedroom. Up until the day I found her dead she used to wash me in a basin. I had no independence.

We lived in a Jewish area, but the Jewish families resented her because she was Catholic and she'd divorced a Jew. I was bullied all the time at school. I used to be pushed around in the playground, I never had any friends because strangers weren't allowed in the house. Mummy made me go to school in proper official uniform – shorts, long socks, the hat, everything, nobody else used to do that. She would come to school at lunch-time to feed me sweets and cakes through the school fence. She used to take me there and collect me; every other child could stay out late, playing, but she would make me come in and go to bed at 6.30. She wouldn't let me wear jeans or trainers, she thought it was common.

The week before she died she knew she was going to die. She'd had tests in hospital after a heart attack, then she got terrible pains in her chest; she drank and smoked quite heavily, and she couldn't walk without getting breathless. I got used to the fact that she used to go by ambulance for tests twice a week. I've still got the letter she wrote when she knew she was going to die. I used to help her take her tablets, two blue pills, two brown every day. Her final letter said 'Doctor Andrew' on the front. Inside she wrote, 'We've come to the end of two blue, two brown: Mummy won't be taking those tablets anymore.' She said I was a very good boy and that she was putting a token of her love in the letter. It was a pound coin. 'Be a good boy and look after yourself. Lots of love, Mummy'. She was thirty-nine when she died; I was ten.

After Mummy died, I tried to make contact with my father. He had come to the hospital the day she died. He tried to take me away with him, he wanted custody, but the police came: they wouldn't let him. I didn't want to go with him anyway – I hated him, I knew he was bad. After her death I found so many documents: the injunctions against my father saying that he'd hit her and molested me.

I knew where he lived from what my mother had told me; he lived with his mother. My grandmother Lesley, she was a little, old, frail, miserable cow. He lives with her still. She'll never die, she'll live until she's 150. He is a bitter old man now and living with her is a prison sentence for life. They always hated each other, they screamed at each other, now he's got to nurse her till her death. He has never married again, never even went out with anyone.

The only good memory of my grandparents I have is of my grandfather, Lesley's husband – he was alright, he used to discreetly slip me a pound note, but she never knew. My grandmother was a horrible old Jewish woman. She hated me, she hated my mother because Mummy was an Irish Catholic. Both sides of my family were riven with religious hatred and prejudice. I found letters from my Catholic mother's mother in Ireland saying never contact me, I never want to see your child, because my mother had married a Jew.

I was the one who found my mother dead. I had heard her screaming in the living room; it was about 2.30 in the morning. I ran into my older brother Simon's bedroom to get him up. He was seven years older than me. He told me to shut up and he punched me. As I ran into the living room, she fell off the sofa. She was blue. I'd seen mouth to mouth on the telly so I tried to give it to her, but all that happened was she was wheezing. I ran out and told the neighbours – they called the ambulance. The ambulance men tried to treat her, then took her in the ambulance; I wasn't allowed to see her. We weren't allowed in the ambulance.

Then it all goes blurry. I remember going into the intensive care unit and being told she was in a coma; that they didn't think she was going to wake up. There was a nurse, Linda Lea, she mothered me for the week I was in hospital. I kept her badge. I used to write to her, sent letters at Christmas time. But what's the point? She never really knew my mother.

I sat there for days next to my mother in intensive care. She was unconscious. I never slept. They sent me to the children's ward to go to school there. Then, after about a week, they took Simon and me into a room and said that while they were talking to us there, they were switching the machines off. They said we could have an hour to sit with her, they gave me a lock of her hair; I've still got it now. He didn't want one.

The next minute there was chaos: social workers were there, the police were there, my father was there shouting, 'I'm your father, you're coming to live with me.' So we were taken up to the intensive care ward, we were there for about an hour. Then they told us we were to go home and people were going to come and see us tomorrow.

That day I was just crying and crying and crying, I was devastated. My mum had sheltered me from the world. I didn't know what was happening. I never saw Simon cry once. I go to my mother's grave whenever I go to London; I put a new gravestone there. He doesn't go. When they came for me the next day they asked if I would like to go to a children's home for a few weeks, meet other children, maybe be looked after by another family. So I think they didn't really want me to stay at home. But I didn't want a new mum, a new family. So there and then they decided that Simon should have custody.

I remember at Mummy's funeral, it was a Catholic funeral, all the neighbours and her sisters, they were all there. They sent flowers, loads, and wreaths – I've still got all the cards, they even came to the grave. But my father came too, and his mother, and his sister and her family. I went berserk at the grave, I screamed at my father and his family for coming. I screamed that I hated them all, that my mother didn't want them there. From that point I had to grow up very, very quickly.

Before my father, she'd married a Spaniard first and they had my stepbrother, Simon. He had a bedroom of his own. He used to beat me up, he was a bully. My mother's sister had come over from Denmark: she wanted custody of me too, but the social workers thought that wouldn't be fair because I was so young. They asked me whether I wanted to go into foster care, but I refused point blank. My father tried to get custody, but there was no chance; that's why Simon got custody. Simon may be a transvestite now, or he may have had a sex change. I don't wish anyone dead. Except Simon: I wish him dead. He tortured me until I got out.

Mummy had been like a film star to me. I think her parents had a chain of dry cleaners, I think they may have given her money – you know, get-out money, take this and never come back. My father paid maintenance, in cash, twice a year. He had accounts in many different names: he was a street trader, a market trader, selling sunglasses, socks, underwear. So Mummy had jewellery and she had a mink coat, like a film star, Two days after she died, Simon sold all her clothes and jewellery. She had cash hidden in the house, he took everything he could find.

I had nothing. He was hardly feeding me. No breakfast. At night if I was lucky he'd just give me beans. No toast. I had school dinners but basically whatever I could find in the evening, maybe a packet of crisps. No real food. So I stole my mother's Magen David (Star of David) necklace, a watch, and a gold coin and a ring. I knew where she had hidden them, under a drawer and in a cupboard. It kills me: I sold it all, for food, for nothing. I sold my grandfather's medals. But I needed emergency money for food. That way I could buy chips from the chip shop. My brother didn't give me any food or money to buy it and I needed to survive.

Simon resented me. He didn't want me but I was a meal ticket. He got money from social services for looking after me and maintenance from my father. He didn't even talk to me. Mother had told me she was about to throw him out of the house, just before she died. He had told her he was going to dental college and she was paying for it, but a week before she died she found pictures of him modelling, gay modelling, and she was furious. He'd been doing that instead of going to college. She told me not to worry about him bullying me because she was going to throw him out. But she died.

Then Simon moved into my mother's bedroom and I moved into his. I was still going to school, still in shorts and long socks. I still had no friends. I started doing charity work, holding jumble sales for the local hospice when I was twelve, thirteen. Looking back, even then I was an entrepreneur. I'd knock on doors asking for jumble. I've still got certificates and letters from the hospice, thanking me. And for a twenty-four hour famine I did for Christian Aid. I wanted to help people. I was very, very lonely: I had nobody, I had nothing.

Simon was never there, there was hardly any food in the cupboards, never any food ready. He'd go out all the time, leaving me alone in the house at night. Social services came very, very rarely and when they did, I said everything was alright because I didn't want to go into care. He'd put on a performance for them – he should have been an actor.

Then Simon started hitting me. He used to beat me up, kick me, throw me on the floor. One night he left me with an alcoholic woman – she was supposed to be looking after me, but she sat on the floor drinking my mum's alcohol out of the sideboard, so I locked my bedroom door and climbed out of the window. It was a ground-floor window. For about three months that's how I'd survive when there was no food. He'd lock me in, but I would climb out every night and I'd go to one of my mother's friends and they'd give me food. They knew what was going on: they told me, come round here whenever you like.

But they didn't report it to anyone, they didn't want the problem. Everyone knew, all the neighbours. Once, when he was beating me up, someone did call the police. They came round and told him off, he beat me up again. One night when I climbed back in, he was sat on my bed waiting for me. He told me I'd been opening my mouth and causing trouble, and then punched me, threw me on the floor.

It was getting unbearable. The next week when I wanted a bath, he wouldn't put on the hot water. I asked for it again.

So he came in when I was in a cold bath carrying a kettle of boiling water. He poured it over my foot. I ran out, with just a towel, screaming. It was night-time, very dark. A neighbour took me to hospital: they bandaged the blisters, they dressed it. I told them how it happened. So they got hold of a paediatrician. But I lied to him – I still didn't want to go into care. The doctor talked to my brother, who told him I was naughty and disobedient. I was sent back.

About a week later, I walked into Simon's bedroom and there was a man in bed with him. Simon told me to get out. When I was about thirteen, loads of guys started to stay over in the house. Then Simon started to make me have sex with him. He'd to come up to me, say he was sorry, that he loved me, then I had to give him oral sex. He'd come into my bedroom and start telling me he loved me and did I love him? He was like Jekyll and Hyde. He'd hit me, then he'd stroke me, straight from being nasty and violent; it was just because he wanted sex. It was revolting. I was physically disgusted, I hated it.

One day I went into school with a black eye. Simon had done it. Then everybody was all over me: they asked me, did your brother do this? I kept on lying. From then on the social workers started to come round more often but there were so many clues they missed. For instance, I had been clever. When my mum was alive I had been in the top set for everything. Now I was in the bottom set. I was on self-destruct. I was a bad child.

Maybe it was because when she'd been alive, she controlled me completely, smothered me and never let me loose. Maybe it was the pressure of the secrets I was keeping, the horrible life I was concealing. Perhaps it was just that I wanted to fit in and not be the wimp any more; I started swearing at teachers. I was concentrating on being bad and as a result, I started having friends. Then I broke into a flat in our neighbourhood, didn't take anything of value, but the police came to the house, took my fingerprints and I was cautioned. All this time the sexual abuse was going on, sometimes three times a week, sometimes every day.

Trouble seems to find me. When I was fourteen, I went to York with the friend of my mother who fed me from time to time. On the way back on the train there was a drunk who started pestering her, annoyingly; he frightened her. So although I had my own problems and I shouldn't have been worrying about somebody else's, I offered to go with him, take him home on the bus, just so that he would leave her alone. We got up to his flat in a high-rise council block. He got his key out – he was shaking, struggling to get the door open. I said I'd do it, took the keys; he stood behind me. I opened the door, he led me in, shut the door and that was it. Suddenly he wasn't drunk anymore.

He assaulted me, got me to do things, lay on top of me. I was really frightened. I realised he must have planned this. I remember the windows, the curtains were all nailed closed with pieces of wood underneath. Somehow I got the adrenalin to throw him off me. I ran to the bathroom and sat on the floor with my back against the door and my feet against the bath, wedging it shut. He was banging outside, shouting at me to open the door. Then there were thuds and I felt the door cracking. I realised he was axing the door down so I grabbed a chunk of wood from the bottom of the window and smashed the glass.

I got out of the bathroom and then I pelted down the stairs, maybe six flights, and out through the streets, naked. A man at a bus stop saw me, said 'Are you alright?' and handed me a boiler suit jacket to wrap around myself. I kept on running. Then I heard police sirens. I turned a corner and hid down an alley, crouching in a corner, but they found me. I was like a cornered animal, I couldn't say anything. They asked me what had happened. I wouldn't say anything, I wouldn't let anyone touch me. They took me to the police station: the police doctor came, but I wouldn't let him examine me. They took me to hospital, but I kept saying I want to go home, I want to go home. I begged them not to come to the front door with me, or tell Simon.

But I had no keys, and by the time I got home it was four in the morning. I was hammering on the door. He woke up, saw the state I was in, and said 'What the hell's happened?' I wouldn't tell him. I locked myself in my bedroom and lay there shaking all night. The memory of the way I'd been attacked kept going round and round in my head.

Simon went out the next day. He just left me alone, without asking me anything. He had no interest in me or what had happened to me the night before. Nothing. But while he was out the police came – people in plain clothes, people in uniform. They said: 'You're safe now, you won't be going back home ever again.' They thought my brother had done it. In the end I told them everything. I told them about the bullying at school; I told them about the assault by the 'drunk', and I took the police back to the flat and they told me his name. Turns out they knew about him: he had already tied down an eighty-year-old and raped her and got away with it. And he got away with what he did to me. 'Lack of evidence,' they said, in spite of everything I told them and evidence like the axe marks on the door.

But maybe they knew I couldn't give evidence in court. I was la-la by then, an emotional wreck. I'd switched off from life: I didn't know who I was, I didn't care. I didn't want to be alive. I had nobody, nothing. They took me to a psychiatric unit for assessment. I started banging my head on the wall. I wanted to hurt myself, to make myself bleed to numb the pain I was racked by. I wouldn't sleep, I wanted to die. I stole some paracetamol and took them. But I told them, and they gave me some chalky stuff, disgusting, to make me vomit.

Then after three weeks, they came in to see me, saw the state I was in, I suppose, and everything happened very quickly. Nurses and a doctor put all my stuff into bin liners:

they said I was a danger to myself and a suicide risk. I begged them to let me stay, I didn't want to go, but they took me to a secure unit.

They told me I was a danger to myself. So this was supposed to be for my own good, to protect my safety. But it was a terrible place. There were two emergency social service beds for young people like me, who needed protection, the rest were all Home Office beds for young offenders. I had one of the social service beds: I'd only been placed there because I was a danger to myself. But it was brutal. I was sexually abused by one of the boys there, beaten up badly by a group of the other boys. The staff just used to turn their backs; they didn't protect me or look after me. I became hysterical there. I was on strong medication, I was la-la. I used to talk to the wall at night hoping they'd think I was mad and take me somewhere else.

I was there about a year. One day at dinner a boy started saying horrible things about my mother and called me 'the little buggered boy, the little raped boy'. The staff were just sitting there doing nothing. I thought, I've had enough, and I threw my food on him. The staff dragged me out of the room and started beating me up. They were shouting, 'Why are you fighting, Andrew?' then they'd bang my head on the floor and shout, 'Why are you banging your head on the floor, Andrew?' Then they said, 'We'll give you a ten-second start and if you can get out, we'll let you go.' They were just playing with me, there were walls all round. I must have only run three metres when they jumped on me and held me while they beat me up. I just went loony then.

They brought in a psychiatrist and he called an emergency meeting. I told them I'd been writing a secret diary. I gave them it – I thought they'd throw it in the bin. It was filled with my thoughts, why was I there? What happened, the times someone hit me. At the meeting there was the Director of Social Services, two social workers and a Ward of Court person, a solicitor – and I was called into the meeting at the end. They told me the reason I had been kept there was a lack of funding to send me anywhere else. I would be leaving the next day. But that night they'd leave the door open. Tomorrow I'd go to a children's home.

It was a small community home for about twenty young people and it was full of losers. Car thieves, burglars, they were all aged fourteen to seventeen. I was fifteen. I thought they were horrible, they used to pick on me as well. I used to run away every night and just spend the night walking round the graveyard and the church. I was very screwed up.

They had staff from the secure unit taking shifts to be with me one to one, trying to get me used to being out in the community. But it was no good: I was gone. All the same, I went back to school. I'd missed the last two years, but I still wanted to take my GCSEs. I did three exams and I got a B in Commerce. Amazing, considering I'd been doing no work and I'd been away from school for two years. I was very chuffed. Maybe I was still clever.

So when I was sixteen I got myself enrolled in college, doing a BTEC in Business and Finance. Education was very important to me. Whenever I ran away and was reported missing the police knew where to come to pick me up because I'd be in college. They found another children's home for me, specially for kids leaving care – a sort of terrace house. But it was in such a horrible rough area I didn't spend a single night there. I used to pretend I was living there when they checked up on us every week because they would give me an allowance for staying in this house. But in fact I ran away to live somewhere else. And the only place I could run to was back home with my brother Simon.

There was no sexual abuse now; I was older. Now I could try to defend myself and answer back. But he still used to beat me up: punching, throwing me against the wall, the floor, banging me against the wardrobe. That lasted a couple of months. But my mother had an insurance policy which paid me ten thousand pounds when I was sixteen, so then I was able to rent a bedsit. I began partying, started to do drugs and alcohol, and blew all the money.

I got a job: I went to work with a friend of my mother. It was import/export, basically what I do now. I discovered I was really good at it, really fantastic. But about that time I began to realise I was gay and I didn't want to accept it. At this point I was going la-la again. I was working hard, but partying all the time, out until five in the morning. When I was seventeen I took a major overdose. I had some really, really strong painkillers; I took a load of them.

It was a serious suicide attempt. I didn't like the person I was. There was nobody else to be proud of me. I had nothing: no family, nothing to be there for. I phoned my boss to say good-bye. I said: 'I just want to thank you for everything, for helping me. I won't be seeing you again.' I didn't tell him what I'd done, but he guessed. He got someone round to break the door down and they found me there unconscious and called an ambulance.

I was in hospital for about five days. When they let me out, I went back to work and told my boss I was gay. That night I went home, but on the way I went to a bridge across the dual carriageway and tried to jump off. While I was standing there, out of my mind – I suppose I'd had a total breakdown – someone called the police and they got me down. I was taken to hospital and handcuffed to a chair; I was nine hours in casualty. My boss came with one of the other directors. They told me later I'd gone back to the mental age of eight, the last time I had any happy memories in my life; they said I was acting like a child. I wanted to leave, but I was sectioned and taken to the psychiatric ward for six weeks under constant watch, with someone constantly in the room. My boss got me moved into a private psychiatric hospital: it cost him £25,000. It was better than the NHS, but I was just a vegetable. Initially they wanted to give me electric shock treatment but they ended up feeding me very heavy sedation instead. No one talked to me about why I was in that state, about anything that was going on in my head, anything that had happened in my life; they just fed me medication.

Now everyone in the Jewish community knew I was gay, they all disowned me. I went to the local pub and someone spat in my face. I had no friends at all, I was a loner. I went to the gay clubs and bars, getting drunk for company and taking drugs. The tablets didn't make the problems go away. I used to have dreams I was falling and falling. I needed to talk to someone otherwise I knew I'd go mad again.

I needed to speak to someone, but not any one that knew me. So I rang a local helpline but it was all doom and gloom, all about if I wanted to die. I think I hung up on them. Speaking to someone like that would make you top yourself. Then I rang ChildLine. I opened up to them for the first time about being abused, about being gay and wanting to be dead. 'Everything nice gets destroyed and nobody likes me or wants to know me,' I said, 'I deserve this, I was a bad boy.'

The ChildLine lady said to me: 'Don't be daft, don't be silly, you don't deserve any of this.' She asked me where I was and whether I was safe. And I think I hung up then – I was frightened that someone would trace the call or somebody would call the police. But they didn't. I never rang them again. In my head I thought it's too late, they can't do anything to help now.

At night I used to ring the local radio and talk about whatever topic they were discussing, just for company. Then one night they were talking about being sexually abused and I rang. This time, I used a different name and I told my whole story. I was on the phone for about forty minutes. The minute I put the phone down, it rang. It was one of my Jewish friends, he'd recognised my voice. I panicked – I just put the phone down on him.

I'd started heading out of London at the weekends. I was off the rails – partying, sex, drugs and rock and roll – but at least in a new town I had no history, no past. And I was telling people the truth, that I was gay. It was a brand-new start. A couple of months later I changed jobs. The guy was a crook and it went bust but I did a deal with one of the shareholders to invest in me instead. I was fantastic at what I did – I used to take all my depression and aggression out in business.

At this point I thought my life had been ruined: I'd lost part of my life because of other people. I wanted to do something about it. Why should I have been punished, put into the secure unit, when I was the one who had been abused? I went to see my mum's old solicitor and he told me I had a case for unlawful imprisonment. I'd been made a Ward of Court so I should have been in the secure unit for just four weeks for assessment, not twelve months. He told me I was allowed to view my file. It took me six months to get hold of it; they don't like you doing that. They put me in this room with a file. I ripped three-quarters of it out, hid it down my trousers and left. My solicitor looked at it all, then a few days before Christmas he called me and said I had a huge case, that I would get a very big settlement. He knew I didn't have any money to take it on, so he agreed to a no win, no fee situation. He wanted fifty per cent of the settlement – he was talking hundreds of thousands. And he said he'd have to instruct a firm in London. It would be very high profile and once we started, we wouldn't be able to stop; it would be in all the papers. I'd have to be prepared for my whole life to come out; I'd need to be behind it all the way. At that point I said yes.

Then I panicked. I took lots of drugs – cocaine, ecstasy, speed, everything. I went into a huge depression. I didn't even have enough money to buy flowers to put on my mother's grave; I'd done it every Christmas Eve except this one. I went to friends, came back on 27 December, went out partying, took a huge cocktail of vodka and ecstasy and speed, got home at three in the morning with two friends, got them a drink, left them in my living room, then I decided I was going. I didn't care, I was going. I left them there, went into my bedroom, took my CD player and my Barbra Streisand CD (she's just amazing, since then I've spent ten thousand to see her in Madison Square Garden) and then I walked to the top of the road. There was a dual carriageway with a bridge over it and I decided to jump. And I knew once I'd jumped off it, I was dead.

I rang one friend to say goodbye. Then I went to the bridge and sat there with my legs hanging over the parapet. And the next minute there were loads of people all round, flashing lights, trying to talk to me. I was hysterical, I was berserk: I was there three hours. The police were trying to talk me down. In the end I was tired out. I didn't want to jump any more but I thought because of my past, if I climbed back over everyone would think I was an attention seeker and I'd be locked in a loony bin. Already I had one leg over the barrier. I thought, I don't want to kill myself, but I've already gone too far. And in a split second, I'd leaned over to climb back, turned round, looked at everybody and just jumped. It was a drop of sixty feet.

But I lived. I broke nearly every bone in my body, shattered both ankles, broke my back in four places, broke my legs in three places, shattered my wrists and my face hit the ground last. Now paralysed, I was kept in hospital for eight months, with no one thinking I would ever walk again. I had sixteen operations, but after all that I came out a new man.

Lying there in hospital I started to go through my whole life. I came out a stronger person. The doctors didn't think I'd survive, or even if I did, they thought I'd end up a vegetable, certainly never walk again. But lying in that hospital bed, my head slowly cleared. I learned how to put all the rotten stuff to the back of my head, so it wouldn't come back every day and every night. I don't want to die, I thought. I want to succeed: show my mum I haven't given in, make her proud of me.

For the first months the police rang the hospital every day because they wanted to arrest me for drugs and alcohol. And maybe because they'd had to close the motorway. But the hospital wouldn't let them near me. I came out of hospital and saw a psychiatrist privately: he wanted to put me back into a psychiatric hospital to assess me. Don't bother, I told him, I've assessed myself. Instead I went back to my business and it started to go very, very well. I said to myself that's what I can focus on; that's what I can make a success of. And with a business partner I've built it up to an eight million pound a year company.

A year after I came out of hospital, a friend of mine invited me as a guest to the ChildLine Ball, where I got speaking to one of the volunteers. I said I want to help children. Now they've asked me to take on some serious fund-raising and I've agreed. I really want to make a difference by raising a lot of money for them.

Why? ChildLine couldn't help me. I was too frightened to ring up when it could have saved me from all that pain, too scared to ask for help when I was being abused because I thought my brother would be told, the police would be called, and I'd be taken away and punished. Now I wish I had been taken away from him and given a new family instead of being tortured for seven years but at the time I didn't want to go to another family. I didn't want a new mum and dad: I wanted my mother. If I couldn't have her, I didn't want another one.

I knew if I told people, they'd get involved and that was the last thing I wanted. When I was young, I didn't understand ChildLine works differently – listens to children, does what they want, finds out what's best for them. If I had rung them earlier I might not have ended up in that secure unit; I might never have jumped off that bridge. But in those days I don't think I fully understood ChildLine and how it works. And by the time I did ring, it was too late. Whatever they said, I couldn't hear. I didn't want them to try and persuade me to live: I just wanted to die.

And yet now I have everything to live for. I have a partner, we love each other deeply, and we are going to get married. If only I had realised that life has so much to offer: you just have to keep your hope alive, never let it die. ChildLine can keep that flame of hope burning, as long as children ring them in time. The reason I've got involved with them now is that I never want another child to leave it too late; to be too frightened to speak out in time. In my day people didn't want to talk about such things as abuse. Why wasn't my father arrested? Or my brother? Why were they, and all those others, allowed to get away with what they did to me? I've seen on the official injunction I found when Mummy died that my father had molested me. I think in those days even the police were too frightened to take up a case like mine. But I would say to any child now, call for help, don't just wait, because it will only get worse. You may think it will go away but look at me, all that pain in my life, how it exploded and took me with it. It nearly destroyed me. I am so lucky to be here today.

ANDREW, the hero of our last life-story, survived by a miracle. Not, alas, a miracle wrought by ChildLine: he rang us so late in the unfolding tragedy of his life that we were unable to help him. But at least now he believes that it is crucial other children contact us as soon as disaster hits them. And, thankfully, indeed, there are many suicidal children who ring us in time.

Eight children a day ring ChildLine because they want to die. Yet more contact us online to talk about their suicidal feelings. We were so concerned about this cohort of children that we printed a special report investigating what drove them to these feelings and when they turn to drastic action.

There can be many reasons for a child to feel life is not worth living. Bullying and abuse top the list. Whatever the reason, some who ring in utter despair can be moved to glimmerings of hope, if they contact us in time. But in our special analysis of suicidal calls, we reported that if they leave it too late, as Andrew did, they have already entered a tunnel of darkness in which they are impervious to any outside persuasion. It's as if they blindfold their eyes and block their ears. They contact ChildLine only to leave a permanent record, a last suicide note.

Our policy is to protect the confidentiality of the calls we receive, unless a child's life is at risk so these suicidal calls give us very difficult decisions to make. If we attempt to trace every suicidal child, and they deny it, we may have forfeited their trust and they may never contact us again. So next time they try, they may die without us. If we don't trace the call, and having spoken to us they commit suicide, that way also ends in a young death. Our teams wrestle with this dilemma week in, week out.

I met such a child, by chance, when I was visiting a psychiatric hospital in the South West. An intelligent, attractive boy in his teens, he said he had rung ChildLine twice. Unlike many children I meet, who tell me how helpful our counsellors have been, this child was furious with me.

He told me that ChildLine had sent the police, without warning him, to his home at dawn. I was perplexed: it didn't sound the normal way we worked in partnership with children but he didn't tell me why he had rung us.

Then by chance I met one of our most skilled and experienced local directors, Paddy Shannon, who until recently ran ChildLine in Northern Ireland. He told me of a very difficult decision he'd made a few weeks previously. A boy had rung ChildLine to say he wanted to die. Our counsellor spoke to him at length and ascertained that the boy had done nothing dangerous to put his life at risk.

But a few days later the boy had rung again and this time the counsellor guessed the child had done something very dangerous. The police were called at once, the boy was rushed to hospital, and he had indeed taken a lethal cocktail of tablets. Without swift intervention he would have died. As it was, the hospital were just in time to save him. It was the boy I had met. I hope he will live long enough to forgive us for saving his life.

Bullying also takes its toll. It has been estimated that sixteen children a year take their own lives because bullying makes them feel life is not worth living. And neglect, one of the most hidden and most difficult kinds of abuse to diagnose, can also utterly undermine a child's self-esteem. Isabel's life was put at risk, but thankfully, she rang ChildLine. This is her story.

CHAPTER EIGHT

ISABEL'S STORY

I don't know my dad at all, never have, because my mum and dad split up when I was about two. All I know is that he was quite simple – very laid-back, my uncle said, not very driven. They lived in Durham. I don't remember anything about the house there because we moved to Exeter quite soon after they split up. I've seen a photo, and I know I look like Dad – very, very much so. He had straight dark hair, like mine, dark eyes – the Spanish look I have. I've got a picture of him holding me when I was a baby and he looks just like me, only I've got dimples and he has a beard. Whereas my mum and I are completely different: she has curly hair, brown, and green eyes.

I suppose I'm curious about my dad, in a way, but it doesn't really affect me, the way it does some people. I have tried to find him, through the Salvation Army, but they drew a blank. I don't feel my life would be transformed if I found him but I know that my childhood might have been very different, if he'd been there for me.

My mum, Debbie, married him when she was pregnant with me. She was just eighteen, he was ten years older than her, but funnily enough they had the same birthday. She always said he still managed to forget it, never gave her a card or a present. Which says something about him, not perhaps the most reliable person. But anyway, he's out of my life.

I don't know how Mum felt about having me – I don't even know if it was an accident or not. Having me when she was so young, I must have made things harder for her. Her life would have been much easier if she hadn't had me. But she always told me she loved me when I was very young. Not when I was older. From the time I was about ten nothing I ever did was good enough for her.

My first real memory is when I was five, at school. The most popular girl in the class – Ellen, I'll never forget her name – was hitting me over the head with a bag of crisps, which burst. She cried because the bag burst and the teacher told me off for breaking it. So I wasn't allowed any juice and biscuits, and she was allowed extra. Juice and biscuits were the one thing I looked forward to all day: I didn't ever have crisps at home, we didn't have enough money, so juice and biscuits were my luxury. So I was very upset and angry: it had been all her fault, but I hadn't been believed. It was quite confusing. I thought it must have been because she was popular and from a normal family that she was believed.

We weren't normal, I always knew that. Mum was a single parent, which was quite rare at the time. And we were poor. Everybody else smelled better than I did: we couldn't afford things like fabric softener and my mum wasn't keen on washing our clothes, or cleaning anything so the other kids would say I smelled and my house was dirty. And it was.

My clothes came from the charity shop or the market. To be fair to my mum she tried to work, to get jobs so as to keep us off benefits, though then we might have been better off. She did factory jobs and she was trying to do a degree at the same time. When I was six she got work in Leeds, so I was living with her partner. I remember thinking it must have been because Mum didn't love me any more. Her partner, Angela, I saw as a second mum.

That was another thing that made me different, of course. Mum was gay all through my whole childhood. I remember when I was about eighteen she introduced a boyfriend to me and I thought, blimey, a man. Hang on, couldn't you have done that while I was at school? Because I got so much grief at school because she was a lesbian. Everyone said because she was, I must be, of course. And because of the way she looked, that was different, too. She's very tall, nearly six foot, and she used to shave her hair underneath. She would wear Dr. Martens and faded jeans – stereotypical, I suppose. None of that made me popular.

When I was eight years old she split up with Angela and from then on, we moved around a lot in temporary accommodation. In one year we lived in twelve different places. Often it was to move in with a different partner. The one consistent thing in my life was that I kept the same primary school. The school itself was OK. I was very intelligent for my age and I remember my mum being called in by the head teacher to say they didn't know what to do with me: I was too intelligent, I was correcting the teacher, and they wanted me to move to a different school. But I didn't want to. Even though I was still bullied because I had messy hair, because I had second-hand clothes, Dr. Martens, and because of the way Mum looked. The bullying stripped me of my confidence, made me feel worthless, and I was very alone. But still, school was the only continuity I had in my life.

When I got to secondary school I dealt with bullying differently. We were all introducing ourselves on the first day. When it was my turn I stood up, I said: 'My name's Isabel and my mum's a lesbian. If you don't want to be friends with me because of that, then that's your loss. But now you all know, you can't use that against me.' The teacher nearly fell off his chair. It was difficult enough for him, being a man in a girls' school, without me being controversial.

In any case, it didn't work. The bullying didn't stop: I was still too different. I was one of the only white girls in the class and I didn't have the right clothes, the expensive branded trainers. Then my mum went one step further: she got a bloody tattoo, which only made it worse. It was on her arm and she'd wear vest tops to pick me up, just to show it off. I would have loved her to be like everyone else's mum but she wasn't. So I'd get called names – 'Dirty', 'You smell', 'You're a dirty lesbian'.

When I invited friends back to our flat, they saw the state it was in and they'd tell everyone else. It was bad, the lowest standard of council housing. The walls were purple, it was cold – no central heating, a gas fire in the living room. On top of that, we had three cats. My mum wasn't clean and tidy at all, it was pretty dirty. We didn't have carpets or a table to eat off, there was broken lino in the living room, concrete in the bedroom. The cat tray was filled with newspaper and cheap cat litter: it was full of crap and rancid.

In primary school at first I thought all this was normal but when I was about ten and stayed with other people, I realised they lived differently: in clean houses, with a table they could eat around as a family. So I rebelled: I became a clean, neat freak. Because of the name calling I would bath sometimes three times a day; I'd wash and iron my clothes, but they were still covered in cat hair, which didn't help with a black school uniform. I only had clean sheets on the bed if I changed and washed them. But although I'd decided to be the complete opposite of my mum, I had to accept that was the way she was.

In spite of everything, I did admire her. That's what you do, as a child, you do look up to your parents. And by the time I was eleven she had finished a degree in art. She was very good – very, very talented. She had her charcoal paintings stuck up on the walls, they were absolutely amazing. Then she got a job working in a factory. It was real minimum wage stuff, it paid practically nothing. So she took on other jobs as well: she worked in an accounts department, sometimes she did night work. She was trying hard to earn enough money to put food on the table. Mum was vegetarian: the food was basic, but I never went hungry. And she gave me the example to work hard, which was good.

But from my first day at school I had to deal with constant bullying. Even as a strong person it grinds you down: you don't feel you have anyone who listens to you, you don't feel anyone's your friend, you're always waiting for what will happen next. And nobody did anything on my behalf. I spent years reporting it to teachers and it didn't help.

So I only had Mum to turn to. That was the only relationship I had. At home there was the two of us, no other family, and she made a promise to me that there would be no secrets between us. But one day when I was about nine my mum went to hospital – she said it was something to do with her teeth. But about a year later I found a letter in all the mess in the flat which referred to laser treatment for cancer. It had been extremely serious and she hadn't told me. I was so angry that she'd broken her promise and I told her. She just said she couldn't find a way to tell me. I made her promise it wouldn't happen again. But it did: a few years later I found out because she told me, when she was drunk, that she'd had to go back to have more treatment. That was too much. It totally destroyed my trust in her.

At that time nothing in my life was working out. From the time I was about eleven, my behaviour at school had got really bad – there was no point in trying to work hard because nothing I did was ever good enough. My teachers said I was bright, intelligent, but I just didn't work hard enough even though I really did. What nobody found out was that I'm dyslexic, I transpose letters. My writing had problems, spelling was bad, (I still get i's and e's the wrong way round) but because I had a good vocabulary, they just thought I wasn't trying, that I was lazy. Mum didn't defend me, she sided with them. So I thought if I'm going to be put down anyway, I might as well misbehave. At least that made the other children respect me. I made silly remarks to the teacher and if I was told off, I'd answer back. That got me a few surface friends, not real ones.

There were times when the whole class would gang up on me, a real pack mentality. They'd all write notes about me, and pass them around and make sure I found them. 'Isabel's a lesbian', 'Isabel smells', that kind of stupid childish stuff. And sometimes it was worse than childish: threats of violence, people were going to beat me up if I walked home alone. And I was sometimes knocked around, sometimes people would start fights and beat me up, but normally I'd run quickly enough to get home.

I stopped complaining about the bullying because it just wasn't worth it. People always knew when I told anyone and then it got worse because I was grassing them up. By this time the relationship with my mum wasn't good. She'd had two or three partners – they were turbulent relationships, loads of rows and sometimes violent, things were smashed – and at the weekends she would drink heavily.

When she was drunk she was very unpredictable and she had a poisonous tongue. I remember one day she went to the pub and I was sitting on the balcony in the early evening when she came home. She was very drunk, staggering drunk. I asked her if I could stay on the balcony with my friends, three or four of them who lived nearby in the flats – we were just talking together. She said yes and went to sleep. When she woke up, she started to roar at me: what did I think I was doing, sitting out there with my friends? Get them out of here! So from then on, my friends didn't want to come back and I wasn't allowed out to play with them. I used to sit at my window and look out, watching them playing together; I felt totally alone.

I was getting more and more unhappy, more and more

Diana, Princess of Wales, speaking at ChildLine's tenth anniversary in 1996.

Crookham Court School in Newbury. L to R, teacher Anthony Edmonds, owner Philip Cadman and co-founder the Rev. Roy Cotton: all responsible for terrible crimes against children.

Top: The Princess of Wales meets ChildLine's first trustees, shaking hands with Ian Skipper OBE, with Sarah Caplin and Vernon Davies.
Bottom: The moment Charlotte tells the Princess: 'It was my job to suffer.'

ChildLine
THE FIRST YEAR

FOR
CHILDREN
IN TROUBLE
OR DANGER

ChildLine
the second year

ChildLine
The annual review 1995

ChildLine ANNUAL REPORT

1991

I just wanted to say thanks again. It means a lot to have someone listen to you and take you seriously for the first time in your life. I just hope that one day I'll be able to help other people the way ChildLine has helped me.

ChildLine

Annual Report

1993

ChildLine
Annual Review 2005

ChildLine can only exist with help from our valued friends like Ant and Dec, Wet Wet Wet and patron HRH the Countess of Wessex.

Left: For twenty years ChildLine was an independent charity. Now part of the NSPCC, with a new online counselling service, we can help even more children.

Landmark events: The legal conference attended by Cherie Booth and Hillary Rodham Clinton, and the BT–ChildLine awards for Services to Children, presented by HRH The Duchess of Kent.

Politicians and popstars helped ChildLine raise funds. Sir Tom Jones and Dave Stewart recorded 'All You Need is Love', Prime Minister John Major hosted a reception and Ken Clarke and Nottingham's children celebrated the opening of a new base there.

The Wilcox team: Desmond, Rebecca, Esther, Emily, Joshua. Over the twenty-five years we have all changed. This was taken in our country garden in 1999.

isolated. People at school didn't want to come home with me either, because of the state of the place. But I didn't really realise what was wrong until I went to somebody else's house. When I went to one friend's, the difference was incredible: it was clean, it was tidy. And they had nice furniture, a table where they'd sit down together and eat normal food, sausage and chips, where as we'd have lentil bake. Which I did quite like, when I got it, but that wasn't often because Mum was never a three-meals-a-day kind of person. So I did a lot of my own cooking when I was hungry and I would clean the whole kitchen, which was in a pretty disgusting state, for a pound. And I used to clean out the cat tray; that was my job.

I spent a lot of time being bored. My mum was always reading a book: she's artistic, academic, but then she goes through these periods of binge drinking, when her life gets difficult. Looking back, I think she did love me, but although she did her best, she just didn't know how to be a good mother. At eleven you don't understand that.

In the end I couldn't stand the way we were living any more. Violence was always in the background, constant arguing going on. You'd overhear things, snippets – I remember listening at the door and my mum shouting at her partner, 'Go on then, hit me, hit me, hit me!' and a window got smashed once. I was frightened of her when she had a drink, frightened of what she'd say or do.

I think she had an awful upbringing herself: I remember she'd tell me when she was a child the food was always locked away, she was always hungry. she was beaten, she was hit, her own mum was mentally abusive to her. There were six or seven children – two girls and five brothers – and the boys were like gods, the girls an inconvenience.

In 1992, when I was eleven, I'd had enough. The constant arguing, the lack of support, the lack of cleanliness; I wasn't sleeping. I thought I'd be murdered by somebody at school. All the bullying, all the arguments going on so late at night;

I was really, really miserable. So I went to social services. I walked – it wasn't far – and I knew where it was, I don't know how. At reception I asked if I could speak to somebody – I was quite upset. They took me to one of their meeting rooms and a man, the duty social worker, came and talked to me. I told him I didn't want to stay at home; I didn't want to live with my mum any more. The only response I got from the social worker was that he went away, came back with a giro cheque for £35 and told me to go and stay with a friend (I didn't even know how to cash it). And that wasn't what I was after in any case. They didn't assign a social worker to me or come home with me, no follow-up at all.

A day later I ran away: it was cold, it was winter time. It was a school day, but I met my friend and told her I'd had enough – I couldn't handle going in to school, all the bullying. And I couldn't stand it at home: the night before there'd been a lot of arguing. So together we found a derelict house and we stayed in there all day. At night she went home and I got on a bus to try and find a friend, Tony. He'd told me there was an empty house near his and I thought maybe I could stay there; he'd said the back door had been left unlocked. But when I got there, my friend wasn't at home. So I wandered around for a while, I had about fifty pence in my pocket. I went into the phone box and I started to panic a bit.

It was dark, 10 p.m. by then, and very cold. I didn't know about ChildLine, but I knew about the Samaritans because it had been on *EastEnders* and so I called them. I used the last of my money on that call. When someone answered, I said I'd run away from home, I didn't want to go home and I was scared. I didn't have anything for a bus fare, so I couldn't have gone home or anywhere, else anyway. But they said because I was under eighteen, they couldn't help me so I was even more scared. I felt there was nobody.

As I was leaving the phone box, I spotted the ChildLine number. It was on listed on the board at the back, the red colour of the logo caught my eye. I'd never heard of it, but the name says it all. And the number was there: 0800 1111. I nearly didn't ring because of the response I'd got from the Samaritans but I was desperate by then. It was freephone, which was good because I didn't have any cash at all (the Samaritans phone call had taken my last). I got through the first time. If I hadn't, I wouldn't have called back.

A woman answered. She asked how she could help me. I explained I'd run away from home and I was in a phone box on my own. She said she would just put me on hold for a moment while she spoke to someone. It was quite quick. A lady counsellor came on the line. She asked me what had happened. I told her. It was like a miracle, because she listened. She didn't offer me money, she didn't think I was being a silly child: she seemed to understand. When I was explaining about the bullying, she didn't think it was just something I would have to put up with. Instead she was very concerned because it was so late and I was on my own. She said she would try and find somewhere for me to stay, then she put me on hold, after she made me promise not to go away. It seemed like ages, but she kept coming back to say she hadn't forgotten about me, she was just talking to the place. Then she explained that it was a children's refuge, and that the refuge would ring my mum and say I was there, but they wouldn't tell her the address.

ChildLine told me the refuge would send a taxi and that the driver would have a prearranged password. It took about half an hour and all that time the counsellor stayed on the line with me. Which was good because it was pub chucking-out time and a drunk came out and started banging on the phone box. He was shouting something slurred, but the counsellor kept me calm, told me not to look at him and he would go away. And he did. If she hadn't kept speaking to me, I would have been really scared. When the driver came, he told me the password. So I told the ChildLine counsellor and she said, 'That's OK, you can go with him.'

The drive took maybe an hour and half. I didn't know what to expect – I was tired, hungry, scared and very confused. But I was so relieved someone had listened and taken me seriously.

When we got there it was just like a big house – living room, kitchen, laundry. The careworker gave me some toiletries and some towels, then showed me where my bedroom was and where I could have a wash. It was clean and tidy, but above all, it was safe. She said she had rung my mum and told her that I was all right. Then she said to go to sleep and that they'd talk to me in the morning. I felt really safe and secure – the bullies couldn't get me there, my mum couldn't grab me back, finally someone had listened to me and that was a great weight off my mind. I slept quickly, and well.

When I woke up, I had breakfast: cereal, toast, very different from home. And afterwards a key worker who they'd assigned to me took me into the office and talked to me. I had to go through everything that had happened, including the social worker. They asked if I was ready to speak to my mum and I said no – I knew she would have been very angry. It was always about her, never about the reason why I'd done it, or how I felt. They didn't try to persuade me. I know now that Mum had been worried and she was upset but I took a couple of days to try and work out how I was feeling, to be confident in myself that I wasn't making a mountain out of a molehill; that my life really was shit and I wasn't exaggerating. And I wasn't: my mum may have been trying her best, but I had a horrible time at home and at school. I didn't have any peace, anywhere.

I could only stay in the refuge ten days and the key worker explained that then she was going to take me back to social services and this time they wouldn't be able to fob me off: they would have to find a foster placement for me. Five days later, they found one. Out of the frying pan into the fire. It was very strange. The lady had four children of her own and two foster children. I wasn't allowed to mix with other foster children, to form a friendship in the house, even though we shared a bedroom and I went to school with one of them. Basically I slept there and I ate there, it wasn't welcoming. I was there a few months, they weren't happy months.

I remember a meeting at the foster home with my mum when I told her it wasn't that I didn't love her, I just couldn't go on living as we had been. I was in foster care six months, with my mum visiting once a week. Then I was chucked out because I'd been socialising with the other foster children, which was against the rules, and also because my mum was interfering so much. In spite of all the chaos in her life, she wanted to completely control me. She didn't want me to have the pocket money they were giving me and she wanted the curfew to be stricter. So I was just put back with my mum, with a social worker and an outreach worker assigned to me.

The outreach worker was in her mid-thirties. She was supposed to talk to me, make sure I was OK and take me out – 'befriending', the idea is. But in reality she would drop me off at the cinema, pay for me and go away, or she would be on the phone, or she wouldn't turn up at all.

Things with my mum got worse and worse. She was drinking, we had constant arguments and the flat got bad again – filthy dirty and untidy. The bullying at school was worse than ever: it became more physical, things were thrown at me, my hair pulled, I was pushed against the wall. So I became more and more isolated. Mum never gave me the freedom to make friends and play outside. I was really unhappy, but when I left messages for my social worker, she would never get back to me.

During the five months I was home again I was ringing ChildLine to tell them about the bullying and also the situation at home. They listened, they were really supportive and they gave me advice, but I already had a social worker and everything they suggested to make life at home bearable I tried, and failed. In the end it seemed pointless to carry on trying to make things bearable.

So I ran away again. It was a weekend in May, in the

afternoon. I had nowhere to go so I went straight to a phone box and rang ChildLine (I had to try a couple of times before I got through). I was in tears, very upset. I managed to get the words out somehow, to tell them my story, why I'd run away. They said they would try the refuge again but this time there was no place for me. The counsellor was very worried: 'Is there no way the social worker could help?' she asked. I said I'd tried and tried, but I just couldn't get hold of her. The counsellor calmed me down a bit and suggested: 'Why not go home, and then on Monday try to speak to her, maybe go to the office or get the school to try on your behalf?' I said I would. But as I was walking back towards my home, I just couldn't face it, so I carried on walking. I was wandering around in a bit of a daze, I didn't really have a plan – I'd reached the point of not caring what happened to me.

At about 7 p.m., I reached a little park – a kind of gated garden – so I just climbed over the gate and lay down on the grass. I just had jeans and a top, but I put my coat over me as a cover. Soon it got very dark. I was terrified. It was absolutely freezing and the ground was wet. I was also scared someone would hurt me.

But frightened as I was, I couldn't face going home. And I had nowhere to go. Even if I'd stayed with a friend, I knew my mum would have tracked me down and she would have been even more furious. The arguments with Mum were escalating – she was angry with me, maybe with herself, because I'd run away. Everything was a fight, a battle. Constant shouting. Some days she was drinking and then she was quite spiteful: she'd say stuff about my dad, that he'd drink all our benefit money. She'd say someone had hit her, but I would know that she had goaded them and goaded them, and drove them to it.

Nothing I ever did was good enough for her: no matter how hard I tried, it was never good enough. If I showed her something, she'd find fault with it. She found fault with everything. It always felt like I'd disappointed her. I was in the top set at school, but I would really struggle with stuff. It wasn't until I was thirteen that they found out that I was dyslexic and I was constantly blamed for being lazy. So even though I was cold, wet and frightened, and that night seemed to last for ever, I still couldn't go home.

At sunrise I got up. I was very hungry, really tired and I felt dirty. It was early in the morning, but I went round to a friend's house nearby. They took one look at me and real-ised something bad had happened – I was such a mess. They gave me a change of clothes and a bath. Then I stayed away, wandering around during the day; my mother had no idea where I was.

On the fourth day I rang ChildLine again. This time they said there was a place in the refuge for me. They did the same thing with the taxi and the password: this time there were nine other children in the refuge and the mix was very differ-ent. There were two girls who were self-harmers, from Leeds, and they showed everyone what they had done and how to do it, and then they just ran away again.

I was there for the full ten days, then on the last day one of the workers in the refuge took me back home to pick up some clothes while Mum was at work. We'd prearranged it and there was a pile of new clothes waiting for me. If we had enough money to buy them now, why didn't I have the clothes before? I'd never had so many. It felt like a bribe from her, a manipulation. I thought, if I take these, will I have to come home? But the social worker said take them, so I did. I took them in black bags. We went to the social services and my key worker went in with me and threatened them that it would be illegal to take me back to the refuge. And at 6.30 I had a foster placement.

It was miles away, in West London: away from everyone I knew. I was the only foster child, with Annie, a foster mother, and her partner, Dave. She was very fat, with a huge beer belly – I thought she was pregnant. Straight away they told me we were going on holiday for a week, to Wales. It was very odd: I didn't know them at all but suddenly we were all staying together in a caravan. It was near the beach; they had to buy me things like a swimming costume.

We got on fine together. Annie was not the best in the kitchen. There was lots of takeaways, microwaved meals – I'd never had them before so it was a novelty. Dave was an electrician so he would drive me to school in his van. I also did a spell of work experience, stacking shelves in a chemist. It was a long day, eight till five, and a long drive there. Annie worked in a pub so I was alone a lot. I would go up and play cards with the neighbours who lived upstairs. They really did mother me, in the right way. I'm still in touch with them – I call her my aunty, though she's not.

Later I found out that social services had given my foster mother money to spend on me, but she hadn't spent it all: she'd kept some back for herself. I discovered that on my sixteenth birthday, when my social worker told me how much I would get (it was £500 for a party and presents), but Annie must have kept most of it herself. All she bought me was a cake.

By this time I was seeing a boy called Matthew. I'd been having sex for about two years, just, I think, because it made me feel that at least someone liked me. And I had no men, no father figure in my life. Girls didn't like me because I was so different from them but I didn't have problems having boyfriends so long as I didn't say no to them. Nobody knew or cared that I'd been having sex since I was fourteen. So on my sixteenth birthday, although I didn't realise it, I was pregnant. I'd been on the Pill, (I'd been to the clinic with a friend to get it, everybody was on the Pill), but I was unlucky.

Matthew was nineteen. He was working as a builder, he was a friend of a friend and he was nice to me. Not long after I met him my period was due and it just didn't arrive. So I went for tests and the doctor told me I was pregnant. I told Matthew, and I said I was going to keep the baby, no matter what and it was up to him what he did. He could think about it, but he said he wanted to stick around. So I rang and told my mum. She was OK. And then I told the lady upstairs, and she said she was really happy for me.

Then I had to tell my foster mum. She went through a whole rigmarole, saying how stupid I was, she was saying I'd ruined my life. Then she manufactured a huge row with me: she was really in my face, screaming and shouting. I think she was furious with me because she couldn't have children of her own. She just wanted me out of the house.

Matthew said I could stay with him at his parents'. Annie's partner Dave drove round with my things, only half my clothes. Matthew had to tell his dad I was pregnant. His dad told him I should get rid of it – abortion would be the best route for all of us. Matthew didn't agree. But when I heard, I sat his dad down and told him I was still going to get an education and a job. He was quite shocked. His attitude changed completely. 'Oh, right,' he said. I think I was so determined he had to respect me. He must have realised with all the things I'd gone through I was quite grown up and actually he has turned into a doting grandfather.

But I needed somewhere for the baby and me to live. So when I was five months pregnant, social services found me a mother-and-baby hostel: a very small room, with a kitchen and bath. Which would have been fine, but after I'd been there a month someone stole all my clothes and food from me and I really didn't have much. So I didn't feel safe there. Then they found me a counsellor, helped with benefits and took me to a doctor.

I was still going to school: I really wanted to get an education and I knew my baby would need me to be good at something. But I was still being bullied by the gang. The worst was when they cornered me and said my baby was going to be kicked out of my stomach. Four fantastic girls protected me and got a teacher, but then the school decided I was a health and safety risk so I had a tutor at home. My English teacher sent me loads and loads of work which I loved doing and she tried to arrange for me to take my exams. I got four A stars in my mocks, but the head refused to let me.

It was this thing about respect – only ChildLine really listened to me and understood. Throughout my whole pregnancy the doctor would talk over my head or past me to my key worker, not to me. So I rang ChildLine three or four times. I explained that people were behaving as if I wasn't there, and the key worker wasn't supporting me. They suggested I should find time to sit down and explain what was happening to my key worker because she might not have realised. So I did, and she hadn't. So that was much better. I had made the assumption that adults just let me down; ChildLine gave me the confidence to speak out and change it.

In May I had a baby boy, Justin. I went into labour around midnight, while I was staying with Matthew's parents. At first I didn't want to wake his parents. As the pains got worse, I went and took a hot bath by myself. At around six in the morning I woke Matthew and told him I'd been in labour for six hours. His dad drove me to the nearest hospital, but there was no room there, so they drove me to London. When we got there, I was nine centimetres dilated. It took only an hour and a half for Justin to arrive after I'd reached hospital. Lucy, the mid-wife, was brilliant, I didn't have any drugs. My mum arrived and was amazing – held my hand through the whole thing. Matthew flitted in and out on the phone. Lucy told him when Justin was arriving. He was a big baby, eight pounds eight.

I was so tired, I just wanted to go to sleep but I saw that my mum kept looking at him. I told her: 'It's all right, you can pick him up.' She said: 'But you haven't held him yet.' 'That's all right, I'm just too tired,' I said. So she was the first person to hold him.

Justin Angus Wilson looked like a plucked chicken, like any other baby. A bit jaundiced, with dark hair, he was too big for all his babygrows. I stayed in hospital overnight, the night nurses were horrible. I wanted to breastfeed but in the night they whipped him away, changed his nappy and gave him a bottle. So he wouldn't breastfeed.

For two weeks I stayed with Matthew's parents, so I had some help. The midwives visited me at home: they were very abrupt with me, really rude to me, insinuating I couldn't cope. 'Why haven't you done this? Why haven't you done that?' Each time they made me feel stupid or inadequate, I rang ChildLine. They calmed me down, reassured me that every new mum goes through these things and they told me to talk to my health visitor, so I did and she was great.

Straight away after Justin was born I made an application to the local college of further education to do a BTEC in Business and Finance. I'd worked out what I could do: it was hard with no GCSEs, but I found an evening course that would take me. So I went to meet the tutor, in this great big tower block with no lift. I had Justin with me in a buggy, so I had to drag him up all the stairs and the tutor looked at me, looked at the baby, looked at the application and saw my age then said: 'You won't be able to do this, not with a baby, not at your age – it's too difficult.'

So I left, bumping the buggy down all those stairs. I felt really deflated – I had wanted to make a difference. The confidence I had when I went in there had just gone, completely gone. Once again adults had undermined me.

So I went straight to a phone box, with Justin in the buggy, and I rang ChildLine. The counsellor told me that I shouldn't let anyone else determine the way I wanted to live my life. She said if there was no policy or rules saying I couldn't take the course, that I should persevere. And she was saying that I shouldn't let what anyone else said get in the way – I should focus and remember why I was doing it. Finally she asked did I think I could do it? And I said yes, my application was still there and whatever the tutor had said, I thought I could do it easily. So she said go ahead then and prove him wrong so I didn't pull out of the course.

I was really nervous that first day, even finding the room. Although I was the youngest person there, I found the work easy. My strength was on the legal stuff; I sat next to someone who was working in an accountancy firm and his strength was the financial side, so we'd help each other.

While I was taking the evening course, Justin was at home with Matthew and his parents. My mum told me she would like Justin to stay with her overnight. I was really worried: I didn't trust her, we'd only just started to get our life together and seeing how she had neglected me, I didn't think she could look after him properly. So I rang ChildLine again.

The thing is they give you ideas that might not occur to you otherwise. They don't try and force you, they just suggest things and ask whether you think it would work out. This time they suggested that I could go and stay with Justin at my mum's to see how she looked after him, to make sure he was safe. I didn't want to say no to her but I had to know he was being looked after. I thought it was a really good idea, definitely worth a try, and it worked out well. Immediately I saw how fantastic she was with him and it gave me a break as well. The flat was cleaner when he was there and I made his bottles up for him. And he was only there overnight. So I could trust her now. A part of me was asking, how could she do all this for him, and not for me? But it was much more important that things were good for him than to go over the past.

At college I made some really good friends, completely different to me. They'd already taken their GCSEs, they were in jobs, they were older. It was fine, no bullying at all; that stopped when I left school. It was a two-year course, two evenings a week, but in the second year I did a course in graphic design and I also worked in a pub. Even with all this extra work I still passed my BTEC with Distinction. And when I got my certificate, I marched right up to the tutor. 'Do you remember me?' He looked at me blankly and I said: 'Maybe I should have brought the baby with me.' Then he remembered.

It was a good moment. I said to him: 'You told me I shouldn't do the course, but someone very wise told me I could, and so I persevered and now I've passed with Distinction. So maybe you should be more careful in the future because next time someone like me might not have the advantage and support of someone wise to talk to.' At this, he just mumbled and turned bright red.

Having that qualification was the equivalent of three A-Levels. I did apply for university to read psychology, but there was only one with childcare and they didn't accept me. So instead I got a job as a receptionist for a media company: £13,000 a year. I enjoyed it. Justin was at a childminder's and then his grandad picked him up. From there I went to work in the accounts department. I loved that – I learned so much – and then I got a job at an architect's.

Then in 2004 I met my husband, Oscar. We hit it off straight away. I'd never married Matthew – we'd meant to, but in the end he called it off. He left me to be with somebody else. But Oscar and I moved in together after we'd known each other about a month. The great thing was that he got on really well with Justin. Oscar proposed on my birthday in 2004 and we got married in 2005.

There were warning signs. On our honeymoon he came in drunk quite a lot and then he'd start arguments. He wouldn't drink every day but when he did, he'd go on three-day benders; he wouldn't come home. I was worried at first, but then I got angry. He'd make Justin promises and break them. It was just like my childhood with my mum. Then one night he got physical: he grabbed me. I was covered in marks on my neck and my boy was standing there but he was too drunk to notice so we ran to neighbours and they rang the police. It took them two hours to get to us, then they arrested him and took him away. They took photos of me with all the injuries.

The next morning they showed him the photos, and he was absolutely devastated. They said in this case they wouldn't charge him unless I wanted them to. He was genuinely horrified at what he'd done, so I decided not to have him charged, but I said I wasn't having him back to live with us. No way would I put my child through the childhood I myself had had, so Oscar just came back to pick up some stuff. I went out – I didn't want to talk to him – but when I came back he was still there. He told me he had found a perpetrators' course.

It was supposed to make them aware and to take responsibility. I had no idea whether it would work, but after all, my mum had changed when she knew she had to. So I said to Oscar: 'You can sleep on the sofa if you take the course.' It was really strict. I couldn't even let him eat an alcoholic chocolate, that was the rule. It was three years ago and he hasn't had a drink since.

Things have gone really well for me. I got a job I loved and cared about. For six years I was a fundraiser for a big children's charity. Now I have moved on to become the fund-raising manager for a smaller charity, where I can work part-time because I have three sons now. I've already told Justin about ChildLine – I'm bringing them all up to know about ChildLine. When Oscar's dad died, knowing how much he loved his grandad, I said Justin could ring. He was so distressed, he couldn't talk to us so I gave him the number. I don't know if he did call, I wouldn't intrude.

I must have made nearly a dozen calls to ChildLine. Each time I spoke to someone different but it didn't matter because it was ChildLine I trusted and they were all fantastic. They helped me turn my life into something positive. Without them I would be dead. When I ran away and spent the night in the park nobody else knew or cared about me.

Who knows what would have happened if I hadn't got through to ChildLine?

Without the counsellor telling me not to lose hope, to stand up for what I wanted, I certainly couldn't have taken the college course. That has made so much difference. Now I have enough qualifications so I'm not stuck at home on benefits, and I have a job I believe in. ChildLine gave me the confidence to be a good mum and be very strong with my husband Oscar, so he's turned his life around, too. And ChildLine made me realise that I can stand up to people when all the bullying could have undermined me so badly that I felt I had no chance – they listened.

ChildLine were only interested in what I had to say, it was unconditional, and they took me seriously when nobody else respected what I thought, or asked what I wanted. They gave me the confidence to take a chance in the end – to trust my mother – and take positive steps to ensure she had a relationship with her grandchildren.

If I hadn't got through to ChildLine when I was on the street, on my own at night, anything could have happened. Without ChildLine I might not have done anything with my life at all. I would say to any unhappy child: take the chance, ring them. They can't change your life for you, but they can help you change your life yourself.

CHAPTER NINE

A CULTURE OF ABUSE

I magine that a multi-millionaire paedophile decided to buy himself a present: a boys' boarding school. That he then ran the school, as he himself explained, 'as a hobby', with a population of children who were entirely at his disposal. And in the pursuit of his 'hobby' he was totally unscrupulous. He deliberately set out to attract the most vulnerable boys to his school, boys who would find it more difficult to ask for help if they were abused. For example, foreign children, disabled children, and children belonging to service families whose parents were far away and out of immediate contact. To make sure service families could afford the school fees, the paedophile dropped them so low that they were covered by a Ministry of Defence grant, even though that meant he made a loss. And he offered special education to other vulnerable children – for instance, those with emotional problems or dyslexia.

Next, to give himself complete freedom, the paedophile insists on making all the decisions in the school himself:

hiring staff, firing staff, making all the educational decisions, the lot. He deliberately hires teachers without references, among them other paedophiles, who had been allowed by a previous school to 'leave quietly'. To make sure he can lure children into his reach, he decides that he himself will be in charge of the tuck shop and handing out pocket money. And he has his own flat on the premises, entices children there at evenings and weekends, and he leaves sweets and money lying around, spread over the sofa in his bedroom.

And finally, to make sure nobody can interrupt him in his 'hobby', he does not appoint any school governors. No outsiders have the right to enter the school, to check on the welfare and quality of life of the boys. Social services cannot enter the school, even though the official government Inspector's Report was appallingly bad, calling the school dilapidated, dispiriting and dangerous, saying the buildings were unsafe, the classrooms were shabby and badly equipped, and the educational standards were poor. But when parents went to their MP and complained to the Department for Education, they were told nothing could be done so the paedophile reigned in the little kingdom he had created, 'as a hobby'.

This may sound like a nightmare, but it is not imagination: it happened. The paedophile owner of the school was 74-year-old Philip Cadman. White-haired, stooping, hesitant and diffident, he conveyed the impression of being doddery and harmless. That impression was disarming and misleading. The school he owned, which housed nearly 100 boys, was Crookham Court in Newbury and there he reigned supreme. This horrifying situation happened not 100 years ago in an age of Dickensian squalor but in 1989, a time when ChildLine had already been in existence for over two years and when *That's Life!* had been constantly campaigning for better protection for children.

In fact, the paedophile Cadman's reign only came to an end because Peter, a teenager who had just left the school, rang ChildLine. They advised him to write a letter to me, asking for help.

When he wrote to me, Peter was a naïve, vulnerable seventeen-year-old. I well remember opening his letter which was written in biro, in a big, childish hand. It was short, but its message was so powerful that I remember putting the letter down on my office desk where it lay for days, like an unexploded bomb. In it, he told me that the whole boarding school was rotten to the core. He said the millionaire paedophile, Philip Cadman, had been abusing him for years. Peter had told his parents, they had gone to the police and Cadman had been arrested but with no corroboration, the police had let him go. And though the parents had tried everything – gone to the police and their MP as well as the Department of Education – they were told nothing could be done without evidence. They did their best to find the corroboration and the proof they needed but Cadman blocked them at every turn. At seventy-four he was clearly not so doddery that he would allow himself to be deprived of his 'hobby'.

It beggars belief that if one boy, Peter, had not had the courage to write his letter to me, paedophile Philip Cadman would have continued for years unchecked, turning generations of children's lives into hell and wrecking adult lives as a result, and nobody could have stopped him. But that is what happens when an institution is corrupted and when those who should take action are either unable or unwilling to take on the overriding responsibility to make children safe.

Peter's letter was forwarded by ChildLine to my office in the BBC's Lime Grove Studios in West London. Don't think it was a glamorous set of studios, like MGM. Or a shiny new glass-and-metal palace, like Channel 4. Lime Grove was an odd, rambling set of buildings, much of it dating back to the 1930s. It had once been the film studios where Jessie Matthews danced and sang, and where Alfred Hitchcock made his film of *The 39 Steps*.

When the BBC bought Lime Grove they made every kind of iconic television programme there, from *Panorama* to *Top of the Pops*, and from *Muffin the Mule* to *Steptoe and Son*. It was a maze of prefabs and metal galleries, a rabbit warren of offices and dressing rooms. The panelled offices where the film industry moguls once worked were still there, investing the building with a 1930s graciousness, like an old lady's mansion flat.

I used to write the *That's Life!* script in one of the panelled offices, sitting at a heavy oak table covered with the cups of tea that were my constant fuel. I remember wrestling with a complicated script one evening, while next door I could hear the *Nationwide* researchers bullying and cajoling a parrot who stubbornly refused to talk to them.

Lime Grove Studios are no longer there: it's a housing estate now and nowhere is there a plaque saying Jessie Matthews danced here or Tom Jones gyrated there (but he did – I once saw him in the BBC Club, looking like many TV stars, far smaller than I had imagined and with his original nose). First as a researcher, then as a producer, I used to wander laden with documents past the reception with its iron-grilled unused lift, along drafty corridors and up rickety metal steps to my office in a tiny commandeered terraced house, which had been engulfed by the BBC. There were dozens of corridors and hundreds of pigeons. Cats used to curl up in odd corners, too, probably feasting on generations of mice.

They – and we – were lucky to survive our working lives there. It turned out the whole building was riddled with asbestos and I once looked up from my desk to see Health and Safety officials striding through our office to test the air-conditioning unit for Legionnaires' Disease. It had the worst canteen in the BBC, which was saying something. Eccentric as it was, we who worked there loved it: there was creativity in the very brickwork. When, inevitably, it was sold to a developer and pulled down, those who had made some of the pioneering programmes there had a farewell party to give it a good send-off.

The *That's Life!* office was busy and cramped. It was filled with desks covered in papers, telephones ringing, typewriters chattering, researchers and reporters all shouting questions to each other. My desk was piled high with viewers' letters and research reports. Peter's letter arrived on the top of that pile in early 1989, forwarded to me by ChildLine's Director of Children's Services, Hereward Harrison.

By that time I had read many letters from abused children. Even so, Peter's letter shocked me. In it, he told me about Crookham Court and the abuse that flourished there. He said: 'I have been abused by Philip Cadman for years, but I kept it to myself. I feel as if I'm the guilty one, I feel so down about it.' Then he aded that he had watched our items on child abuse when ChildLine was launched and heard how abusers threaten and frighten children into silence. He was determined not to let that happen to him, to try and bring Cadman to justice. 'I'm going to do everything in my will to do what's right, no matter what people say. I'd be grateful if you would help me in this case,' he ended.

I read and reread that letter for three weeks, horrified, and intimidated by the scale of the abuse it revealed. Already we had heard cases of abusive teachers who had been allowed to leave a school 'quietly' so as to protect the establishment from scandal but nothing so evil as a school being run as a paedophile's playground, his personal hobby.

Each time I read Peter's letter I realised what a ferociously difficult investigation this would be. If we were to broadcast Peter's allegations, we had to discover enough proof to stand up in court. Sexual abuse is a secret crime. We must find stronger evidence than the word of one child. But Peter had also alerted ChildLine and in both my roles, working as Chair of ChildLine and as a journalist for the BBC, I felt we had to respond. He had shown such courage, I knew we must act.

Hereward rang regularly to chivvy and spur me on while I made up my mind how to approach the investigation. Because there was a culture of abuse in the school, the children were imprisoned in it, so Cadman held all the keys. Somehow we had to find a way of giving the boys the confidence to tell us what was really happening. We would need to talk to the children in the school, find a way to cross the threshold.

The first step was to put our toughest, most experienced producer onto the investigation. Richard Woolfe was the obvious choice. As a researcher he had handled every kind of investigation for *That's Life!*, from the most light-hearted to the more serious, and he took every challenge on with energy and focus. He discovered that a group of parents had tried to create an action committee to protect the children. Cadman had never taken them seriously, ignoring their suggestions that he was clearly out of control. What's more, Richard discovered that Cadman's policy of employing teachers without references had paid off: there were other paedophiles on the staff. One of the boys had complained that the English teacher, Anthony Edmonds, had regularly sexually abused him.

When a child complained about the abuse, Crookham's headmaster, Michael Gold, had confronted Edmonds about the accusation. Edmonds had appeared shamefaced and had not denied it so he was forced by the headmaster to resign. Even then Cadman gave him an excellent reference and wrote a letter defending him to the Department for Education and Science saying the child must have been 'confused'. Another teacher, Bill Printer, taught French. He, too, was suspected of abusing boys. Printer was a giant of a man, with a huge bellowing voice: children were terrified of him. In his case, none of the boys had dared to speak out.

The parents' Action Committee were so deeply unhappy about the culture in the school that they had called a meeting.

Afterwards they gave our investigator Richard Woolfe the Minutes, which make extraordinary reading. At the meeting, some of the teachers had made their feelings clear. One called the school an 'evil environment' and resigned because he said the children were not safe there but it was equally clear that nobody had the power to make the children safe.

Fortunately the parents were able to present Richard with enough guidance for him to identify the teachers who were not involved in any abuse. The staff painted the whole picture for us: they warned us that at the age of seventy-four, Cadman created an image of a slightly demented old man but this was deliberately done. In fact, in sacking any staff who threatened him and by appointing others who would never been given jobs in any other school, he could run his 'hobby' exactly as he chose.

Richard's first task was to discover whose word he could rely upon. One ex-teacher, Ian Mucklejohn, was especially helpful. Mucklejohn had already complained to one of the teaching unions about Cadman's total incompetence as a teacher, describing how in one class the boys had pinned a paper to Cadman's back which said 'I am a thickie' while they threw pellets across the classroom. Another teacher had collected forty complaints about Tony Burgess, the violent, intimidating caretaker, who swore at the boys, prodded them with a screwdriver and on one occasion, stamped heavily on a boy's foot. Whenever he was criticised, Cadman defended Burgess.

Some of the parents told Richard that on one speech day they were furious when Cadman encouraged the boys to run a bar, so they consumed vast quantities of alochol and were found being sick all over the school. The matron, Yvonne Walton, had done her best to cope, expressing concern that Peter, who had written to me, was known by the other boys as 'Caddy's Bum Chum'. The abuse was the stuff of graffiti around the school and taunts in the playground. And while the adults might have had problems gaining evidence, the boys knew exactly what was happening in the rotten heart of the school.

In all this chaos, Michael Gold, the headmaster, seemed almost sane. Grossly overweight and said to beat boys with far too much enthusiasm, he was also forthright in his opinion of the school. It was, he said, a 'den of iniquity.' Gold had already forced the English teacher, Anthony Edmonds, to resign. Gold himself was not implicated in sexually abusing any of the boys so it was hardly surprising that while we were investigating the school, Cadman sacked him as headmaster. Cadman even went to Reading Court to obtain an injunction to prevent Gold from entering the school.

That gave us our opportunity. We knew that Cadman himself would never have allowed us into the school to speak to the boys but we realised that he would have to be away at court and out of the school on the morning he went to Reading to obtain his injunction. So at our request, Gold's last act as headmaster was to invite me, as Chair of ChildLine, into the school to talk to the boys that morning.

I will never forget that drive to Newbury. Three of us went together to Crookham Court – I took Hereward Harrison and Richard Woolfe with me. Our journey to Newbury was extremely tense. I'd had long experience of confronting conmen, some of them aggressive and hostile but this was on a different scale. There was so much at stake now and so much could go wrong. Suppose the caretaker, Burgess – who we knew could be verbally and physically violent – threw us out? Suppose Cadman decided not to go to court after all and was standing at the front door, barring our way? Even if we got in and were able to talk to the boys, suppose I failed in my attempt to persuade them that they could trust us, that they had the right to safety; that we were there to protect them and that they should talk to us? If we failed, how many generations of boys would be condemned to suffer more physical and mental wounds that would be with them for life?

When we turned our car into the drive of the school, the sprawl of buildings looked as shabby and run-down as I had expected. There was no sign of Cadman, or of Michael Gold. The matron had called the boys together and they gathered in the hall to listen to my talk. I remember how they sat – looking at the floor, awkward and embarrassed, never meeting my eyes. So I started gently, introducing myself, Hereward and Richard to them, talking to them about ChildLine and reminding them that any child could ring about any kind of problem, even something as shaming as abuse.

But I hadn't much time: Cadman could return at any moment. So I moved on, talking now about the impact of abuse, deliberately using language I thought would be understandable and demystifying.

'The thing you have to remember is that abuse is never a child's fault. The most horrible thing about sexual abuse,' I told the boys, 'is that it makes you feel disgusting, as if you've done something wrong and you're to blame for it. It's as if you went for a walk across a field and you found a cowpat as big as a mountain, and you fell into it. When you climb out of it, you think you smell disgusting. You feel horrible. So then you rush home and have a bath, and all the crap disappears down the plughole. And there you are, pink, clean and sweet-smelling, so it was the cowpat that was disgusting, not you.

'Abuse can make you feel like that: you feel horrible. But then you talk to someone about it, and they say the abuse is disgusting. but you're not. It's never the child's fault. Never. So that's why it's really important for young people who've been abused to talk about it. Because for some reason talking about it is like having a bath – you feel clean and sweet-smelling again. And ChildLine is there for you to talk to. Do you know the number?'

Hereward had brought with him dozens of ChildLine stickers and leaflets with our Freephone number 0800 1111 printed in red all over them and we handed them out to the boys. They seized them from us and leapt away, like young goats frolicking in the sun. Suddenly all the pressure and embarrassment had gone. What I didn't know, but what Cadman later revealed, was that he came back from Reading Court to find his flat entirely plastered with ChildLine stickers and posters. The boys had no doubt what I was there to tell them and they instantly located the rotten heart of the school and put their talisman, ChildLine, there.

Was I right, does talking about abuse remove the feelings of disgust and defilement? Not all the feelings, not entirely. Meeting Peter more than twenty years after he left the school, he is suffering still. He continues to bear the scars of the abuse Cadman inflicted upon him. Peter has grown up to become an attractive man now, with his own family, but his eyes are still guarded and when asked a question, he hesitates, unsure, unconfident. When he thinks about his abuse, he still feels guilty and confused. Although he now has two lovely children of his own and a clever, pretty wife, he can't summon up the anger he needs to put the blame, the responsibility where it should lie: with Cadman. The anger has turned back upon himself.

I told him what a fantastic achievement it had been for him to blow the whistle and expose the wickedness at the heart of Crookham Court School. So why should he still carry such a heavy burden of guilt?

Peter told me: 'I never had a lot of self-confidence as a boy, and I still don't have. That awful period of my life still gives me flashbacks. There's programmes on television I can't watch because they bring back memories; sometimes I know I talk in my sleep. I still carry the scars – I'm uncomfortable taking the kids swimming, or having a bath with them. I wonder, would I feel like this anyway? I'm never going to know, am I? Now I have two kids of my own, I don't know what I'd do to someone if it ever happened to my two.'

His face was blank with remembered pain that for years he could never reveal. Then he told me his story. 'Looking back,' he said, 'I see now why Cadman ran the school the way he did, so he could persuade families like mine to send their children there. I knew they had made sacrifices to send me and my brother there. And they were away abroad practically all my life.

'My father was in the navy and like most people in the Services, he travelled all over the world. I was born in Singapore in 1970, my brother David was born in 1973. My mum had to run the home and she was very strict – I was always frightened of going to her to say I'd broken a window or had a hole in my shoes.

'When my parents were posted to Hong Kong in 1983, they needed to find a school for us in England. Dad looked into the grant you got in the Services to cover education: it wasn't a very big grant, not enough to pay for an expensive school. I remember going with my parents to different schools to have a look at them. Some of them cost more than the grant, so they were out of the question. I understand that we went to view one where someone was injured in a PE class and Mum and Dad didn't like that one because they didn't think we'd be safe there. Ironic, isn't it?

'I remember going to see Crookham Court for the first time and the moment my dad slammed the car door, a drain-pipe fell off the wall. So it was a bit shabby but the fees were dropped for Service families so that they were low enough to be covered by the grant. One of dad's friends had a son who was also starting there – that and the budget persuaded them to pick Crookham Court.

'David and I are not the brightest. I have lots of trouble spelling – I suppose I may have dyslexia, although I've never been tested for it. Anyway, I went there when I was just thirteen. My first day I spent running around and feeling excited, but then later on I remember crying and being homesick. I told my parents I wanted to come home and they said I'd get used to it.

'It wasn't all bad. I'd always wanted to go to a boarding school – I read a lot of Enid Blyton books, so I had a picture of what it could be like, adventurous, and making lots of friends. And in some ways Crookham was like that: a very close school, everyone looked out for each other. In a way the boys made it a happy school. There was a bit of picking on people, as you might expect, but not a lot of bullying. And when it came to education, actually I think I did better there than when I was at state school, where I was buried in a big class. I certainly got more attention at Crookham, where there were only twelve or thirteen boys in a year.

'Philip Cadman owned the school. Caddy was doddery and vague, a bit of a joke. By the time I went to Crookham, he'd stopped teaching. I don't think he was ever any good as a teacher but he ran the tuck shop and handed out my pocket money every Friday night. He had a flat in the school where he lived, so he was there all the time. Boys used to go to his flat in the evening – they'd steal whatever they could nick from whatever was around, drink, sweets, and for me it was money. There was always money lying around.

'Caddy sexually abused me for years. It began a few months after I started at the school and it went on for four years, from the time I was thirteen until I was seventeen. It made me feel confused, not knowing whether it was normal. Maybe, as Caddy told me, a part of growing up. At the time there was the AIDS crisis and he did warn me that was how that got passed around. At first I could stand it when it was happening to me: I haven't got any self-respect, I never have had. No confidence, I suppose. I was getting money out of it, anything I could nick, or I would nick his safe key and we used to rob the safe, but only what we needed – £20 or £30 quid.

'But then I wanted it to stop. On quite a few occasions I told him I wanted it to stop. At first he'd say yes, but then it would just carry on. I remember him chasing me around the room one time. But I couldn't tell anyone, or ask for help – it was something you kept to yourself. I didn't want my parents to know, so I just got more and more depressed.

'After I left the school, a teacher called Alex Standish did some digging. Standish took my mum out, with my sister, and told them about some accusations that had been going on; said that the boys had been calling me "Caddy's bumboy" and the matron had been worried about me. The accusations were that something was going on between me and Cadman.

'It was a Sunday when Standish went out with my mum and told her. She was horrified and contacted my dad. At the time my dad was away, so he was taken off his ship by helicopter to join us. I went to the police station to make a statement: I told them Caddy was abusing me and what he'd done to me. I thought, a bit naïvely, that he'd get arrested and that would be it. He'd be tried and be sent to prison. But all that happened was they went and spoke to him, but because there were no witnesses – it was my word against his – nothing got done about it, although the police certainly tried.

'I had thought it was just me getting abused, but then I found out about my brother David. David was still at school after I left. He was sexually abused by Anthony Edmonds, an English teacher. He'd told my mum and dad, and they told me about it. Mr Edmonds had abused David in the school, and he'd taken David to Wales because Mr Edmonds had a property there that needed restoring, and he used that as an excuse, saying that David could help him. And he abused David there. Then I was angry. Standish said it was happening to other boys as well, but the police said there was nothing they could do. That was when I decided to write to you.

'I rang ChildLine first and I spoke to a counsellor called Peter. And then I wrote to you because I had watched you on the telly talking about it, saying that if children don't ask for help, it gets worse. I addressed the letter to you at ChildLine.

I remember saying that something had got to be done; that I wanted to do the right thing and speak out, whatever anyone thought, because that's the only way to put these men where they should be, in prison. Otherwise they'd just carry on abusing more and more boys.

'I remember writing the letter. When I'd sent it, I thought that's that then. I expected results. I had no doubt that somebody would get back to me. And you did. It took a little time, but you asked me to come and see you in the *That's Life!* office. I remember coming to see you, it was quite overwhelming. As a family, we'd very rarely gone up to London, so that was the first thing. And when we got there, it was nothing like I'd imagined. I suppose I'd thought of something much grander, maybe a big modern office and loads of staff. But you were sitting in this poky little office, with four or five people around you constantly asking you questions, and the office was really busy. I met Richard Woolfe, the producer who was doing the research into Crookham Court.

'I talked to you, and him, for an hour or so. I told Richard everything, almost. Everything I could bear to make myself remember. And I said I wanted you to encourage other boys to talk about the abuse they'd suffered because staying silent turns your life into hell, like it had for me. Then I went home again, waiting to see what would happen. I had no appreciation of how much time and trouble it would take to put the programme together – I expected to see it hit the news straight away and be on the the front of the paper the next day. But of course it took weeks.'

Peter was right: the investigation did take weeks. There were so many hurdles. First of all, we had to be sure the BBC would support us. The common allegation flung at us by critics (and eventually, by the defence lawyers when we got to court) was that we were conducting 'trial by television'. I remember ringing John Birt, who was then the Director of News and Current Affairs at the BBC (and later became

Director-General) from my dressing room one Sunday night when I was between rehearsals in the television theatre. I outlined what we knew so far, explained the police were powerless because they had already failed to obtain evidence and asked whether we should take on the investigation. He thought for a moment and then said: 'Yes, that would be right.'

After our visit to Crookham Court, the next step was to try and meet the individual boys. With the help of the parents and of the school matron, Yvonne, we made a list of the children they thought might have been abused. One by one, I contacted the boys' parents and asked permission to take them out of the school and interview them. Ringing the parents out of the blue and having to explain why I was calling was incredibly difficult. At that time we had no evidence, so the only way to confirm whether their sons had suffered was to speak to the children themselves. It was tough on the parents, but they all agreed. And of course it was even tougher for the children.

I knew that with the prison walls of the school still around them, the children would be terrified to speak out; that is the effect of a culture of abuse. We had to meet them in a neutral place so we chose a local hotel, and Richard and I met them all. The moment they realised they were safe to speak, that their parents had given permission and that we had nothing to do with the school, they were free to speak. And they did.

They told us tragic stories. Of being abused in the English teacher Edmonds' study and then being returned to their beds and lying there crying, desperate to ask for help, but not daring to ring their parents. Of the self-disgust, the confusion. And it was not just abuse by Cadman and Edmonds. Bill Printer, a third teacher, was added to our list: the six-foot five giant of a man who used to intimidate children by bellowing at them. One child told us: 'They called me "Printer's Bum Chum". He took photographs of me and raped me – he'd give me whisky.' And another who had been abused by Printer said: 'While we were alone in a classroom, he hit me while he was abusing me. I felt I was disgusting, that I had let my parents down.'

Then we learned that Printer had already been asked to leave by a previous school. I spoke to the Headmaster of that establishment who told me that one of Printer's victims there had cleverly tape-recorded the teacher asking for sexual favours in return for money and then taken the recording as evidence to the Headmaster. Even with incontrovert-ible proof, fearing any police investigation would harm the reputation of the school, the Head made a deal with him: he allowed Printer to leave quietly on condition he worked in a girls' school. And Printer left, to find the perfect teaching job for a paedophile: in a boys' school, working for Cadman.

Cadman reminded me of a spider, trapping boys as if they were flies in his web. One child told us: 'Caddy could make me do what he wanted – I felt disgusted with myself.' Another said: 'I went into his room to use the telephone – I was very upset about something. He made me sit next to him and then he abused me. In the end I threw the telephone at him so hard it broke and ran away. I cried all night in bed; I couldn't sleep and from then on, I thought about it every day. I had constant nightmares. It was as if I had a dreadful secret inside.' Another said: 'The other boys called me "Caddy's Bum Boy". It was like having a wound that wouldn't heal. That man shouldn't be anywhere near children, he should be in a cell!'

Once the boys had told us what had happened to them, we had to pass on the information to their parents. That was painful, for them and for us. I remember one mother coming to meet me and asking for a private conversation. The only room I could find was a storeroom filled with cardboard boxes. We propped ourselves up on the piles of boxes while she told me of the abuse she herself had suffered as a child. What happened to her son brought back her own worst memories and filled her with guilt. I told her not to blame herself for what had happened to her boy. These teachers were clever, ruthless criminals: they groomed the parents and the boys.

And the Ministry of Defence had much to answer for. When parents discovered abuse and asked to remove a boy, they were told that if a child left the school before the end of the year, the parents had to repay the whole year's grant: £4,000. Which was of course impossible.

Our plan was to script what the children had told us, keeping them anonymous. But we couldn't broadcast what they had said without expert guidance. *That's Life!* was regularly given legal advice by Michael Bloch, QC, who used to give us a rough ride whenever he thought we were skating on thin ice. (Michael later became a Trustee of ChildLine.) This time the ice was terribly fragile: everything depended on the strength and courage of the boys who had talked to us. Cadman could well afford to sue the BBC and we were accusing him of extremely serious crimes. If he sued us for libel, the damages would be huge if he won. And he would be exonerated, too. So it was crucial that the children would be strong enough to give good evidence in court.

Michael Bloch interviewed each child and then, separately, Hereward Harrison did so too, to see if in their expert view, the boys were truthful and telling their stories in a way a jury would find credible. The boys passed both interviews with flying colours.

So now it was up to me to turn the tale of Crookham Court into a script. We changed the names of the boys because legally we had to ensure they remained anonymous, but nothing else. The piece began with the terrible report the school had been given by the Inspectors. We described the dangerous buildings and the inadequate teaching, emphasising the fact that the owner of the school – Philip Cadman – took full responsibility and nobody could restrain him. And finally we revealed that he and Anthony Edmonds were both paedophiles. We quoted each child's description of the abuse they had suffered, the torment of guilt and shame they had experienced. And we pointed out that Cadman, knowing a child had disclosed abuse by Edmonds, had still given him an excellent reference when he resigned. At the time we believed that Edmonds was no longer teaching.

It had been our longest, most difficult investigation. My tension showed in the programme – my voice was half an octave higher than normal. Listening to the children's stories, I remember our audience in the Television Theatre was utterly still: I could feel them listening, appalled, as this unbelievable story unwound before them.

The programme broadcast on the Sunday night. On the Monday morning I came into the office as usual. My phone rang, it was an irate mother. We were wrong about Edmonds, she said: he had certainly not left teaching, as we had said in the programe. He was an English teacher again and she knew where. She named her son's school. And, she said furiously, we must also be completely wrong when we claimed he had sexually abused any children. Mr Edmonds was by far the best English teacher her son had ever had, all the pupils in the school liked him. She was adamant. The man she knew could not possibly be a paedophile. I tried to explain that, as Ray Wyre had told me, 'Monsters don't get close to children. Nice men do.' At the time Ray was the country's leading therapist working with paedophiles and he knew more about their methods than anyone else but that didn't convince her.

In our next programme we named Bill Printer as another child abuser and we told viewers that we'd been wrong to say Anthony Edmonds had left teaching: he was back in another school, thanks no doubt to the warm reference Cadman had given him.

Then we described the pressures put on the boys and their parents. One child had told us he'd been threatened, 'Nobody will believe you, they'll say you're lying.' We revealed that the Ministry of Defence had insisted boys had to stay in the school the whole year otherwise their parents would have to pay back the whole fee of £4,000. (As a result of our programme they immediately changed that policy for the Crookham Court parents.) Social services wanted the right to inspect an independent school for quality of life. (As a result of our programme, David Mellor, then Minister for Health and responsible for the Children Act 1989, gave them the right, which has recently been withdrawn.) After the programme a man came to Lime Grove to tell us that he too had been abused twenty-five years ago when he was at boarding school. He was abused by his housemaster, Philip Cadman.

The boy responsible for our investigation, Peter, came to the Television Theatre in Shepherd's Bush to watch us recording the programme. He told me: 'When we came to the studio again it was overwhelming, the cameras were everywhere. I remember going into the Green Room in the TV theatre in Shepherd's Bush and that's when we first met Val Howarth, who ran ChildLine. After the programme, we all expected something dramatic to happen, for the police to take action, but nothing happened at all.'

It was a tremendous anti-climax for us, too. We had put together, we thought, such a strong case. But although the local Newbury police came to talk to us, they didn't seem at all enthused by the idea of taking up the case of Crookham Court School again, even though I pleaded with them to protect the children. I told them that I believed Cadman would continue abusing boys. They were incredulous – 'He'd never dare, now.' But he did.

After what seemed a lifetime – in fact it was two months later – we heard that Cadman, Edmonds and Printer had all been arrested.

Edmonds pleaded guilty. Not out of nobility, not because he wanted to spare his victims from the ordeal of having to give evidence in court, though that was the effect of his plea, but because when he was arrested, he was allowed one phone call. So he rang his mother in a panic and said: 'Destroy the diaries.'

But the police heard him and got there first. They found his diaries. Like many paedophiles, he recorded his crimes so that he could mull over them, enjoying them repeatedly. In his diaries he described 1,200 assaults against children, 111 of them against Crookham Court boys. Painstakingly and methodically, he also recorded the sums of money paid to each child. That was Edmonds, the enthusiastic English teacher the mother had rung me to defend. The same Edmonds who was passed from one school to another, three schools in all, each time leaving with glowing references.

The two other teachers, Cadman and Printer, both pleaded not guilty. Which meant the boys had to experience the full horror of our adversarial judicial system. They had to give evidence in an open court, describing in detail to total strangers the sexual abuse which caused them immense pain to remember. As an extra cruelty, none of the children was allowed any counselling before the trial because if they did, there was a risk that the defence counsel would use that to claim they had been 'coached' and told what to say. So their memories remained unhealed wounds.

And because they could only answer the questions they were asked, they couldn't tell the jury the full story. We interviewed one of the boys after the trial and he told us, 'That time in court was the worst time in my life, as bad as the abuse. I wanted to tell them about the pain I went through, the physical pain so that I can't go to the toilet properly now, and the mental pain. You can't forget any of it. This will stay with me all my life. I feel I'm to blame, because I was the one it happened to.'

While being cross-examined by the defence barrister, one boy was made to try and read a transcript of an interview he had given but he was never given the opportunity to tell the court that he was so profoundly dyslexic he could not read. He told us, 'I couldn't understand, it was too difficult to me. So I just wanted to get out quickly.'

Another burst into tears as he was asked to give all the details of the abuse he suffered. Alas, as one lawyer told us, 'To the jury, a crying kid is a lying kid.' John Spencer, Professor of Law at Selwyn College, Cambridge, explained why such cruelty was commonplace in abuse trials. Since the child is often the only prosecution evidence, he told us, 'The only defence is to break the child down, muddle the child or attack the child's evidence.'

And that is easy enough to do in the intimidating, confusing atmosphere of the courtroom. I was a witness in the trial of Cadman and Printer and had to give evidence myself. It was an ordeal. I remember every detail.

At the back of the courtroom sat the paedophiles. Not the ones on trial, but those who came for the spectator sport because they were hoping to enjoy as much detail as the children could be persuaded to reveal. I only hope the children themselves were not aware of these ghouls.

I had been well prepared. One of the trustees of ChildLine, the philanthropist Ian Skipper, was so concerned ChildLine might be attacked in the course of the trial that he arranged for me to meet the eminent barrister, Michael Mansfield. Mansfield was, and is, a charismatic figure. He strode into his chambers, gown and hair flowing in the wind, like Charlton Heston leading the troops into battle. Obviously he was not professionally permitted to 'coach' me by asking me any questions I might actually be asked at the trial but he cross-examined me instead about the value of counselling abused children. Tough though it was, I realised that I could take my time, reject the suggestions he made to me and answer in my own way. He explained to me that when I was asked my address, I could ask the court's permission to write it down, rather than say it aloud. None of the boys knew that. If they knew there were paedophiles in the courtroom, how worrying must that have been for them? It occurred to me that if I, a professional broadcaster, could feel so intimidated at the thought of giving evidence, what must the boys be going through?

Because I was to be called as a witness, I was not permitted to listen in on the children giving their evidence, although I was told that one of them sobbed uncontrollably in the witness box and another was so small the jury were almost unable to see his face as he tried to peer over the top of the box. When my turn came, subpoenaed by Cadman's defence barrister, I realised the lawyer's purpose was to use me to undermine the boys. I was cross-examined by a barrister who argued that I myself was so obsessed by the subject of child abuse from my work at ChildLine that I managed to implant the idea in the boys' minds. By hypnosis, I wonder, or telepathy?

I found an opportunity to try and explain to the jury how humiliating it must be for the boys to give evidence in an open court. 'If you asked me to tell you, here in the courtroom, in detail, what my husband and I did in bed together, I would be embarassed and humiliated, and yet we are both adults. We love each other and what we do is quite legal. I can only imagine what it must be like to be a child, and to try and describe an act which I know is criminal and which fills me with disgust and shame to remember.'

Indeed it had been an almost intolerable ordeal for them. Peter told me: 'On my way to the court for the trial, I was very nervous. We'd gone through so much. All it took was for someone to say "Not Guilty", and they'd go back to the school and everything would carry on. I had to give evidence for two or three hours. I can't remember the cross-examination – I think I must have blocked it out from my mind. But I do remember after it was all over, I was told I was good. I had been told not to lie, but I don't lie anyway. I was told if I didn't understand anything to say "Pardon" to give me more time to think. So I did, quite often.

'I had to walk past Caddy in the dock. After I'd given evidence I was worried that he wouldn't be found guilty. It would all have been an awful waste of time. That was why I'd rung ChildLine in the first place, because he deserved to go to prison. Knowing what he'd done, the thing that got me was the number of years the abuse went on for, without anyone knowing or being able to stop him.

'What really got to me was that when all that had happened in the past, the parents had just taken their kids out of the school, or teachers had left, with no one being told the reason. It just wasn't right, it wasn't the answer. I know it screwed me up. It's no good just sweeping it under the carpet, that just leaves the kids carrying the whole thing secretly, being screwed up with nobody on their side to help them. It needed to end.'

The jury went out to consider their verdict. The verdict came through on a summer's day when the *That's Life!* cricket team were playing a charity match in the New Forest. As I was watching, my phone rang. I listened, and as the verdicts were read out to me one by one, I stood up and began to run towards the pitch, filled with joy and overwhelming relief. The cricketers stopped playing and our team began to run towards me. All of us cared so much. This was so important to these children, and to *all* children. As I heard the three guilty verdicts and passed on the news to our team, we all hugged each other in the middle of the cricket pitch and then I ran to my car to drive to Reading.

Outside the court I was caught by a local television reporter.

'You were accused in court of trial by television, Miss Rantzen. How do you respond to that?'

'The judge exonerated us of that accusation,' I said. 'We all believe these cases should be heard in court and that it's up to a jury to come to a verdict. But without the evidence we put together, this could never have been tried at all. We had to find that evidence and it was only because of the courage of the children who gave evidence in court that these men are where they deserve to be, in prison.'

With the teachers in prison, Crookham Court School closed down. Cadman and Printer briefly lived there when they came out, then Cadman died. The buildings began to rot and decay but the school left a legacy for the boys who had been abused there, who were left with flashbacks, nightmares, a feeling of shame. But for other children, there were some reforms to the judicial system. The *Childwatch* programmes, and the work by enlightened judges and lawyers meant that video-taped evidence was now allowed into courtrooms. That meant children were no longer forced to confront their abusers in the courtroom but they are still denied counselling. They are still forced to undergo live cross-examination, still prevented by our adversarial system – which was designed to frighten adults into telling the truth – from telling their whole story so that the jury hears the truth. Other countries do it differently, and far, far better.

But at least in the Crookham Court case we got the crucial guilty verdicts, which saved more generations of boys from abuse. Peter told me: 'My parents wanted to bring them to justice, so they were pleased when they were sent to jail. They all deserved it. Printer was nasty – a bully. He'd raise his voice and use his height to intimidate boys. Edmonds did it for his own kicks. And all Cadman's threats that nobody would believe me turned out to be rubbish. I got support from everyone at ChildLine, and from my family while I was going through the trial, from everyone involved in the investigation. Nobody except Caddy's lawyer during the trial ever said you're having a laugh, you're telling lies.

'After they'd been sent to jail, even though good came out of it, we decided not to go public, not to talk about it. Mum and

Dad always said, don't go round talking about it. But I don't really care that people know, as long as I'm helping someone else. If any other children are given the courage to ask for help because of what happened to me, that's what makes it worthwhile. That's why I wrote to you in the first place.'

Some months after the trial, Diana, Princess of Wales, came to ChildLine. Feeling somehow they needed to be rewarded for their courage, I invited Peter and his brother David to meet her there. I told the Princess's team a little of their story. Peter told me: 'We were quite nervous. I remember David and I were in a room by ourselves in the ChildLine office, wondering what to say and how to approach her. Somebody kept popping in and updating us as she walked around ChildLine, meeting people. We heard your voices, we knew you were getting closer and closer. Then the Princess walked in. She was stunning, smiling, and very tall, beautiful – just the way she looked on the telly.'

Everyone at ChildLine was on their best behaviour that day, trying to stick to royal etiquette. But the boys had chanced their luck and brought a camera. As Diana came into the office, she saw the camera in the middle of the table. She looked at the boys, smiling, and asked: 'Whose camera is that?' 'Mine,' said Peter. We half-expected the camera to be confiscated by her protection officer, but instead Diana asked: 'Would anyone like a picture?' Of course the boys were thrilled. That photograph is on Peter's bookcase today. He told me: 'Sometimes people notice it and ask me why it was taken. I don't tell them. I just say "It's who you know" and they leave it like that. But I would like to talk about it now, because now I really believe abuse is not something to hide or be ashamed of. As Hereward always told me, when I admitted how guilty and ashamed Caddy made me feel, it's never the child's fault.'

CHAPTER TEN

SUFFER LITTLE CHILDREN

There are many reasons why children can become so securely locked in that no matter how great the pain, they cannot break out of the prison of silence. In families, it may be that they love their abuser too much to risk losing him, although they loathe and fear the abuse itself. In organisations, like a school, a children's home, or a church, it may be that there is a culture of abuse. They may be abused by people they believe have so much power, or who are united in a conspiracy, so that the children are completely unable to ask anyone for help or take control of their own lives.

Crookham Court School had that culture. But at the time I investigated the school, I had no idea that one of the founders of the school, the Reverend Roy Cotton, went on from the school to commit a lifetime of crime against children. And, alas, the Church of England provided the perfect shelter for him. For since the *That's Life!* investigation, more fascinating facts about the school have emerged, and its links with this particularly ruthless paedophile.

If you look up Crookham Court School on the internet (www.crookhamians.co.uk), you will find a website for old boys. It includes the school crest and explains what the various symbols mean:

Welcome to the Old Crookhamians website.
The Official Web Site for Old Boys of Crookham Court School, Thatcham, Nr. Newbury, Berkshire, England.

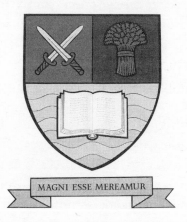

MAGNI ESSE MEREAMUR

The School Crest
The School Crest was devised by Roy Cotton, and the original, hand painted Crest which hung in the dining room, was designed and painted by the father of founder-member Chris Brett.

*The motto: **'Magni Esse Mereamur'** translates: **'Let us deserve to be great.'***

*The third section represents the **two head teachers who founded the school**. It depicts an open book resting on sea waves. The book is said to represent Roy Cotton, who gained an MA from Oxford, and the waves represent the naval career of Robert Smithwick, who retained his title of 'Commander'.*

Of the two founders mentioned on the website, one, Commander Smithwick, had a naval career of some distinction.

The other, the Reverend Roy Cotton, had been a teacher and had studied to become a priest. When he left Crookham Court he went on to enjoy a career in the church. A career as a priest, a choirmaster and a paedophile.

The Church of England has been a source of inspiration to millions, all the more reason for Church leaders to protect their followers from predators like the Rev. Cotton. But they failed.

Before Roy Cotton ever came to Crookham Court, before he had become a teacher, and certainly before he became a priest, he had already been convicted for sexually abusing a choirboy. At the time he was twenty-five years old, an ordination student, hoping to join the Church. Instead, he was kindly and gently advised by the Church to try a different career.

You might think after that experience, being caught and convicted of molesting a child, he would find another job which kept him well away from children. But no. Paedophiles inevitably try to find work which puts them in direct control of children. And Cotton did just that: he went into teaching. Imagine his delight at meeting and impressing Commander Smithwick. And then to become the co-founder of a boys' boarding school, Crookham Court School.

Paedophiles are addicts, of course. And Cotton was determined to gain access to the objects of his lust, young boys. So it is not surprising that soon enough there were allegations about his behaviour with the boys at the school. They were so serious that Smithwick dismissed him. He left quietly. No scandal. No police involvement.

So where did Cotton go next? Back into the forgiving Church. Did they know why he had left? They did. But even though it was known that boys had complained about him, Roy Cotton was ordained and then spent years as a priest and choirmaster in the Church of England, blithely continuing to sexually abuse boys. Because he was a priest, he could commit crimes against children who were powerless against him, whose families trusted and looked up to him. His position in the Church allowed him to gain their trust, and gave him easy access to the children.

How is it that organisations set up on the highest moral principles – churches, boarding schools, children's homes – not only allow themselves to be corrupted, but seem to protect those criminals who infiltrate them? A psychiatrist once gave me an insight into the behaviour of organisations.

It was only a few months after ChildLine was launched and my family took a holiday together on a boat. Among the other passengers was a group of psychiatrists from Florida. When I told them about the creation of ChildLine, they were fascinated but they told me to beware. One of them said: 'The first day an organisation is created, it exists for the sake of its clients. From day two, it exists to protect itself.'

When they are threatened, organisations go to great lengths to protect themselves, often sacrificing individuals in the process. That's why schools prefer not to report paedophile teachers to the police. We have seen how the Catholic Church covered up criminal priests over generations, causing huge suffering, and in the end tremendous damage to the reputation of the Church itself. And small wonder. For decades, when children were abused by priests and tried to ask for help, the Vatican responded by shifting each priest to another parish, and by covering up and concealing the crimes to protect itself.

But of course that is not unique to the Catholic Church. Indeed, working in the Diocese of Chichester, the Reverend Roy Cotton, as a High Church Anglican priest, was allowed to be a choirmaster with easy access to children, even though he had already been convicted for sexually abusing a choirboy.

Phil Johnson, one of Cotton's victims, was groomed and abused by him, and now tirelessly campaigns to alert the Church to his crimes. Phil Johnson was born in 1965 and grew up in Eastbourne. He told me:

'Roy Cotton preyed upon me and he groomed my parents skilfully and ruthlessly. They were religious people and they were tremendously impressed by his education, by the interest he took in me and, of course, by the fact that he was the vicar and the choirmaster.

'We were an ordinary family, not well-off, not much money to spend. My earliest memories are living in a council house next to a railway. It was a red brick semi, with a little front garden which had a concrete path up the front. And a little back garden with a path straight up the middle and vegetable plots either side. I used to steal the strawberries and peas, which taste amazingly sweet straight from the plant. I'd blame it on the birds, I never admitted it was me.

'My parents were quite rigid disciplinarians. They married when my mother was sixteen and I was born very soon after that. I look very like her. She was slim and attractive, though she dressed in a rather frumpy way: she wore glasses and never had the money to buy nice clothes. We children were brought up in hand-me-downs, everything was borrowed.

'Mum and Dad both left school at fourteen, so they had no formal education, but neither of them was stupid. My father was a skilled electrician. Nowadays you have to have a degree to do his job. My father did whack me from time to time, but nothing serious. Once he threw me downstairs because I called him a wally. I still do, from time to time – it's a family joke.

'We left that house when I was four or five and moved to another council house on a brand-new estate. It was bigger, at the end of a terrace built in 1969; my parents still live there. We had to move because as more children were born, we needed more space. The new one had three bedrooms. My father comes from Irish Catholic descent and he was brought up as a Catholic. My mother's family was from Sussex, they were church-going High Anglicans. There was an issue about them marrying: they couldn't marry in Church, so they married in a Registery Office.

'I went to a Church school in the early days, St Andrew's Church of England Infants' School. It was part of an imposing Victorian red-brick complex with the church in the middle. There was a strong link with the church, of course. The vicar would take our school assemblies at least once a week, and we'd go to carol services and Easter services in the church. My great grandmother had been to the same school and she was an ardent member of the congregation. My grandmother, great grandmother and a great aunt who used to look after me sometimes were all great church-goers.

'At the age of seven I changed school and went to the local county junior school, half a mile down the road. But there were still strong connections, strong links back to St Andrew's Church, and the vicar kept the connection going with my new school too, organising carol services and so on. The street where I lived was built around a square and there were lots of other children living there who were the same age as me. Three of the boys were members of the church choir so my parents thought it would be a good idea if I joined, too, because I was quite a good singer and there were loads of other activities organised for the children in the choir – trips and things. So I just sort of fell into it, not from any burning desire to be a choirboy, but it seemed quite a good idea to my parents.

'I got into choir very easily, I didn't have to audition. The choir was run by the vicar, Roy Cotton. He had come to the church in 1974. He was an odd-looking man – extremely fat around the belly, but with very thin arms and legs. He was about five foot ten, with dark hair cut fairly short, curly on top, and I remember, the way children do, that he had terrible dandruff. He wore heavy thick glasses with tortoiseshell rims, and wore black trousers, a grey shirt and a dog collar. Out of vicar dress he was partial to short-sleeved shirts, shorts and sandals. He smoked very heavily and drank a lot, always smelt of fags and whisky. By then he was in his late forties but looked older. I see him as vividly now as I did as a child.

'And I had to see a lot of him – the choir took up a great deal of my life. There was choir practice on Fridays, Mass or Eucharist on Sundays, Evensong on Feast Days and weddings on Saturdays. Loads of them. In June or July, you might do three weddings a day so it took up a lot of time.

'After a while I was made a server, which meant I had to do week-day services as well, almost every morning. It was my job to ring the bell to call people to prayer. Cotton gave me more and more responsibility. And he got to know my parents really well – not, of course, that they ever really knew him, although they thought they did. He was always in our house. The church was two miles away and one of our neighbours used to take me there. But I was one of the vicar's favourites and because I had to take on additional duties, he would take me home. And then he'd meet my parents and have a cup of tea with them. They thought he was a very good influence on me: he was very well-educated with a Masters Degree from Oxford, so they respected him. And as things began to happen with me, he began to see them more and more. For instance, on weekdays when he would take funeral services because the crematorium was quite close to where we lived, he took to dropping in on my parents on the way back. So he infiltrated the family completely.

'Without asking me, he'd make arrangements with them so that I had to see more and more of him. Each time I got home, they would have arranged that I'd be doing this or that. Additional services, or educational trips to learn church architecture – to see the church at Sompting, for instance, because it has Saxon towers. It was just an excuse to spend lots of time with me.

'At first I didn't mind – it was all educational and harmless. I was quite clever and I respected his knowledge – he knew a lot about things I was interested in. As my parents had so little formal education, I couldn't ask them questions because they didn't know the answers but when I asked him, a book would come out and be shown to me, in his house. It was all about control, really. But I liked that knowledge he shared with me.

'And I liked the attention. I came from a very working-class family but when I went out with him, we'd eat out at restaurants, where I could never go with my parents. The best we could do as a family was share a plate of chips in a pub garden whereas with him, you could order anything off the menu. He once ordered me steak with stilton on the top, which tasted better than anything I'd ever eaten before. Mum was a terrible cook. She used to foster children, she used to give them spam, instant mashed potato and baked beans. It was horrendous. So with him it was like being in a different social class and he was quite well-connected, so he knew people who could get me new school uniforms and things because he'd do a deal somehow. And I had discovered from wearing hand-me-downs that second-hand clothes can be very stigmatising. Other boys tend to notice.

'For the first year Cotton didn't do anything inappropriate to me. He made sure he had everything in place first, that he had thoroughly groomed me and my parents before he started anything. The next stage was studying sculpture, and that's when other things began to happen.

'Every summer he'd take a group of scouts and choirboys on minibus tours across France, visiting all the cathedral cities in Northern France, for instance, or Lourdes, or the Loire Valley. Later, he'd taken them on to the Vatican and Venice. It was always in a twelve-seater minibus and he'd drive. Usually the group would only be boys, although sometimes he would include a couple of girls.

'By 1976 when I was ten, I was his little helper. So he asked me to help him prepare the next trip, unpack last year's tents and so on. We worked together all day one Saturday. And when at last I had finished, he insisted I was dirty and needed a shower. I'd never had a shower. In our house we had a bath once a week and shared the water. We all had the same water.

So I wasn't accustomed to having a shower but he insisted, so I did.

'I went in and started to shower, and then as soon as I was in, he came into the bathroom, too. Then he said: "You haven't got a towel," so he brought one and just stood there with it, out of reach, watching me in the shower. Then there was a strangely horrible moment when I wanted the towel and he wasn't giving it to me – it was a very uncomfortable moment. But it passed. I took the towel, dried myself, dressed and went home.

'About this time he introduced me to sculpture. He would talk about the sculptor Michelangelo and what a genius he was, and how he could show all the muscles under the skin. Next, when I looked at books with him, it always had to be in his front bedroom. And while we were there I'd be given gifts as well: books to start with, then anything I needed for school like a set of compasses. They would always be presented to me in his bedroom.

'Next, we would both have to lie on the bed to look at his books. Then he would take my top off to show me Michelangelo's muscles. Then he would undo my trousers and trace the muscle with his hand. But nothing sexual, yet. And of course at ten you have no idea what is going on.

'Bit by bit, things escalated. But the first thing that was really disturbing happened when we were lying on the bed studying geology. We were just having a conversation, but then he became really affectionate with me, started to talk lovingly. Then suddenly he rolled me over on my back, got on top of me and French kissed me. I remember his stubble, his tongue forced in my mouth. And I couldn't understand what was going on. I was really troubled. I thought about it over and over again. All I could imagine was that maybe he had some sort of disease that made him do that. And that he had put his tongue in my mouth because he was trying to pass on the disease to me. That left me completely confused.

'I didn't tell anybody. I really don't know why, it was just too strange and horrific. I tried to avoid going into that room but however I tried to avoid him, it was hopeless because I'd come home from school and find that he'd already been there and arranged outings with my parents, so I couldn't get away.

'I passed the 11 Plus – I was the only one from my street to get a place at grammar school. So I was alienated from all my peers. And my loneliness was a huge opportunity for Cotton. He said he was very proud of me. So now he used to take me under his wing in earnest. He got me my school uniform and a horrible brown fold-over briefcase. And a blazer. And log tables. And a geometry set. And a dictionary. And a nice expensive bicycle to get to school, a twelve-speed racing bike. And a Pentax and lenses. All things my parents couldn't afford.

'The next trip we did in 1977 was to France. I was taken on this camping trip, I was eleven. My parents didn't pay, it was a gift from him. It was my first big foreign trip. I'd never had a holiday, not even an overnight with my parents, so this was the first time ever away from home.

'It was a long trip, four or five weeks' camping, moving around from one campsite to another in this minibus. And I got a stomach upset. Then in the shower block I lost my watch, which upset me. Then I got lost for a few hours, wandering around town, not knowing where I was, separated from the group. Cotton drove around looking for me. Eventually I stopped at an army barracks and told them I was lost. They took me in and looked after me; they let me sit in a tank. But as a result of all this, I was really upset.

'That night we were in a big tent, in compartments – I was always put in the tent where Cotton was. I felt ill – I was having nightmares about having been lost – so I got up in the night and I went to him for comfort. I needed a hug. So he held me. He said: "Does that make you feel better?" I said: "Yes, it's like having a great big teddy bear." So Cotton took this as a signal anything was on. He took me into his bed and he was aggressively sexual with me.

'From then on he created a code: TB standing for teddy bear would be code for anything sexual. He'd introduce TB into sermons, the bedroom became the Tibby Room. Nobody else would know but he would look at me in a room of 200 kids and talk about something we had talked about on the bed. And it made me freeze, horrified in case someone else would know: he could intimidate me in a room full of 100 people and nobody else would know.

'From that point on it developed sexually on a logarithmic scale, more and more often. And he would make excuses for me to stay over at the vicarage, so I'd have to stay overnight with him. It made me frightened, I hated it. But there were still parts I liked: the attention and the learning. And Cotton had got me smoking and drinking from a very early age. It was another secret. So he had a hold over you.

'The only way I had for dealing with the rest was to try and remove myself from my body. I would dissociate, I would freeze. I would count the books on the bookshelf, anything to remove myself from what was going on. And not move at all. He would drag me onto him, make me do things to him. But I wouldn't: I wouldn't show any complicity, any approval. But if I tried to resist, he'd just continue until I was sore and bruised. When he finished he'd go back to his room. So in the end, you just wanted him to get it over as soon as possible.

'So it went on, for the next seven or eight years. I had fallen out with all the other boys, the ones who lived near me and the ones in the choir – they all thought I was Cotton's favourite. I had to sit in the minibus next to him, up front. And I went to the grammar school so they thought I was a snob. But at school I was rejected, too: the bloke from the council estate, my nickname there was Scumbag. And that suited Cotton. I was completely friendless, I was very alone. I still don't have any close friends, I find it incredibly hard to trust people.

'I had become aware it wasn't only Cotton. A local bishop who had confirmed me, Peter Ball, was his friend and I was taken to see him and stay over there. I got very suspicious. There was another boy there who had committed arson in his school and caused massive damage. He was fifteen or sixteen, and somehow instead of a custodial sentence he was given into the care of Bishop Peter. When I was there with his monks Bishop Peter was treating this boy like a puppy: petting him, showing him off, like a trophy, like a cuddly toy. (I found out years later that Bishop Peter had to resign from Gloucester in 1993 because he'd been cautioned for performing a sex act on a seventeen-year-old in a shower. Once he touched me up in front of Cotton, and Cotton just watched. There are a number of complaints against him on the record in Lambeth Palace.)

'When I went to stay with the Bishop, I slept there overnight and Cotton came into my room. It was late in the evening. I knew what he wanted, and I was very shocked. I said, "You can't do this, there are people around." But he said, "That's OK, that's fine," like everybody knew about it. Then he groped around, touched me and went away. So then I was sure the Bishop knew.

'The next summer trip was to the Loire Valley. We went in the old purple Ford transit minibus: Cotton was driving, me sitting up in front next to him as usual. We went to visit an old friend of Cotton's who had spent time in England, his name was Père Nicholas. He was a Catholic priest, but very unconventional. He lived in a sort of commune, with lots of teenage boys around. And there was a young woman in her twenties living with him. They were very affectionate together.

'We all slept in a hall. That evening, Cotton selected a few of the boys to take away, one at a time. When it came to my turn, I was taken upstairs to the attic, which was an old dark loft with photographic lights. Immediately I got there I was very concerned because on the walls were large black-and-white prints of boys, all completely naked. Not pornographic, the pictures were "artistic" like the Nazi propaganda pictures of the perfect Aryan. But one was of a boy I had seen downstairs and in the picture he was posing with ribbons.

'I was very, very scared. Cotton told me to undress. I refused. He tried to take my top off. I wouldn't let him. The other priest was there, watching. In the end Cotton jumped on top of me, put all his weight on me to hold me down and kissed me full on the mouth while Père Nicholas took photographs. Who knows what else would have happened, but I managed to kick a lamp over and in the kerfuffle I escaped.

'All of this together made me believe that everyone in the Church knew what was going on and that they were all in it together. So it was no surprise when in 1979 Cotton took me to see Father Colin Pritchard. Pritchard and Cotton had been students together. The excuse to go was that they needed statues repainted in the church and Cotton recommended me because I was very good at that sort of thing: I was artistic.

'We stayed at Pritchard's vicarage three nights. Cotton came into my bed and again told me that would be fine, so I thought Pritchard must know. One night we went out to a friend's: there were half a dozen people there, all men. We had a big Chinese takeaway meal, my first ever, and Pritchard introduced me to a Gin Sling: Gin, Cinzano, lemonade. I was fourteen. He kept plying me with this concoction and I drank a vast amount.

'I have no recollection of leaving this place. I only know that I woke up the next morning back in the vicarage, in the bed, completely naked. I didn't sleep naked normally. And I felt as if a horse had kicked me in the head. My clothes had disappeared. There was a horrible black silky dressing-gown hanging up, so I put that on, and went downstairs and found Pritchard there doing a crossword. I asked him: "Where are my clothes?" He said: "You were sick all over them so we had to wash them." I didn't believe him. I said: "I'm sure I would have remembered that."

'Instantly he got furious. He said nothing, not a single word, he just slammed me against a kitchen cupboard, grabbed my genitals, cutting my penis so I was left bleeding and seizing my throat in an iron grip. He glared at me, his face only inches away. It was like time had frozen; I don't know how long he held me there. And then he went back to his crossword. I went to the bathroom and found my clothes. No sick, not washed. I really don't know what happened that night, with all those men, but I was really scared. I said to Cotton: "We've just got to go." He was angry, but we left.

'I remember going back to school on the bus and thinking, I really must do something about this. I remember watching the traffic lights and thinking, I've got to talk to somebody but I thought if I did it would be front page of the *News of the World*. I thought it would blow up, destroy my family. So I made a conscious decision to tell nobody. If only ChildLine had been there, if I had been able to talk anonymously I would have. That is the moment I could have escaped and brought them to justice.

'From then on there was a lot of intimidation to keep me quiet, all kinds of threats. Cotton would create secrets, like the alcohol and the cigarettes, and imply that if I told, he would tell. I tried to avoid ever seeing Cotton but to my horror, "as a special surprise" he arranged for a trip to Greece alone, just him and me. I had no choice. The plane tickets were there waiting at home. And while we were there, he did whatever he could with me, although he wasn't in the best of health. Overall he abused me for the best part of nine years.

'Not only me. Cotton abused my baby brother Gary too, who is five years younger than me. But I didn't learn how Gary had suffered for years. I feel terrible about it, I had no idea – I thought it was just me. I don't know how he did it and kept us apart.

'As children, Gary and I were very close: we shared a room, with a bunk bed. There was no room even for a wardrobe, so we kept all our clothes in two suitcases under the bottom bed. Gary is really musical. He can play any instrument by ear, he can write music. So naturally he joined Cotton's choir, too. And Cotton took him under his wing to teach him piano. When I was eighteen and went away to college, he just substituted my brother for me. I didn't even know.

'I came back home for the summer when I was nineteen. By then Cotton had moved to another parish, Breede with Udimore on the Kent-Sussex border. My parents insisted that I must go and see him there and take my brother with me in my car. I did. When we got there, we sat around chatting with Cotton, and then he got out a bottle of whisky and began to ply us with it. That's when the alarm bells rang, because it was very clear what Cotton had in mind. I said to Gary, "Come on, we're leaving," even though by then I was very drunk, with half a bottle of whisky inside me and it was driving rain. I bundled him into the car and drove away as fast as I could.

'At that moment I had a huge sense of elation, I thought I'd saved my brother. And I thought, that's it, I'm finally in control, free of the worst Cotton could do to me. I was relieved, excited, released – driving away as fast as I could in my own car. And the inevitable happened. I crashed the car. I skidded, crashed into a level crossing, the car left the ground, the exhaust broke, dug into the ground, and the car wouldn't move.

'I got Gary to run to some roadworks to get their little yellow lights to warn any other cars. Then a police car pulled up. They didn't want to get out of the car, with the rain coming down in buckets. If they'd arrested me, I would have blurted out everything to them. But instead they said they'd escort us to Battle and from there, we got back to Eastbourne.

And still, in spite of everything, Gary and I never talked about it. But as soon as I went back to college, Cotton went on abusing him. It wasn't until years later, in 1996 when we'd both seen a story about abuse by a priest on television, that we talked at all. We both stopped and watched the programme together and I could see from his face it had hit him. It became very apparent. So I said, "Did anything happen with you and Cotton?" He said nothing, just went ashen and then broke down. He sobbed for an hour – I felt horrible and just didn't know what to do. But that's when I went to the police station. I was expecting to get some help, but I didn't get it.

'When I told them why I was there, they sat me in a waiting room in the child protection office. I remember there were pictures on the walls of children being abused. Children they were trying to identify. I thought it was very inappropriate, putting me in there. But anyway, I told the police my story.

'When I finished, the police officer said to me, "Do you have children? Do you bath your children? Do you put them to bed?" Suddenly I felt I was under suspicion. They took statements from me and my brother. They put a woman detective on the case, but then they told me she'd been signed off with stress and was transferred to traffic. So they assigned another officer to the case, but he didn't even check to see if Roy Cotton and Colin Pritchard had criminal records. If they had, they would have discovered that although at the time there was nothing on Pritchard, Cotton had a conviction and Peter Ball had a caution, but they failed to check.

'They treated my brother and me completely separately. I had three or four interviews with the police, each one lasting two hours. But eventually after a year had gone by, I was presented with my statement to sign. I couldn't believe it. It was so brief, just three sides of A4 paper. I protested. Where was the detail? The trips? The gifts? I had a huge amount of circumstantial evidence. They just said it was not admissible. They arrested Cotton and Pritchard in 1997 and they were bailed. Then in March 1999, I got a letter saying the CPS had decided that there was not enough evidence to take it any further.

'I was depressed, angry, pissed off. I felt that nobody had done a thorough job and brought these men to justice. And that's when I decided to take things into my own hands. In 2000, I published a magazine and called it "The Secret Life of an Eastbourne Vicar: The Truth About What Went on Behind this Eastbourne Vicarage Door." I gave as much detail as I could, hoping that other survivors would come forward – I wanted Cotton in court. But very disappointingly nothing happened: the Church took no action at all. Now I'm told people did come forward. One person immediately disclosed to his mother and she reported it to the neighbouring church, but they have no record of it.

'At last, in late 2006 somebody else came forward in Northamptonshire who had been abused by Colin Pritchard. This time the police there investigated it thoroughly. A man and his brother had been abused by Pritchard. What's more, he had been brought on a trip to Eastbourne, where he had been abused by Cotton – the mirror image of what had happened to me. So a detective came from Northamptonshire to Sussex to investigate if anything was known about Cotton, and there although the Church had no records, and nor had the police, they managed to find a draft letter from the Church's child protection officer to me. So that led them to me.

'The Northamptonshire police were brilliant – thorough, caring – and did an extremely good and professional job. Pritchard was charged, tried and convicted of indecent assaults and acts of gross indecency. And he was sentenced to five years. Unfortunately, just before Cotton was also due to be arrested and charged, in 2006 he died.'

Over the last couple of years Phil Johnson and Colin Campbell (who works for the BBC) have been researching Roy Cotton, trying to find out how he had got away with so much abuse in thirty-five years as a priest. And it started so early.

They have discovered that he was born in 1929 on the Isle of Wight, went to school in Sandown and did his National Service in the Navy. He worked as a teacher in 1947 in St Catherine's Home on the Isle of Wight, which was a Church of England Home for children who were recovering from illness. In the same year, he applied to the Church.

Cotton attended a selection conference and was recommended for training as a priest. He went to study at Ripon Hall, in Oxford. From 1951 to 1954 he was an assistant scoutmaster in Oxford. And in February 1954 he appeared at Abingdon Magistrates Court, where he was convicted of indecent behaviour with a child in a one-on-one music lesson with a chorister and was sentenced to one year's probation. (A letter from the Scouting HQ in October 1968 referred to this as an 'indecent assault on a young boy' and stated that he must under no circumstances have any connection whatsoever with the Scouting Movement.)

He had been due to be ordained six weeks later but it didn't happen, then. Although in March 1954 a letter from Bishop Allen, the principal of his college Ripon Hall, says, shockingly, that his conviction need not hold him back and he could still become a priest: 'I have said to him that it need not necessarily prejudice his ordination for all his life. He was in any case a rather weak immature character.'

So he went into just the right career for a man convicted of sexually abusing a child he was teaching: he became a teacher working in boys' boarding schools. For three years he worked as a schoolmaster in an independent school, Lysses School in Fareham. But he hadn't changed. According to a Facebook Old Boys page and Friends Reunited, there were two complaints against him. Not that they stood in his way. In summer 1961 he was appointed Reader (Lay Preacher) in the Oxford Diocese. It was at this time that he met Commander Robert Smithwick. Together, Cotton and Smithwick decided to set up Crookham Court School.

Five years later, he left, dismissed by Commander Smithwick. Why, when it was such a perfect job from his point of view? In 1966 there is a letter from the Bishop of Portsmouth to Commander Smithwick, which says that given that Cotton wants to be ordained as a priest, he needs more information about 'the sad story of Roy's dismissal by you. What I am concerned about is that possibly you have information which I ought to be aware of and I should be grateful if you could write to me about it. I have been aware all the way along of the incident twelve years ago when he was put on probation. As far as I am concerned I would want to write that past off, unless there were good reasons for not doing so.' There is no response from Commander Smithwick on the files.

But it's not difficult to work out why Cotton was told to leave. In 1966 there is a note from 'GT', copied to the Bishop of Portsmouth, saying that Cotton 'came to see me on May 4 at the Bishop's suggestion. I found him in a state of considerable distress and tension. His partner in the school in which he works, Commander Smithwick, has given him notice to leave as a result of allegations made or insinuated by boys at the school.'

Clearly new allegations of an old crime. But then there is a letter from the then Archbishop of Canterbury – Archbishop Michael Ramsey – who agreed with the Bishop, 'you would do right to consider ordaining him to a title in the carefully selected parish which you mention.'

How do you carefully select a parish for a convicted paedophile? Especially when there have been more recent allegations from other children? What must the Archbishop have been thinking of, giving such appalling advice?

Alas, they followed his advice. The Bishop of Portsmouth wrote in 1966: 'I find no truth whatsoever in the allegations which have been made. I referred it to the Archbishop and he thinks I should do right to ordain him to a carefully selected parish.'

And since poor Cotton had suffered so deeply, being accused by all these children, the Bishop kindly recommended that he should not be put through a Selection

Conference because 'he has been pretty desperately hurt by the turn of events, and I believe it could be wrong for him to have to go over and over the whole story again. Over these last twelve years he has been taking boys away to the Continent and there has been no breath of suspicion.'

There is very little else on the files relating to Cotton. He was indeed ordained in 1967 and became a curate in St Margaret's Eastleigh, near Portsmouth. In June 1971 he was given a parish, in Harting, in Chichester. And then, silence. Official silence. Because from 28 June 1971 to October 1998 when he resigned during a police investigation, there is not a single record in Cotton's file. Neither the Bishop of Chichester nor the Bishop of Lewes have a single note of his existence. Not his name, not his phone number, even though he twice moved parishes. Nothing. Not a complaint. Not a request for holiday cover, nothing. Not a single piece of paper.

Roy Cotton retired in January 1999 because Phil and Gary Johnson had complained so vociferously about the abuse and Bishop Wallace Benn believed he was guilty and told him to resign. But in fact even after that he was given permission by the Church to carry on officiating at Sunday services, weddings and other services, and applying to work as a choirmaster – he even tried to take choirboys away on trips. He died in 2006.

But that didn't end Phil Johnson's fight for justice. He was determined to make the Church recognise that they had allowed a paedophile to act as a priest for thirty-five years. We will never know how many children suffered as a result. Phil himself has discovered eleven victims. There may be many, many more. After all, that doesn't include the boys he abused at Crookham Court, whose complaints caused him to be sacked.

Finally, in 2011, Phil and Gary Johnson received a letter of apology from the Church of England and a very large sum of compensation. The letter, signed on behalf of the Bishop of Chichester, is addressed to Phil. It says:

'I am writing to offer you and your brother an apology. I

can only reiterate how deeply sorry I am that you suffered abuse by Roy Cotton and also by Colin Pritchard. Such abusive behaviour is wholly wrong, offends all our values and is indefensible. It should never happen. It is with heartfelt regret that I repeat my apology as Bishop of Chichester in respect of the decisions taken in the past and for mistakes, failures and lack of knowledge on the part of those who held positions of responsibility in the Diocese. I acknowledge that, in the light of his conviction in 1954, Roy Cotton should not have been ordained priest in 1967. Errors of judgement were made about him and his fitness for ministry and I accept that, had the Diocese taken opportunities to investigate his past, the police might have decided to pursue a prosecution prior to his death in 2006.

'I acknowledge that the history of this matter had resulted in further stress and suffering for you and your brother, and for that I am sorry. Please be assured that as a Diocese we are doing and will continue to do all in our power to seek to ensure that no one else suffers as you and your brother have.'

Today Phil says: 'The apology was extracted from the Church as part of a legal settlement. They didn't offer it, the Bishop himself didn't sign it – I don't regard it as sincere. I now believe that the Church I put my faith in, my family put their faith in, has been completely self-interested. The most incredible thing is that they seem to be completely unac-countable, even the Freedom of Information Act doesn't apply to them.

'When I was abused I was completely helpless, caught inside a culture that protected my abuser. Because as a child I believed that everybody was in it, they all knew about it, I felt completely powerless to do anything: I was trapped. If only there had been something like ChildLine at the time, I could have spoken to them anonymously and I would have felt safe, without a devastating comeback on my family. I couldn't possibly have told my parents or people in the Church at the time. If I had, my fear was that it would have broken up the family. When my brother and I did tell the family in 1996, it caused immense distress – my father thought I shouldn't have told anybody. He thought it would make my mother very upset, and she was.

'And yet it was only because Cotton and Pritchard were clergy that they were able to get away with it. Clergy have a position of unquestioned trust and the abuse of that trust is the worst kind of abuse there is. These are the people who preach to us, who teach us, and yet they don't practise what they preach. I had to make a witness statement at Pritchard's trial, and in it I tried to sum up the impact of what had been done to me and my brother. This is what I said:

'I was sexually abused for nine years by my parish priest. It was not just that I was abused, every aspect of my life was controlled and manipulated, and my parents were influenced and persuaded by Roy Cotton. Every decision that was made about my life, my education, my friends and my free time were manipulated to ensure that the abuse could continue and develop.'

'It did also confirm my suspicions that there was collusion and cooperation between some members of the Church of England clergy in the abuse of boys like myself.

'The effects of the abuse that I suffered at the hands of these men continues to the present day. It is not something that you can forget and it is extremely difficult to forgive anyone for it, you just have to find ways to cope with it which usually involves suppressing your true feelings and emotions.

'When your earliest sexual experiences are with overweight, middle-aged men who are older than your own father, they stay with you forever. You can be in a perfectly normal, loving relationship when someone touches you in a certain way and suddenly you are ten years old again. The memories come rushing back, as if your body has an indelible memory of your abuse that you cannot overcome.

'The two police investigations that I have been through, totalling over four years of my life, have also been extremely disruptive. Over the years, I believe that these issues have damaged my education, my marriage, my career and my confidence and self-esteem. The duration of the abuse and the time that I have spent trying to deal with it have taken up a huge part of my life. Since I first went to the police in 1996 there have been four years of investigation, interviews, statements and mostly disappointments. I don't know who I would have been if this hadn't happened.

'Throughout my upbringing the Church of England was a large part of my life – it is not now and it is certainly not a part of my children's lives and that saddens me. When you know what these priests have done, how they have colluded and lied about it, it robs you of your faith in the clergy. When you know that the clergy do not practise what they preach, the hypocrisy robs you of faith in the Church. But ultimately it just robs you of faith.'

When Phil was abused, ChildLine did not exist. He got in touch with me because he discovered his abuser, Roy Cotton, had created the school *That's Life!* had investigated. When years later Peter was abused at Crookham Court by Cadman, he was able to contact ChildLine and the abusers were brought to justice.

Could a child today be imprisoned in the same kind of culture of abuse? Yes, indeed. As long as there are organisations whose first reflex is self-protection, any cry for help will be swiftly stifled. Will such a child have the courage, the desperation, the trust to ring ChildLine? I do hope so.

MANY INSTITUTIONS have failed to protect children over the generations. One of them is the law. In 1986 I was warned that when abuse cases came to court, juries never believed children. In fact, Richard Johnson of Incest Crisis Line once told me, 'The only evidence the court will accept is the dead body of a child.'

After the *Childwatch* programme things began to change. In 1989 a committee headed by a remarkable judge, Tom Pigot, pointed out that children can be fact be extremely reliable witnesses. And in a recent crucial Court of Appeal decision, a little girl of three was described as a compelling, competent witness and as a result, her rapist was convicted. But still the little girl had to undergo a live cross-examination in which she was asked to define what truth means. Is that a sensible way to obtain justice for children?

Some welcome changes have been adopted in our court-rooms. Since ChildLine was launched twenty-five years ago, video-link equipment has been introduced, which has allowed children to give evidence via the link without being stared down by their abusers. And there have been other, small reforms. But the Pigot Committee nearly twenty-five years ago recommended small children should never have to give evidence in open court and that the cross-examination should also be recorded. Isn't it high time that reform was also adopted in our courts?

Alice's story shows how much of an ordeal a trial was – for the victim and the whole family – and how close it came to disaster because the lawyers were frightened her daughter would crumble under cross-examination. If they'd had their way and the trial had been stopped, a callous, determined child abuser would have escaped justice.

CHAPTER ELEVEN

ALICE'S STORY

I don't know whether my marriage suffered. They say this kind of trauma can have that effect. But after all, in 1984 when Daniel and I married, we were both very young. I was twenty-one, he was twenty-four. He was an engineer and I was working as a nanny – children have always been my great love. I'd trained in Leeds and I'd always, always wanted to work with children. My father was in the Army – army life is very sociable so I did lots of babysitting. If I'd been brighter, I might have been a teacher but I'm very dyslexic and went to thirteen different schools. So I was never academic, but I managed to get the right grades to get into college and do the NNEB (Nursery Nursing Examination Board). It was the first thing I excelled in. The first thing I did from start to finish, so that was great.

Then I saw an advertisement in *The Lady* magazine: a family with two little people and a baby on the way needed a nanny. I would have use of a car, the job was in London – everything sounded perfect, so I applied. I remember exactly what I was wearing, very carefully chosen of course to make a good impression: a cream dress and jacket. I walked into the sitting-room on the day of the interview and there were Esther and Desmond. Of course I was in awe of Esther in 1981 – *That's Life!* was at its height. She had quite a big bump, so it was obvious that the new baby was to arrive quite soon. And I met Emily straight away, their oldest daughter who was about four years old. During the interview, we played games on the floor – it was very easy to interact with this adorable little girl.

Esther asked me her trick question, which was about smacking, and I obviously answered correctly that I didn't believe in it. So I passed the first interview and then I was called back to spend a day with the family. That's when I met two-year-old Becca, who was adorable, too. We went for a walk in Kew Gardens – we had a very nice day. I was absolutely delighted that I got the job: £40 a week and use of a car.

Four months later I met Daniel at a leisure centre, playing badminton. We went out for three years and then we got married. Emily and Becca were our bridesmaids, Joshua (the bump when I first met the family) was our page boy.

My own baby, Samantha, came along three years later. By that time I was working with a different family, but still with Esther and Desmond at the weekends. They had a seven-day working week, so they needed support over the weekends. And I used to bring Samantha with me to work, which they always encouraged.

Before Samantha was born, about two years into our marriage, Daniel and I moved. Next door to our new house was an elderly couple, the Gillings, who invited us round to their home to meet the neighbours. They gave us supper and made us very welcome. Bob Gillings worked nights for British Airways, so he was around during the day and he offered to walk our two little dogs for us. They had a trim garden with a little pond, which they were very proud of. Cynthia worked full-time for the local hospital and my two girls were both born there.

When I got pregnant, the Gillings were both delighted. They had no grandchildren and longed for one, they said. This, they told us, thrilled, would be the next best thing. Cynthia immediately started knitting cardigans and hats for the baby and she was my very first visitor. She met Samantha the actual morning the baby was born (it was easy for her to pop in because she worked for the hospital). She wanted to be called 'Auntie' and Bob wanted the children to call him 'Uncle'. Uncle Bob was the first person waiting at home for me to take pictures of the new family: Daniel and me with our gorgeous new baby.

Looking back, the Gillings completely groomed me, although I never saw it at the time, of course. They won my trust by always offering their help. I got to the stage where I was grateful to them because I knew I could rely on them, they were on hand from day one. I never had to get a feckless teenager in to babysit, the way I had myself, because I had lovely, trustworthy Auntie Cynthia and Uncle Bob. But they never liked babysitting in my house, they always suggested that I should bring her round to their house instead in her Moses basket, and then in her travel cot. We would go out confident she was in good hands.

As time when by and when Anna – our second daughter – was born, they were even keener to look after the girls for me. More pictures were taken, more knitwear given. Whenever I had to go out, shopping and so on, they immediately offered to have them for tea. Bob made a special step so that the children could climb over into their garden. 'Come and feed the fish,' Uncle Bob would say, or 'Help me water the garden,' ' or 'Let's go and visit the lady up the road.'

And from the time she was eighteen months old, Sammy always came back with a little present because Bob worked for British Airways: the colouring books and crayons were the freebies they used to give children on the planes.

When the property crash happened in 1991, my husband Daniel lost his job because his company went bust, so we had to sell the house. We moved away from the house next door to the Gillings and went to live with my parents. Bob and Cynthia were very upset but I reassured them. I said we'd only be three miles away and we would come back every week to have tea with them. And we did.

By this time Samantha was four and Anna was eighteen months. I can't say the children were happy about the idea of visiting them, so I would jolly them along, reminding them about the little presents they got each time and the sweets the Gillings would so kindly buy for them and the delicious tea. Every time we arrived to have tea, Cynthia asked me if I had any shopping to do, and I'd say that would be great, to be able to whizz to the bank or the supermarket. 'No need to take the baby with you,' she'd assure me. 'You can get on much quicker without Samantha and she'll have a much nicer time with us.'

Soon Samantha started school, and every day when I picked her up at the end of the afternoon she would burst into floods of tears. Now looking back I realise she never knew which day we'd go round to Bob and Cynthia's and she was dreading it, knowing it was always after school. But at the time I was worried that she might be bullied and so I spoke to the school about her unhappiness. But they always said she'd been absolutely fine there, with all her friends. Also I had noticed that there was redness in the girls' vaginal area: they were very sore, Anna was very uncomfortable. I took them several times to the doctor, three or four times, and they said the girls had worms. So I got the sachets of anti-worm stuff, but it didn't get better.

In 1993, when Samantha was five, Esther and Desmond offered the family a summer holiday staying for a month in their cottage in the New Forest. That year I heard that Cynthia had broken her leg and was a bit depressed, so while we were staying there, I rang and invited both the Gillings to the cottage for a picnic. It was a beautiful, hot, sunny day. We were making a barbecue by the pool. Daniel was not around and I was sitting by the pool talking to Cynthia. She was facing into the pool, I was looking away.

Then I heard the words that were the beginning of our nightmare, but thank God were to end the nightmare my children had been living through. Samantha was in the pool with Bob when suddenly she called out to me in great distress: 'Mummy, Mummy, Uncle Bob keeps touching my bottom and it's hurting me and he won't stop!' Cynthia behaved as if she didn't hear anything – very quickly she started to talk about something else. When I turned round, I saw that Bob was near her, but I couldn't see exactly what he was doing because they were both in the deep end. I went numb. Shocked. Thought I must have misheard. Didn't know what to do. Stunned, I suppose. I tried to pretend I hadn't heard what Sammy had said, I tried desperately to act as normal. So I said as casually as I could, thinking I've got to get this girl out of the pool: 'We're going to have lunch now. Out we come.' Thinking, we've got to get rid of these people, the sooner the better.

We had lunch. I didn't tell Daniel yet, but of course I kept the girls very close to me. I decided not to confront, or tell Daniel until they'd gone; I couldn't process it. I didn't say anything about it. But I thought the children need never see these people again. I'll cancel them coming to Sammy's birthday party next week. The afternoon seemed to last for ever: we went for a walk and finally they went.

The children never saw them again.

That evening, on autopilot, I put both the girls to bed – told them stories, gave them lots of cuddles, but didn't talk to them about Uncle Bob. I needed to speak to Daniel first. And Sammy didn't mention it at all. When both of the girls were asleep, I told Daniel. He was devastated, as stunned as I had been. We agreed neither of the girls would ever be alone with Uncle Bob again. And we decided that I would speak to

Sammy in the morning. And I did. But when I asked her about Bob touching her, she hid her face. She said in a voice so small it was only just audible that when she went to the loo, it hurt. But when I asked if he had ever done it before, she said no.

I told Daniel that, and then I spoke to my parents who were deeply shocked. But we agreed that the girls should be allowed to forget all about it and we wouldn't mention it again.

But the memory stayed with me. Touching my little girl like that, was it abuse? It was obviously not normal. I was confused, I needed to talk to someone. Esther and Desmond would have been the obvious choice, with her experience of ChildLine, but they were away. So a few days later I decided to ring social services and tell them what had happened. I came away from the phone in tears. But I had made the phone call from the Wilcoxs' home and their daughters Emily and Rebecca had heard me. They obviously knew about Esther's work with ChildLine – she was a volunteer counsellor and the charity's Chair. So they begged me to ring Esther and Desmond and speak to them.

Then the social services visited my mother, wanting to speak to me, and that made her very nervous and extremely angry with me. Were they going to take the children away? You read so many stories like that in the papers. She was furious with me for telling them anything. She said the connection with Esther and Desmond would mean the whole thing would be in the papers. How dare I do such a thing, and how dare I remind Sammy of that dreadful day. I was terribly upset. I seemed to have done nothing right.

But that evening I steeled myself, and rang Esther and Desmond. I just blurted it out: 'Samantha has been sexually abused.' Esther asked me enough questions to understand what had happened in the pool. Her reaction was very depressing. She said in her view, if Bob had the confidence to touch Sammy in those circumstances, with me there and the whole family so close, he must have done it before. Probably many times before. He might even have done it to both girls. She asked if they had ever spent the night in his house. Yes, they had. Both the girls? Yes, both the girls. Then Esther said I must be prepared for the worst; that perhaps he had been abusing both children for years.

She asked if I had told anyone else. I said only social services and they had asked me to get in touch with them again. She said: 'Don't do anything immediately.' Later she explained that she was fearful once a legal process started, I would be prevented from talking to the girls for fear of 'tainting' their evidence (Esther had met mothers who had been put in that terrible position). Instead she told me to speak to both children myself first, to try and map the problem, see how great a problem this really was. That I must find time to make it a relaxed conversation, when we were doing something else, so they wouldn't be silenced by my pain. I had to stay calm. And I must only ask open questions, not put any words into their mouths.

So we arranged to go to the Wilcoxs' home in London. Daniel took Anna for a walk on the Heath, I stayed with Sammy in the kitchen, arranging flowers. But almost as soon as we started to talk about Uncle Bob, the flowers were left on the table and she climbed onto my lap, sobbing. She seemed so frightened. She kept repeating, 'Mummy, Mummy, you'll be cross with me. I couldn't help it!'

Slowly the story unfolded that he had been doing it to her as long as she could remember. She couldn't remember a time when he hadn't touched her, he just always had. She said that he had not only touched her in the pool that day, but in the changing room, too. She showed me where and how he had touched her, and then, sobbing, repeated the threat he had made: that if she ever told anyone what he'd done, he would kill me. That little girl was carrying that awful secret, that awful responsibility: that if she told, Mummy would be killed and that would be her fault.

I did my best to reassure her, to tell her how brave she had been to tell me, and that Daddy and I would always love her. And that Uncle Bob would certainly not kill me. And that nothing was her fault, that she had done nothing wrong.

We tried not to show her how devastated we were. But when we were alone together, Daniel flew into a rage. I told my parents and they were so upset. They kept apologising for having criticised me. Our little Sammy had been sexually abused all her life. Thank God she had been so happy, so relaxed at the cottage, in the pool that she had called to me for help. Otherwise... it doesn't bear thinking about.

Then Daniel talked to our younger daughter, Anna. That was really difficult. How could he ask a two-year-old the question without putting thoughts in her head? He decided to turn it into a game, called 'Anna, who do you like? Do you like Granny?' Yes. 'Do you like Grandpa?' Yes. And so on, until he got to: 'And do you like Uncle Bob?' 'No, he tickles me like this,' and she showed Daniel exactly what he did to her. 'And when he does this, it hurts me.' She showed him what she meant. And she was clearly showing him sexual abuse.

When I told Samantha about her dad's conversation with Anna, she became very distressed. She told me that when Bob started hurting Anna, she used to hit him to try and make him stop. She knew what it felt like herself and she wanted to protect her little sister but she thought we would be cross with her for hitting him.

How could we have been so blind, so trusting? How could we have allowed this evil man to abuse our daughters and force them to keep that frightful secret? And my poor little five-year-old, trying to protect her baby sister. I couldn't bear the thought.

Now we started on a long, hard road. It would take a year to investigate Bob's crimes against our children and try to obtain justice for our children. First, I got in touch with social services again and they contacted the police. They came to meet us and discuss what lay ahead. They were not encouraging. Did we want to press charges? Even if we did there was no guarantee it would ever get to court. The children would have to undergo medical examinations. And they would have to give evidence via a video link. They would have to be cross-examined. Our children were so young. Only one case in ten ever obtained a guilty verdict because children are not regarded as credible witnesses.

I remember talking to Daniel for hours, both of us wrestling in our minds trying to decide what to do for the best, as the rain streaked down the window. Watching us were the faces of our two lovely blonde children – their picture in a silver frame, their blue eyes wide – but now I thought I could see a shadow of the pain they had endured. And we allowed it to happen. Could we really put them through still more ordeals, more traumas? And yet, how would they feel in years to come if their bravery had been met with our cowardice? What would they say if Uncle Bob carried on abusing more children, and no one had the courage to stand up against him and bring him to trial? This man was evil. He was cunning and ruthless. We had to stop him doing this to any other child.

It was an awful decision to have to take but we decided in the end, yes, we would press charges. Our children had the right to be heard. We would be alongside them, supporting them. After all, we would never forgive ourselves if we allowed these crimes to be brushed under the carpet. We had enough guilt to contend with, we didn't need more. So we decided to put the rest of our lives on hold, and do what we had to do.

And so the children were interviewed, separately. After a great deal of pleading from me, I was eventually allowed to be there during each interview, provided I said nothing. Anna was two, Sammy was just six. There were to be no leading questions. If neither of them mentioned Bob's name, the case could not proceed. Anna was given a doll, so she could explain what happened using that. The children both gave brilliant interviews. There was no doubt about it: Bob had sexually abused them both.

The next ordeal was the medical examination. For me it was one of the worst moments of my life, it will haunt me forever. I can remember every detail of our time in the health centre: a social worker, two doctors and a police officer, a six-year-old and a two-year-old. I stayed with the girls when they were being examined, chattering about everything and anything. Anna's third birthday was very soon, so I talked to her about a teddy party, with different teddy bears on each invitation, and I asked her which of her guests would like which one. I was running on autopilot again – I'd got used to that.

The doctors were looking for every mark, every tear, every bruise, each scratch. I hated it. I held my children's hands all the way through, but I hated the whole process. I loathed all those people standing round the bodies of my little girls, examining them internally and externally. I dreaded what they might find. And they did. It felt like a bomb going off in my brain when they told me. Samantha's hymen had been broken and she had internal scarring. There was evidence on Anna's body, too, only the two doctors couldn't agree if the evidence on her was strong enough.

Up to that point I had hoped it wasn't true. I had prayed to God it wasn't true. I believed my child, but at the same time I had longed to be comforted, to be told the abuse was not as serious as Samantha had said. Now we had proof. Every word she had told us was accurate. I think this was the moment I stopped believing in God. It was the fact that Bob, the evil bastard, had wounded my little girl so deeply. That was the moment when hell took over.

But the process was inexorable. Next, I had to spend a day giving my statement. Explaining why I had been persuaded, cajoled into trusting Bob and Cynthia. How Bob had set a trap for me and my family. I cried, of course. Drank endless cups

of black coffee as I re-lived everything. But I was a witness –
it had to be done.

Then, when they had all their ammunition, the police went
to interview Bob and Cynthia Gillings. They told me later she
was quite calm. I think if anyone had accused my husband of
such horrible crimes, I would have been shocked and hysterical. But no, she was quite cool and collected. And Bob just
denied everything. He said it was because I had worked for
that woman Esther Rantzen and she was obsessed with abuse
that she had put all these accusations into my head and filled
my children's imaginations with the same stuff. On and on he
went, protesting his innocence.

The case went to the Crown Prosecution Service to decide
whether to take it to trial. The good news was they decided
Samantha was a strong case, with the statement, the medical
evidence and the fact that I had witnessed him in the pool
when she had cried out for help, it all added up. The bad news
was they decided Anna was too young to withstand cross-
examination. Also, there was the confusion about the medical evidence on her body. So Bob would never be charged with
the crimes he had committed against Anna.

We were very angry. Anna and Samantha had been quite
clear about what this evil man had done to them and yet he
would get away with half his crimes and Anna would have
no voice. It was terribly unjust. Also it meant that poor
Samantha somehow had to be prevented in court even from
talking about how she had tried to protect her baby sister
from him. What a difficult, inadequate legal system we have.

We had no doubt that he had abused Anna, too. My friend
Gina knew the family well and sometimes used to help me out,
taking Anna to playgroup and collecting her, that sort of thing.
And she had several conversations with Anna when they were
alone together in Gina's car. Gina recorded some of the things
Anna said in her diary. She told me Anna had said that Bob had
touched her, and that she didn't like him. And that Sammy had

smacked him and said 'No!', and that sometimes Bob smacked her. And that he had made her cry. But the jury in the eventual trial would never know what he had done to Anna: Samantha's evidence would have to stand alone.

At least Sammy had the NSPCC on her side to help explain the elaborate, mystifying legal system. One of their staff, Frances, came to visit us and spent time with her, explaining the court process. She had dolls to act as barristers and one with a wig was the judge. Although Samantha was obviously a little anxious, concerned to understand and do the right thing, she liked Frances. And she took everything in. But it seemed utterly wrong to me that when the trial happened, I wouldn't be allowed to stay with my five-year-old, while she was being interrogated. Absurd. But at least, after a lot of the discussion, the court did allow Frances to be with her. Otherwise she would have been put into a room with absolutely nobody she knew and then asked to relive the most painful, shameful events that had ever happened to her. Worse than absurd. Inhuman.

Then our world exploded again. The *Sun* newspaper put the story all over their front page. Bob had gone to court for the first hearing. Somehow the *Sun* had discovered that a child had been abused in Esther's pool, that made the perfect headline for them: 'Child abused in Esther's Pool.' They named the abuser, Robert Gillings. But they didn't name us.

Then suddenly a little ray of sunshine broke through the grey clouds that had enveloped us. The police came back to see us, and said that a mother had read the *Sun*'s story about Bob and immediately rang her daughter Millie (who was by now a woman in her twenties) and said: 'Darling, I'm so sorry I didn't believe you all those years ago when you told me Robert Gillings had abused you.'

It was horrific news, that he had been abusing children twenty years before. But at the same time it lifted our spirits because we thought that meant Samantha would have an adult to support her story. The daughter, Millie, was prepared to make a statement to the police, saying exactly what Gillings had done to her. It was just what he had done to Sammy, bribing her with little gifts from British Airways, taking her to watch the fish in the garden pond, where he could abuse her out of sight of the house. But the CPS decided not to call Millie to give evidence. It seemed crazy to me, and to some of the experts I've talked to since, but at the time the CPS lawyers thought Millie's abuse had happened too long ago and couldn't be linked with what Bob had done to my daughters. So once again the lawyers left Sammy utterly alone: it would be her word against his.

I met Millie, a lovely young woman, who felt deeply distressed when she discovered what Bob had done to my children. She felt if only she had gone to the police when she was a child, she might have been able to prevent him abusing other children. That strengthened me in the belief that we were doing the right thing. And she told me what a huge difference it made to her that now, at last, her family believed her and she was receiving help for the terrible damage he had done to her.

Then we discovered Gillings had abused two other children, who had been to their local doctor and described what he had done to them. When they spoke about it, they were teenagers and they told the doctor they didn't want to tell anyone else. How many more children had that man assaulted, how many more lives had he wrecked? At least my daughters had spoken out and made his horrible crimes public so that he could be punished.

Esther helped us again, by putting us in touch with experts at Great Ormond Street Hospital. With their support, Samantha began to tell us – and them – more and more details, which they recorded on video. Children often do that, they told us: start by telling what they think is the easiest to describe and then gradually reveal the truth. The doctors offered the children counselling, which they said would be extremely helpful, but the CPS intervened to stop us. They said if Sammy had counselling, the case might be thrown out of court because her evidence would have been 'tainted'.

We desperately wanted to heal our little girls, but we were caught in this trap. The trial had been set for July, the counselling was due to start in June; Daniel and I just didn't know what to do for the best. In the end we decided against the counselling. We had gone so far down the road, we couldn't risk the case being thrown out, leaving Bob free to carry on with his hideous crimes. Somehow we would find good counselling for the children after the trial.

Waiting for the trial was agonising. I was filled with guilt and shame that I had allowed my children to be so terribly badly hurt; I was in tears every day. The only way to survive was to keep busy – push away those feelings, stay strong for the children and for myself. My close friend, Gina, was always with me and by listening to me, she helped me get through each day. But Daniel and my parents were in just as much pain as I was. We had decided to move house, which under other circumstances would have been an ordeal in itself, but at least this gave me other things to plan for and organise. So in a way it acted as therapy. And the last thing I wanted to do was reveal to Samantha and Anna the torment I was in during those months.

And then, a year after Sammy had disclosed the abuse, we were given a date for the trial. The day came, we put on our best clothes. I felt as if we were all about to enter the lion's den. At noon, just as we were about to leave our home, the police rang. There was a problem: there would be a delay.

Then another phone call. The CPS wanted to meet us the next day. You might think it was to make sure we were happy about the process, and that Sammy was prepared for what was about to happen, and in good heart. You would be completely wrong. They were about to persuade us to pull out: they told us the defence were going to cross-examine Samantha about the tape-recording of her interview at Great Ormond Street. Because she had told them more than she had been able to tell the police they would exploit every difference. How could she withstand that? The CPS had decided that she couldn't. They wanted us to pull out, drop the charges. At this last moment, Bob was to escape justice. Daniel and I had a sleepless night, terrifed Samantha's story would never be heard.

Esther's husband Desmond Wilcox came with us the next morning to the Crown Court as moral support during our meeting with the CPS. Gillings was there. It was the first time we'd seen Bob since that day in the pool in the New Forest. I felt sick. We said nothing to him, of course. We went to meet the lawyers. The CPS told us their fears, described the cross-examination and asked if we thought Samantha could stand up to it. They recommended us to withdraw the charges and pull out of the case. It was a disaster. After everything the children had been through, and we as a family had been through, what about justice, for us, for other children? Daniel and I argued our case with the lawyers. We said there was no way we could back out at this stage: we would tell Samantha to tell the truth, as we had always told her, all her life. We would tell her to say if she couldn't remember. And in the end the CPS agreed that the case could go ahead the next day, at 9.30 a.m.

So at last the day of the trial had arrived. We dressed in our best again, drove to the court, and Frances from the NSPCC was there waiting for Samantha. Sammy and I were not allowed to go into the courtroom because we were going to give evidence. We were put into a small room and to my great relief, Sammy seemed quite calm. Then they called her. At just seven years old, she had to go without me to give evidence in this crucial trial. I longed to be beside her – I was so very scared for her. My heart was in my mouth, had we made the right decision to let the case go ahead? We had already made so many bad decisions, trusting this evil man.

Later I was told Samantha's evidence under cross-examination had been wonderful. She was connected by video-link to the courtroom, so she couldn't see the man who had tortured and intimidated her. The camera only showed her the lawyers who were asking her questions and the judge. But behind one of the lawyers she could see her grandparents sitting in the public seats and that encouraged her. I'm told when the jury first saw her, they gasped. This innocent little child, with long blonde hair and serious blue eyes, in her pretty flowery dress, how could anyone hurt her? She gave her evidence in a clear, high little voice, smiled politely at the judge and stayed strong, even when she was accused of lying thirteen times.

Samantha had given physical details no child of seven could possibly have invented. And yet the woman defending Bob Gillings told the child thirteen times that she was lying. What kind of justice system is that? But my little girl remembered what she had been told all her life. She said no, she wasn't lying, she was telling the truth. My friend Gina is a teacher. Watching it all from the public seats, hearing the defence barrister doing her very best to confuse and undermine that little girl, Gina called the process legal cruelty.

But I was not allowed to hear any of that. From the room they'd put me in I could watch Samantha leaving the court house with a friend of mine. I longed to be able to hug her, to say how proud I was of her. But I couldn't. I felt like a prisoner trapped in this room, waiting for my own execution. Because of course I would have to give evidence and if I made a mess of it, got too emotional, got into a muddle, I could destroy all the hard work done by the police and the prosecution to get this man convicted.

They called me after lunch and when the courtroom door opened, I immediately saw my family, my friends and then the jury. The jury were staring at me – I thought they must be weighing me up, wondering what kind of neglectful mother would allow her little girl to be left in the power of this disgusting man. And then it started. I swore on the Bible, then had to give my evidence and then came the cross-examination: it all seemed to last a lifetime. Afterwards, Daniel, my parents and everybody else told me I'd done well. And they told me Samantha had been a star. But had it been enough? All we knew was that there was nothing more we could do to bring Bob Gillings to justice.

I was allowed to go back into the courtroom then to listen to the doctor giving evidence. As she described the damage he had done to my little girl's body I felt a huge anger. There was Bob, standing unmoved in the dock. I just wanted to run at him, hit him, tell him of the hurt and pain he'd caused both my children.

At the end of that long, long day, at last I could go home and be with my girls. I hugged them over and over again. They seemed quite happy and relaxed but perhaps beneath the surface there was pain and anxiety. I couldn't tell.

The next day there was more medical evidence, then evidence by the police, and then by Cynthia, Bob's wife. She came to defend Bob. I had wondered if she too had been one of his victims. To hear what she said made me lose any sympathy I'd had. She was the last witness.

The lawyers gave their speeches and as always happens, the defence barrister spoke last, leaving the jury with a very negative impression. It was Friday afternoon and the judge said he would sum up on Monday. That meant we had to wait in suspense throughout the weekend and it would start all over again the next week. I have been told that it might have been better that way than the jury having to make up their minds with the defence barrister's words fresh in their memories undermining everything my daughter had said – I just don't know.

But when Monday came, another hot, hot day, I could hardly bear to listen to the judge. His summing up lasted an hour and a half. He kept telling the jury they had to be 100 per cent sure on each of the four counts otherwise they must acquit him. My friends tried to reassure me, tell me the judge had to be impartial, otherwise Gillings would have grounds to appeal. But to me it just sounded as if there was no hope left for a verdict of guilty beyond reasonable doubt. It was my little girl's word against a practised, experienced, evil liar.

The jury went out to consider their verdict. After three hours, they came back. On one count they found Gillings not guilty. I wanted to curl up and die. How could they? But the police reminded us there were three more counts to go. Suddenly, crazily, my sister remembered an appointment, a work appointment she might miss. She asked me to ring them to cancel it. I flipped. I threw the phone down, tipped up the table which was covered with cans of drink and tried to smash up the room. Everyone tried to calm me down and I hugged my sister, who after all had come there to support me. The stress was getting the better of both of us.

After another lifetime we were called back. This time the jury had reached their verdict on the three remaining counts but I couldn't go back into the courtroom. The pain of Sammy's disclosure, the terrible story of threats and abuse my two little girls had told us, the medical examination in front of all those officials, the phone calls, the arguments, giving evidence, hearing my daughter's hymen being discussed in open court, hearing the lies being told and all the time trying to keep going, trying to pretend that life was *fine*, I had nothing left, nothing to face the possibility that he might be acquitted.

My mother stayed outside with me in that little room. She

wrapped her arms around me, we were both crying. I was sobbing into her lap and she was rocking me like a baby. I tried to tell her my fears. What was I going to tell Samantha if he got away with it? How could we ever put our lives together? How will we ever heal? All the fight, all year long, to try and get justice would have been for nothing. Bob had never shown any emotion, no repentance. He would be defiant, full of smug self-righteousness, and he'd have been given the green light to carry on abusing children for the rest of his life. The bastard.

My friend Gina left me and went into the courtroom with the others. On one other count he had been found not guilty, but on the remaining two he was convicted. Gina ran back to tell me as soon as she could. She rushed in, shouting, 'He's been found guilty on two counts!' and ended up on her knees next to me. I fell on my knees, too, not understanding, holding her hands.

'Does that mean he is half-guilty?' I asked her. 'No' she shouted at me, 'He has been found *guilty*! They believed Samantha!' 'So he has definitely been found guilty?' 'Yes, yes, *yes*!' I felt the tears falling again, like a waterfall. I heard myself whispering, 'Thank you, God, thank you!' A surge of people came through the door, hugging me, crying, kissing.

But there was no champagne, no celebration. Gillings had got away with sexually abusing Anna and Millie, and all the other children. Gina went and collected Samantha, then told me afterwards that she had wound down the windows of her car and drove home, shouting 'He's guilty and it's over!', getting some very odd looks from other motorists and waking up the next day with a badly sore throat.

Ten days later the judge announced the sentence. Daniel and my father went to court to hear it. I never wanted to see Bob Gillings again. The judge said the medical evidence of the torn hymen had been caused by him, that there was seriously repeated abuse, that Gillings had befriended our family, got them to trust him and treat him as an honorary grandfather, and that he must therefore be given a custodial sentence to protect the public and other children. He got a sentence of eighteen months.

Robert Gillings was taken to prison in Surrey. Eighteen months seemed to us to be a very small punishment for such a huge crime but hateful feelings destroy you. He was not going to destroy us any more, he had done enough damage. Bob was going to prison and we were going to start a new life.

We tried to settle into our new house in the New Forest that we all loved and start our life afresh but Samantha had been too badly hurt. She developed a phobia about her food, saying she could smell Bob on it and couldn't eat it – it made her physically sick. Now she had nightmares and sometimes wet her bed, which she hated. She would also self-harm. Her sister Anna was getting very angry so it was clearly crucial to arrange counselling for them both, the counselling our legal system had denied them.

It took a long time, but at last Sylvia from social services came to see Sammy. She took her to a group of other children who'd had similar experiences and it worked, or at least the panic with food stopped and so did the bed-wetting and the nightmares. But as she grew older, Sammy needed more help. Anna had help, too, to talk her through the fear that Bob had put in her mind that she would be taken away from us. Daniel and I were given our own support, too at weekly meetings. I remember talking to other mothers of abused children who felt as guilty as I did but they clustered around me, telling me how brave Daniel and I had been. We had believed our children; we had withstood all the lawyers who had tried to persuade us to give up in our efforts to bring Gillings to justice. And those mothers made me feel so much better, much less of a failure. The experiences we all shared were agonising to recall and discuss, we all wept together, but I think we also helped each other heal and grow stronger. Sadly, in the end

Daniel and I divorced but not until the children were old enough to be independent. They'd been through enough without that.

I have so often wished that I could somehow erase all the dreadful things that have happened to the children I love so much but I know I can't. Maybe the experience of what they endured will be put to positive use, to help and protect others; I can only hope so. So throughout these terrible events I made careful notes in a diary and then put the whole narrative down in a book I have created for the children. It took me fourteen years to write it. I would put together a paragraph and then leave it until I could bear to take it up again. For me, writing down what happened for Samantha and Anna to read, so that they would understood how it came about, was in itself a very difficult ordeal. Remembering that dark time brought the pain back as sharp and agonising as it had ever been.

But rereading it, looking back over the whole story, I also know that if it hadn't been for ChildLine, I would never have recognised how serious the abuse had really been. I would have wanted to believe it was just one single occasion, just that one appalling moment in the swimming pool. After all, that's what Samantha told me at first, she was so fearful of what would happen if she told me the whole truth. And to protect her, I would never have wanted to talk to her about it again, just wanted to help her forget it had ever happened. I might even have been like Millie's mother and not believed that kindly Uncle Bob could do such a thing. And that would have condemned my two children, and how many more children, to years of torture.

There are so many things I would like to change about the way my children were treated: Anna denied her time in court, Sammy cross-examined so horrifically, and then the awful short sentence. But at least my children were believed, at least he was found guilty. And at least Robert Gillings was revealed as what he is, a ruthless paedophile.

● ● ●

SAMANTHA'S STORY

Much has been said and written about 'False Memory Syndrome'. Some people have been deeply sceptical that memories can be blocked for years, only to re-emerge in later life, but I was around throughout Samantha's ordeal. I know she was abused. But for her, almost every memory of her childhood has been obliterated. Certainly the memories of her abuse have gone, been buried. Perhaps it's the way her mind has chosen to survive.

Meeting her today, you would never suspect the traumas she endured. Now twenty-five, Samantha has a high-flying job and seems calm, self-assured and in control. She has a natural sense of style: blonde, blue-eyed and tall, she is quietly impressive. Asked what she remembers of the abuse and all that followed, she says:

'I only have one real memory of my childhood, and it's a random one of Uncle Bob and Aunty Cynthia. I was sitting in their kitchen, at a tiny wooden table, eating jam sandwiches off a breadboard.

'And two other rather vague blurry memories. One of a grey cat, and me sitting with it on a sofa. And I also remember Uncle Bob and Auntie Cynthia had a cupboard under the stairs and he gave me crayons he got out of it.

'I do have one memory of getting ready for a swim in Esther's pool, being in the changing room. I think he was there as well, but I don't remember a single sinister thing. I feel as if my memory has been completely wiped so I remember nothing, until the moment when I was sitting in the cottage and my mum saying, 'You're so brave for telling me.' But what I told her, I simply cannot remember.

'I have a few memories of the court case. I remember being in a room with two people behind me, and I was watching a video link, and I think I remember seeing my grandparents on it. And I remember Bob's lawyer – a woman I disliked. She kept telling me I was lying and each time I said no, I'm not. That's what I remember saying; I knew that had to be my response. I remember towards the end of the session they wouldn't let me go to the loo. And then when it ended, eating a cheese and pickle sandwich, which was my favourite.

'I do not have a single memory of the abuse, not a single image. I even had to relearn the facts of life when I was in my teens, although obviously I had been through so much you might think I'd remember. But I feel like I've had my memory completely wiped.

'Throughout my life, my memory has not been very good. Now, when bad things happen, like when my parents said they were breaking up, I remember being shocked and upset for twenty-four hours and crying, but after that I didn't think about it. I think I've trained myself not to think about bad things. And when it comes to early memories, I don't have any, not even good things.

'I don't know when it was that I decided to wipe my memory. I don't know if it was a conscious thing or not. I guess overall it's a good thing, but I know I'm different from other people, but I don't know why. I'm just not connected, emotionally. So with my boyfriend, it's very frustrating for him. I know he loves me very much, but I'm disconnected from him. He doesn't know why, I've never spoken to him about the abuse.

'Also, in a physical sense, I'm not particularly interested. I don't have bad thoughts, not revolted or anything, but I'm quite indifferent. I sometimes see my friends, so in love with someone, and I'm just not. I think I'm incapable.

'I do get angry sometimes and I find it difficult to think clearly or analyse my feelings. I feel detached – I can detach myself from people and places quite easily. People talk about being swept off their feet – that would never happen to me.

'When I read my mother's diary and realised the whole story, I thought wow, I had no idea. At least not consciously, but I suppose it has left its mark. I know now I'll never trust anyone completely. I've never let myself go with my boyfriend. I'd like to, but I just don't have it in me or maybe I've just blocked it out. I am in my own world, I am my own entity.

'I've done well, at school and at university. At school I was physically sick before exams. I've always put so much pressure on myself – I was terrified of letting my parents down. An innate fear. The same at university, only I was doing it for myself there. I think other people my age enjoy themselves more, let themselves go a bit more. I don't know what stops me. Something inside me.

'I would recognise them if I saw them. Her more than him. When I was younger, I used to worry that he might have died and that he might haunt me. I would quite like to meet him in the street now, I'd be the empowered one. If I see old men in the street, I think about him. I'm not frightened of meeting him at all. I've never thought what I might say to him. I'd be curious, but I wouldn't want to interact with him.

'I've never talked to Anna about him or anything to do with the abuse. I'd never want to do that – I don't see how that would help. I'm really bad at talking. I don't see it as therapeutic, I want to keep things to myself. A lot of people comment on how I'm so closed. I think I have talked about it when I was younger – I think I must have had counselling – but I don't remember.

'I definitely think if that hadn't happened to me I would be different. What I've been left with inside me is a bunch of anxieties. First, when I was about seven and we were in Florida, and I thought for some reason I could smell him in my cheeseburger. I was sick. I had other phobias about food. Until I was sixteen I could never eat in restaurants, I hated it. I thought then I'll never have a boyfriend because I could never eat with him in a restaurant, the thought of it made me feel so sick.

'That transferred itself to a fear of eating in people's houses. At friends' parties I had to pretend I wasn't well because I couldn't bear to eat a whole pizza in a restaurant. I had counselling at school for a couple of years to deal with that, then it got progressively better, but then I couldn't drink in public situations. I dreaded it, for reasons I couldn't explain. I had that until I was twenty-one. And to get rid of that I saw a hypnotist to help me with my fear of exams and the fear of drinking in public places.

'I don't have those phobias anymore, thankfully, although I'm left with this mass of anxieties, always there. I just have to get rid of each one as they come along. Now they're centred around my boyfriend, so with him I'm quite controlling, and untrusting, and there's the fear of being let down. It's like a shifting ball, the anxieties; I think they will always be there. That's what I've been left with. Because even though I can't remember it, it did happen. You are a product of your life: I'm always going to have consequences.

'I am very focused now. Essentially I have the life I've always wanted – I've made sure of that. I always worked so hard to make everything just so. So now I've got great work that I enjoy and it's a well-paid job – I live in a nice flat, everything on paper is great. I feel I've got something inside me that other people don't have, some of that's positive and that's what other people see. They think I have everything worked out really well. But some of it's negative, so I can't be happy when I know I should be. There's something inside which is stopping me.

'When I think about the future, I think it's bright. I have goals and a successful career. I've never wanted to make a difference to the world. I want to be financially independent. I want to have a good set of friends, which I have. I got a first-class degree. And oh yes, I have a nice boyfriend, who will be there for me. So I'm very much in line with all my goals.

'I feel that everyone has to have something bad happen to them and I've already had mine, so now I can enjoy whatever comes my way.'

~~~~~~~~~~~~~~~~~~~~~~~~~~~~~~

IT IS INTERESTING how many of the survivors I have spoken to while I have been writing this book have decided to give back what they have received in some way to repay the help ChildLine has given them. When we try to show what good value we give in return for the generous donations we receive (and every penny helps), we say that we can answer a child for £12. What we cannot calculate is the value of the contribution donated to us all by the children we help. Louise is one of them.

~~~~~~~~~~~~~~~~~~~~~~~~~~~~~~

CHAPTER TWELVE

LOUISE'S STORY

From the age of four I lived on an army camp because my dad was a military doctor. He and my mum divorced when I was eleven because he sexually assaulted two of his patients. The Army hushed it up and told him that if he agreed to go quietly there'd be no further action. So he left the Army, stopped practising as a doctor and worked as a salesman. Eventually he gave that up, too and became a fulltime carer for my grandmother Claudine, who had had TB and lived on 24-hour oxygen, though she somehow she managed to smoke like a trooper at the same time.

I was a frail-looking child – mousy fair hair, blue eyes, you'd never notice me at the back of a class. I found it hard to relate to anybody throughout my childhood, I was always an isolated, withdrawn kid. There were a couple of reasons why I was so shy. Living on the camp set me apart from other children but the main reason was the sexual abuse. I was abused by my dad, and by his father, my grandfather.

It had been going on for as long as I can remember – I

must have been pretty tiny when it started. And I know my grandmother was aware of it. She was in the house when it happened. In later years she even helped them. Because after a while my dad sold me to other men and she let the 'customers' into the house.

Dad and Grandad sometimes abused me separately, sometimes together. Dad was my main abuser and it was much more frequent with him. For a long time I didn't realise it was wrong. Living on the army camp I didn't have friends to stay over, or go over to friends' houses, and my dad just made it quite normal. But I didn't like it. It was always uncomfortable, painful at times. I didn't like the way my dad smelt. He said all dads did the same with their little girls, it was just him showing that he loved me. By the time Grandad started I just accepted it. My grandad had also tried to rape my mum, I discovered years later, but she fought him off.

When I was five I told a teacher. I'd drawn a picture. They had asked me to draw a family picture and my dad looked like a scary monster, which is how I saw him when I had nightmares. The teacher asked me about it. And I explained that I didn't like it when he touched me and I pointed to where he touched me. She told me not to make up dirty stories. This was in 1979, sexual abuse wasn't spoken about, but even so. Anyway, when she said that I just felt really confused and on my own. I didn't tell anybody else for another twelve years.

My grandad died when I was eleven but my dad carried on abusing me. When I was about eight, that's when other people got involved. He took me to my grandparents' house in another part of Hampshire. I'd be upstairs in their room and my grandma would bring the other men into the room, my dad would be with me. I don't know who they were. Over the years there must have been twenty or thirty of them. They were just ordinary men, the sort you'd see anywhere. Some I only saw once, some were pretty regular. Sometimes they would call me names, as if it was my doing. Some would say it was what I wanted. Most of the time they wouldn't say anything, just sexually abuse me and then give my dad money.

Sometimes there'd be one, sometimes three or four. They'd take photographs, I don't know what they did with them. Maybe the pictures are somewhere on the internet now. It worried me for a long time; I used to dream about it. You know how sometimes you have that dream, you'd walk into assembly and you'd realise you had no clothes on. I used to dream everyone could see me having these things done to me. It was a paedophile ring; I hated it. I didn't want to go – I threw tantrums, I cried, I sat down and refused to leave the house, but none of it worked. Apparently my mum never knew what was happening. There's a lot of people who should have known what was happening to me. I had repeated infections, gynae problems from a very young age, in and out of hospital, and yet nobody put two and two together.

It messed me up for quite a while. I took my GCSEs and failed all of them. Because at fourteen I was pregnant. I don't know who caused it. I hid it. It was in the summer holidays, so I didn't see many people. I wanted the baby. But at the end of August my dad induced the birth at twenty-six weeks – he was a doctor, he put me on some kind of drip. I felt like life wasn't worth living any more.

My baby Daniel was born alive, but died very quickly. There was no medical care for him. It all happened in Dad's medical room. Dad didn't say a word. He left Daniel with me after the birth. Then he came back and took him away. I don't remember an awful lot about the next few months, it's all a bit of a blur, to be honest. I functioned as much as I needed to. In any case nobody noticed anything. I'd always been labelled as a quiet, withdrawn child.

The next year was my GCSE year: my grades had been dropping over the last couple of years. I had done very well in primary school but then going to high school, when the abuse was really stepping up after my grandad died, things got really bad. I couldn't do my school work. That was the time when my dad had left home and was living with his mum so when I went on access visits it was quite often just me and him, with her downstairs. The abuse was more intense, it was happening two or three times a day; I was a wreck. It caused internal damage so I had to have a hysterectomy two years ago. I still have constant pain.

From the time I was fifteen, I tried to stop the abuse myself. Something in me snapped after losing Daniel. I tried to say no to Dad, leaving tampons around so he'd think I had my period. I'd refuse to take the train to see him but then he'd just drive down and collect me. It was better when I'd go and stay with a friend he didn't know. He always treated me differently from my brothers – he'd buy me presents, he'd take me to the pub and show me off. I was his special princess. And at those times I suppose I liked being with him – he couldn't do much to me surrounded by friends in the pub. But behind closed doors, that's when the fear really came in. He was unpredictable and very violent, mainly with his fists. He used to thump my mum and I was caught in the crossfire: he threw a table at her and it hit me. And he was violent to me when I wasn't compliant in the abuse. He was also a raging alcoholic – he used to drink all the time.

And yet if you met him you would have seen a well-spoken, generous, funny man who would do anything for anybody; that type of guy. That's why he was so popular in the pub – he had a lot of friends.

By 1991, when I was seventeen, I was desperate. The paedophile ring was occasional by then, which made it even more scary because it was so unpredictable. I knew about ChildLine, I'd seen posters; I'd seen it on TV. But it took me a while to phone: I wasn't sure that they would be able to do anything, because talking about it wasn't going to make it stop. So I thought about it for a few weeks.

And then one day the house was empty. I was living with my mum and my younger brother. I used the phone at the bottom of the stairs. It was in the late afternoon. After a few attempts, maybe four, I got through. A woman answered, which is just as well because I think I would have put the phone down if it had been a man. She said, 'Hello, you're through to ChildLine.' I didn't say anything for a few seconds. She said, 'It's OK, take your time.' I said, 'I don't know what to say.' She said, 'That's OK, you can say whatever you want to, there's no rush.' She had a very friendly voice. I told her I didn't know what to do. She asked me what I didn't know what to do about. And I kept saying I can't tell you. I guess that went on for a bit. Then I remember speaking really quietly and just saying, 'My dad's been abusing me and I don't know how to stop him.'

I remember her saying I was really brave, which I didn't feel I was. I know now I was, but I didn't feel like it at the time. She asked me lots of questions, about what I was doing. I said I was at college, talked about who was in my life, who might be able to help me. We decided my college tutor was probably the best person; we talked about when I was going to tell her, what I was going to say to her, and we practised on the phone together. It's a really good technique and it did help. Even though when I told my tutor it didn't go like our practice, it still helped. Then she said I could phone ChildLine any time, if I needed to phone back before I told my tutor, or if I wanted to phone back afterwards, that was fine, too. When I put the phone down I felt like a weight had been lifted off my shoulders, although I was completely terrified at the thought of what I was going to have to do. But having told someone once gave me the confidence to do it again.

So, two days later, I went into college and asked to see my tutor. She had been encouraging work-wise and looking back I think she knew. She never said she knew but she always said, 'You know, you can talk to me about anything,' when we had tutorials. So I just blurted it out: that my dad was abusing me, and about Grandad. Then I burst into tears. She didn't say anything, just came and sat beside me and held my hand until I'd calmed down a bit. Then she said she would help me sort things out.

The same day she arranged for me to see a counsellor and came with me to the first session. I owe a lot to that lady. Then I had weekly tutorials with her and kept her updated with what was happening during the counselling, which was focused on keeping me safe and getting up the courage to tell my mum. It worked, except I didn't tell my mum, my dad did.

I rang my dad first and said to him: 'You have to tell my mum, or I will.' I was stronger by then. So I gave the phone to my mum and he said: 'I've been interfering with our Louise.' 'You bastard!' she screamed and put the phone down. Then there was a whole barrage of questions: it lasted all evening, it was quite bizarre. When did it start? What had been happening? Why hadn't I told her? Then she phoned our church minister and he came over. He was really supportive. Just listened more than anything, and kept repeating to me that it wasn't my fault. I was quite distraught by then, not dealing with it at all well.

The next day Mum called the police. She had to give a statement and then I was taken to a children's unit to give a series of statements. I told them everything except about Daniel, and the paedophile ring: Daniel was too precious and I didn't think anyone would believe me about the ring. The police kept in touch with me over the next few months. Meanwhile, Dad denied everything.

He pleaded not guilty so I had to give evidence in court at his trial. It was one of the most horrific experiences. The courtroom was full of men. And me. I was facing my dad because by then I was eighteen so I wasn't entitled to a video link and there was no screen. He stared at me the whole time. The only good thing was that the judge asked me why I changed my name (I'd done that as soon as I was eighteen). I said: 'Because I didn't want to be associated with that bastard anymore.' That felt good. And the judge didn't tell me off for swearing, which was nice.

The cross-examination even made me doubt myself. Everything I said they twisted and turned it round. And after two or three hours of it, they had me tied up in knots and I just broke down in tears on the stand. The judge cleared the courtroom and got me some water. Then it all started again.

Once I'd given evidence, my dad changed his plea. He was advised to change it because it was clear he was going to be convicted, because I wasn't lying. So he pleaded guilty to incest over the age of sixteen, which is a lesser crime. Still illegal, but he claimed it was a mutual relationship. And I didn't get a say: there was no way I would have agreed to that. It was referred to Crown Court for sentencing.

I went to the court that time, too. The judge spoke to me. He talked directly to me and said that he was sentencing my dad because of the evil deeds he'd done to me and I wasn't to take this into my adult life because it wasn't my fault or my responsibility. And he said he was only accepting the lesser plea because he had to. Dad was sentenced on seven different counts, to be run concurrently, which only came to three and a half years. I thought it would be seven times that. He served twenty months.

I felt that justice hadn't been done. Considering what I'd been through in the courtroom, having to describe in graphic detail exactly what was done to me, even for just that ten-month period of the court case, it didn't feel enough. I was a wreck by the end of it, but years later I realised how rare it is, to get a conviction at all.

I left home a few months later and went to live with an aunt and uncle. I had re-sat three GCSEs at college, done a BTEC in Health & Social Care, and began to think about a career in social work. Then, at the age of twenty, I had a breakdown. I took a huge overdose of painkillers. My aunty found me and I'd been very sick so she took me to hospital and they put me on lots of drips. Then I went into a psychiatric hospital for three months – it helped just to have time out. And I saw a psychotherapist for two years. That helped a bit, too.

I took another overdose when I was living in a hostel for survivors of sexual abuse. I told everyone I had flu, but I'd in fact taken ninety-six paracetamol – they realised that when my liver failed. I was moved into intensive care in a liver unit and a doctor said to me when I arrived: 'Well, you've got what you wanted, you'll be dead by the morning.' I thought, how dare you! I wanted to live then, just to spite him. He wasn't nice to me: I wanted to prove him wrong.

I was there for two weeks and came out to find the hostel was closing down; they were trying to find me somewhere else to live. And still feeling absolutely determined, I moved into a flat, living independently for the first time. And that was the beginning of my recovery.

They'd given me loads of medication to take, but I decided to flush the lot and went cold turkey, which was horrendous. It was like having the worst flu ever: my bones hurt, my skin hurt, I was hot and then freezing cold; I was throwing up, I couldn't even take water. That lasted two weeks. I thought I was dying. And then I started to get better, and I became me again, or whoever the new me was going to be.

I went back to college and began social work training, but it wasn't for me. That lasted a year. Then I started counselling training for three years. After a year I joined ChildLine and trained as a volunteer counsellor. I did that because the counsellor I'd spoken to had enabled me to change my life and I wanted to be able to do that for other young people. And I did. After I'd been there a couple of years I started to take some regular calls from young people. I remember one who was being sexually abused, as were her younger sisters, by her father. Her mum had died. I spoke to her for three months, then she stopped calling. I'm hoping she was able to tell someone. We'd identified someone who would have listened and believed, she said, so we'd done a lot of practising, the way my counsellor had helped me. I still think of her and wonder what happened.

And there was a very young boy I spoke to the week after 9/11. He was having nightmares every night of people jumping out of towers. I spoke to his mum, too. We worked out that he could put on a video and go to sleep watching it. And his mum phoned up a week later and said he'd not had any nightmares ever since.

I worked with ChildLine for five years, but by this time I was also working for the National Association for People Abused in Childhood and got too busy. Pete Saunders, who founded NAPAC, came to ChildLine and asked if anyone there knew someone who could help them start up their support line. Listening to survivors had churned up my own feelings – maybe I tried to work there a bit too soon. It's been nine years now and my work today is very different. Now I'm responsible for developing NAPAC's prison service.

So many prisoners have suffered abuse in their childhood. We've done training and workshops in prison and supported individual prisoners. NAPAC always had letters from survivors talking about their childhoods, revealing for the first time the abuse they experienced. Everyone working with prisoners – prison governors, everyone – knows that prisons are filled with survivors. A whole chunk of the prison population has suffered horrendous abuse when they were children but nobody has worked out how to help them. So what we want to do now is a complete programme there: twelve sessions over four weeks, a really intensive course, and set up a dedicated prisoner support line. Because apart from us, nobody else is dealing with the root cause. Symptoms, yes – drug abuse, alcoholism. They are given therapy such as CBT to stop self-harming and anger management training, but nobody is dealing with the root cause of it all. The Ministry of Justice want us in there because nobody's doing this work at the moment.

I was lucky: I had my tutor, I had ChildLine. I had some really good people along my journey. Most of the prisoners I work with have nobody. I know my mother feels a huge amount of guilt because she knew what my dad was like (I guess he abused her in a sexual way as well). She knew that he'd abused the two patients at the army camp. He's still very dangerous. I was told some years back that he'd died but then I discovered that he'd been arrested for yet more allegations of sexual abuse against a half-brother I never knew I had. I'd say he'll always be a danger to children but he's not on the Sex Offenders Register. It didn't exist when he was convicted for my abuse.

From my point of view, as a survivor and as a volunteer counsellor, I'd say ChildLine is a lifesaver. It certainly helped me to reclaim my life. ChildLine was the first place where I was able to talk about what happened to me: it felt safe. I didn't have to give my name, it was on the phone so nobody could see me; nobody knew who I was and that made it safe. For me, I needed to be in control of what happened – I'd never really had control. The abuse was beyond any control I'd had. And there were times when I used to dream that someone would come in and whisk me away to live with a family where I'd be safe and it was normal. I used to read a lot, about other families, normal families, but actually the reality was that I needed to stay in control. My dad had taken all control away from me.

Even when the police were called in, in fact it was my mum who called them. That wasn't my decision – I just wanted the abuse to stop. I guess the fact that my mum knew meant that it was over, it wasn't going to happen again, so that could have been enough. I'm not saying that going to the police was the wrong thing to do, it just wasn't my choice. It happened too quickly – I think that's why I had the breakdown. The trial was way too quick. And the whole court case was way too much: two days on the stand, it was just horrendous.

I did get my revenge, though. My grandma died just after my dad pleaded guilty, but before he was sentenced. At that stage he told all his drinking friends that he was going to go away for a time because he was grieving for his mother and he needed to get his head together. I didn't know that, but I suspected that when he came out he'd go straight back and carry on with his life. So I got the train to where he lived, and went into every single pub he ever visited: I knew them all. I asked them if they knew where he was and they all told me the same story: poor Dad, he's away, trying to get over his mother's death. So I put them right: I told them exactly where he was, and why. And they believed me. As it turned out, he did go back and tried to pick his life up, but he wasn't welcome so he had to move.

Now I can move on with my own life, doing work I love. It was a horrendous childhood, no doubt about that, but I guess it has helped me now to recognise how other people have been hurt. In prison all I do is listen, believe and allow them to talk, which sounds very simple but is highly effective. It absolutely works, takes away the need for them to numb their memories in the way they used to, by kicking off, or by self-harming or taking drugs. Because I come in under NAPAC's banner, it inspires confidence that I will understand: they feel safe talking to me, knowing that I won't judge them. For some it helps that I'm a woman. For some, it helps if I disclose that I am a survivor, too – that can make it easier for them. So, looking back, I believe that the way I have been hurt, and the way I have been helped, have given me my goal.

NAPAC, the charity that helps adult survivors of abuse, was founded by Peter Saunders. In his day, there were no words for what happened to him as a child. And in his work he is constantly in touch with others who also suffered abuse long before ChildLine was launched. In fact, he was thirty-eight when he first rang us but his life was transformed by that phone call. And through him, NAPAC has transformed many thousands of other lives.

CHAPTER THIRTEEN

PETER'S STORY

'm sure to outsiders we looked like the perfect family. We lived in Bromley, as respectable a suburb as you can get. And my parents were equally respectable, neat and tidy; Percy and Margaret, he an accountant, she a housewife. The house was always spotless. They were very strict Catholics and we'd go off to church every Sunday, the whole family together. Percy was never without a shirt and tie or his pipe; he was tall, clean-shaven, a real charmer. He was a perfect example of old-school politeness: whenever we'd pass a lady on the street he'd take his hat off and I would tip my school cap. When we'd walk to confession, he'd take his hat off as we passed the chapel as a sign of reverence. He was incredibly loyal to my mother, even though she was such a moo to him.

My mum Margaret was very attractive. She had shining dark hair – she didn't go grey, even when she was ninety-two. With her dark eyes and olive skin, she looked Spanish. Dad said she was a real cracker, a gorgeous-looking woman when they met. Margaret had left school when she was fourteen and went into service in a big house in Richmond. She wasn't well-educated, not terribly bright, but she was very practical. She met my dad when they were both in the RAF during the war: the Blitz was on, there was a thick fog and they were both trying to find a church. They started dating: one thing they had in common was they both loved to go dancing together. Mum read a lot, Dad loved music, but I remember that whenever she came into the room and he was listening to something she would make him turn it off.

Apparently, according to my dad, she had changed when she started going through the menopause. From then on, she was a grumpy cow and that bad mood lasted for the rest of her life. We always prayed that she would die first because he was very popular, very sociable, and without her he would have had a good life. But he went first.

Mum was forty-four when she had me, which in those days, 1957, was considered pretty old. I was always told I was a mistake. They had four other children: my oldest brother Tony, my brother Mike, my sisters Mary and Pauline, and me. I can remember in my very early days snuggling up to Mum when I was small, but as I got older she became less and less interested in me. All the same, up until I was seven, I wasn't particularly unhappy. My sister Pauline used to look after me, she was thirteen years older than I was; she made a fuss of me. When she was a teenager, she even took me to school with her in my pram. I remember a nun telling her, 'You've got a beautiful little brother, there, but you shouldn't be bringing him into school.'

Emotionally we were all totally neglected, disturbed, unhappy, but nobody noticed. The only people who came and went in our house were connected with the church – missionaries and so on. We could only make friends with Catholics. When I was three my sister Mary went off to a convent to become a nun – that was her way of escaping. She's a grandmother now, living happily on the South Coast.

My dad was married to the Catholic Church. Mum was consumed by herself. Outside the family people quite liked her, but by the time I was in my teens I realised that she was a hypochondriac, bitter and angry. She always told me that she would end up in an early grave because of me but she made it to ninety-two, as miserable and angry and horrible as ever. She rarely had a good word to say about anybody.

Although Dad was very popular, at home he was pretty violent to us. We were all regularly beaten. Dad really used to lose it with my brother Tony. Tony's dead now: alcoholism took him. If only there'd been a ChildLine in those days. My sister Mary told me recently she thought we were all neglected. These days there's no doubt I would have been taken into care. But in spite of it all we loved Mum, I always will do. I hated the way she was to me and to the rest of them, but we all loved her. Because she was our mum.

One of my relatives, I'll call her Agnes, was very close to me when I was a child. Tragically, she ended up having the most miserable life because she married an evil man. She met Bernard when she was twenty and I was seven, and they got married a year later. Bernard was Catholic, from a good Catholic family. His father had an OBE, his brother was an international sportsman, and he taught at a big Catholic grammar school. So he ticked all the boxes for Mum and Dad. I was well impressed with him – he paid more attention to me than my mum and dad put together. It was the perfect grooming scenario. He would pick me up, hold me; he taught me to swim, took me to the pub and bought me lemonade. I remember caddying for him. As an eight-year-old I remember he bought me toys. Nobody had ever bought me toys except for birthdays and Christmas, but he bought me a Dinky toy. I remember being amazed at how much it cost, when I was getting sixpence-a-week pocket money. Something like seven and six, it was a perfect little model of a security van with gold bullion in it. He made me feel special.

Within the first year they had their first baby and I was their babysitter when they went out for a curry. What I never got my head round is that when I was eight, when I stayed with them, Bernard would come into my bedroom at night and sexually assault me. It happened every weekend. All I ever felt about it was total confusion: I got no pleasure out of it, I thought Agnes must know what was going on. It was such a small house, but nobody ever mentioned it during the day. I really couldn't get my head around what went on.

The abuse went on from when I was eight to when I was fourteen. Bernard was the head of PE at his school, so whenever we met, he used to make comments about me. He would laugh at me because I was a skinny runt at that age. So he'd laugh and say, 'Girls aren't going to be interested in that.' It was embarrassing, humiliating.

Not only that, but from the time I was twelve I was also abused by an elderly priest, who lived in our school. He had a bedroom at the top of this old building and would summon me to his room, sit on the bed next to me, rubbing my leg, patting my bits, and then he'd give me a Mars bar. It never went further than that. Then there was the Head Teacher – you used to have to go and see him if you felt unwell. He would be sweaty and clammy: he'd lay me on his bed and undo my trousers, but that's all he'd do to me. And I know they both did the same to other boys. Maybe more with other boys.

But Bernard did much more when he got me alone, in my bedroom. He used to touch me, masturbate me. I remember the first attack with horror, but I had no idea what was happening and even if I had tried to tell someone, I couldn't have described it. I really had no idea what he was doing or why.

I have quite a vivid recollection of the last time he assaulted me. That was the night his wife gave birth to another baby. At the end of that evening he'd had quite a bit to drink and he plied me with drink so I was quite drunk, too. Then he made me get into his wife's bed. I realised that he was naked and he wanted me to touch him. I said, 'No, I can't, I won't,' and I got up out of bed then rushed out of the room and downstairs. I curled up on the settee as tightly as I could, with my back to him as he came down and followed me. But all he did was chuck a blanket over me and he threw some pornographic magazines at me. Then he left me alone. That was the last time.

But the baby born that night was his son Ed. Years later, when I disclosed my abuse to them, Ed said: 'I wish you hadn't told me that because I know it's true, because Dad did that to me, too.' But that broke our relationship: Ed and I haven't spoken to each other for the last sixteen years.

I think what the abuse had done was render me totally under the control of my abuser. He used sexual violence to subjugate me, dominate me, until I became a wreck emotionally. Nobody noticed. But even after Bernard stopped sexually abusing me, he started playing mind games with me at school. He was taking revenge on me, I suppose, undermining me. He'd take me to one side and tell me I was stupid – 'unlike my clever brother Mike' – and he'd constantly tell me my mother was very stupid and my father was a coward.

Whatever I wanted to do Bernard would attack the idea and pour cold water on it, telling me I was stupid. Once his wife Agnes joined in with him attacking me and then I felt totally betrayed. This was the woman who had looked after me, cared about me, but now she was totally under his control. And Bernard had his way: the years of constant torment left their scars. I became rubbish at school – I only managed two O Levels. So I got the hell out, left school at sixteen and went to work at a bike shop.

But all the same, by 1995 I was teaching. I'd gone into teaching to prove Bernard wrong. In spite of my appalling results at school I'd gone back to college: I'd got a degree and trained as a teacher. Then when my dad was seventy-six, he became very ill, it was cancer. As Dad was dying, I realised that for the first time I wasn't frightened of him anymore. He and I became very close. I was given time off to be with him: I used to care for him, the way he would care for me, he said. Interesting, that he would remember my childhood that way. As I got closer to him, the anger in me that had been locked inside for years, the fury at what had happened to me as a child began to well up, but I still didn't say anything.

We brought Dad home from hospital a few days before he died. A couple of days later, as bad luck would have it, I bumped into Bernard. His wife Agnes had kicked him out many years before because not only was he a monster to me, he was a violent brute to her. He used to knock her about, he'd shove her across the kitchen. She put up with that for years, then they separated. She is a Catholic, too, and in spite of everything she doesn't believe in divorce. Anyway, I bumped into him in an off-licence and he made the biggest mistake of his life. Instead of saying nothing, he asked me how my dad was, not as if he cared, with a smirk on his face. 'He's dying,' I said. Then he laughed in my face and said: 'You didn't have to get that chairlift installed, then.' I said, 'Yes, we did.' Nothing else.

Nobody else in that shop would have noticed. There was no violent swearing, no shouts of rage. There didn't have to be. Because in that moment I knew what I had to do. His callousness, his confidence, as if he still had me and my family right under his thumb, brought all my boiling anger to the surface. Suddenly in that moment I knew why I had felt so dirty all those years, it was his filth. He was a dirty man, he was a fucking pig; he was just a disgusting man and I was going to tell everyone who needed to know. At last, at long last, I was going to spill the beans.

When I came home from the off-licence, Dad was very close to death. The day before he died, we talked. I spent all that day with him, lying on the bed with him, organising things for him. Then he looked at me and said: 'I used to hit you all, I think I got that wrong. It was the way I was brought up, darling.' What could I say? There was no point in trying to undo what had been long done. I said: 'You did what you thought was right and now I'm going to sort this family out.'

I spent that night at my home and I slept really well. When I woke up, I just knew he was going to die that day. I felt a heaviness come over me, a cloud of heavy darkness. I got up and set off. I drove through Richmond Park and then found a quiet place where I stopped the car and prayed for a while. I felt something big was going to happen, something connected directly to all the pain and shame I'd experienced in my childhood.

I started the car again and drove to Agnes's home. She was in the kitchen, baking. I said: 'Agnes, we've got to talk.' She stopped what she was doing, my tone must have cut through to her. 'What is it?' she asked. I said: 'I'm not going to let Bernard come to Dad's funeral.'

In that moment she knew. She said: 'Did he abuse you, darling?' I said: 'Yes.' And at that moment we had a phone call to say Dad had died. I went straight back to see him. Dad had died with a smile on his face and I believe he's in Heaven.

Well, then it all kicked off. Word got back to Bernard that he wasn't welcome at the funeral and his children wanted to know why so I agreed to see them. We sat in Agnes's living room, Agnes and her son, and I said: 'You probably know I'm not having your dad at my dad's funeral. It's because your dad abused me.' They both said they wished I hadn't told them. Both believed me. Ed said: 'Dad did the same to me.' All the same, he didn't want me to do anything.

But I did: it was time. So I reported it to the police – I was in the station for two hours. I gave them a statement, told them everything, and then I left believing and hoping that Bernard would be arrested and charged. Weeks went by. I heard nothing from them.

In the end I ran out of patience. I rang the police and asked what was going on. They told me to come in. Two of them sat down with me and they told me they'd done an investigation, but nobody else had reported any abuse. They told me that the rest of Bernard's friends and family 'are not supporting you'. So they said although they totally believed me, they were closing the case. They said as it was thirty years ago, in any case, the CPS would probably not take the case to court. I said: 'But he's still teaching a thousand boys.' They obviously heard from my voice how angry I was, and how determined. So they said, 'On no account must you go to his school. If you do, you may be arrested.'

I got into my car and I drove straight from the police station sixty miles away to the school. Then I went into reception and said: 'I want to speak to the Head Teacher.' The receptionist looked at my face and clearly realised it was urgent. The Head Teacher came out of his class to speak to me.

I said: 'I must tell you, there is a member of your staff who is a child abuser.' 'You have to tell me who this is,' he replied. I said: 'I will. I'll come back and make a full statement, in front of a witness.' Then he took my hand, held onto it and said: 'Of course you realise this happened a long time ago.' 'Yes, but he's still teaching in your school,' I told him.

The next Saturday I gave a full statement in front of a solicitor. They asked if I would sign a statement for the governors. I said yes. After a few weeks I had a long letter from the school saying that the man had been suspended the next working day. He had denied all the allegations, but had agreed to retire.

What had given me this courage, this determination, when I had been shamed, undermined, humiliated all those years? Within days of my dad dying, I had rung ChildLine. I had been sitting on my bed at home, desperate, knowing I needed help. I was thirty-eight, not a child any more, but I realised that ChildLine was the only place that could have helped me as a child. I had looked everywhere else, there was nothing. And as I sat there, with everything churning in my mind, turning over the Yellow Pages, I saw the ChildLine number, so I rang,

I spoke to a wonderful, wonderful woman – I think her name was Eileen. We talked for about forty-five minutes. I apologised. 'I feel awful ringing – I know you're here for children and I'm not a child,' I said. She said: 'It's OK.' Then she listened to me and said I had survived something awful. I'd just thought I was a shitty person. She said she thought I was very strong to have survived. But we both knew there was nothing ChildLine could do for me now. It was then that the idea of an organisation to support adult survivors came into my head.

So I wrote to the Chief Executive of ChildLine, Valerie Howarth, and I got a very, very warm letter back saying I was right, there was a great need for an organisation for survivors of abuse. She was extremely supportive. I read a book about sexual abuse, *Innocence Destroyed* by Jean Renvoize and I realised for the first time that I wasn't the only one, there were millions of others. Another instant response came from the late agony aunt and broadcaster Claire Rayner. Another agony aunt, Deirdre Sanders, came and met me with Chris Cloke from the NSPCC. This was 1996. In January 1997, we had a meeting at the headquarters of the NSPCC, Weston House in the City of London. We agreed to set up a new charity, NAPAC, the National Association for People Abused in Childhood, and I was appointed chair of the committee. I always wanted it to be a kind of ChildLine for adults: I knew there was a huge need for people to get the kind of strength I'd taken from the conversation I'd had with Eileen, the ChildLine counsellor. In May 1998 we became a registered charity.

Hard as it is to raise money for children's charities and pretty animals, it's a nightmare trying to raise funds for adult survivors. However, we are blessed with many great friends and supporters, from pensioners who donate £2 per month to anonymous rock stars who have given us thousands.

Lord Archer, while he was in prison, through talking to the other prisoners discovered how many of them had terrible memories of the abuse they suffered in childhood, so he recognised the need for NAPAC and donated £10,000 to us. We love people who put their money where their mouth is. The Big Lottery gave us a grant, too, but we always need more. We desperately need to reach out to more survivors, to help many more people on the road to healing, and that takes more resources than we have.

Still, at least we are up and running now with our own helpline for adult survivors. We are answering around 3,500 calls a year and 75 to 100 emails a month. God help us if the numbers went sky-high, which they might if more people knew about us. We always ask people who ring what they think of our service and some of their comments are really moving. 'Thank you for caring and doing something,' 'It was so comforting to talk to someone who was understanding,' 'Thank you for existing,' 'A week has passed since I called you and I have never felt so peaceful and proud of who I am,' 'I feel hope for the first time in my life,' 'A huge thank you for all the work you do, God bless you all,' 'I only wish I had called before, this service has made me realise it's not my fault,' 'I feel so much better about myself.'

They use us in so many different ways. Often it's because memories have been triggered by something that happens within their family, perhaps, or by a documentary they've seen. Sometimes they aren't quite sure what they are remembering: they will say I have a feeling something horrible happened to me. Psychologists will tell you that the brain is amazing in the way it can shut off, file away something it finds too painful to deal with. It was true of some of the people who lived through unspeakable events in the Holocaust: their brain would split off and leave those memories in some place they didn't have to visit.

Then sometimes they will ring because the memories have

suddenly come back and it's like being hit by an express train. It could be because there's been a family wedding or a funeral and they happen to meet their abuser there. That's very common, especially as the abuser is often a family member who thinks his (or her) victim will have forgotten. It could be that they have a child themselves who reaches the age at which they were abused and it becomes overwhelming (that happened with me, too).

We hear from the survivors who need help. Most of them have been left in a very bad way. Not all of them, obviously – they haven't all ended up in prison or addiction units. Superficially they may look successful, in their business or their family life, but beneath the surface they are really hurting, still suffering. If only they'd been helped at the time when they were children – been believed, been reassured that the abuse was not their fault. But in their day, most of them had no way of asking for help. I know what a difference ChildLine has made, but in my day when it didn't exist, I would just have been slapped down if I'd asked for help. But then of course I didn't have the words to explain what had been done to me, anyway. It would be no exaggeration to say that the call I made to that wonderful woman back in 1995 (what I'd do to be able to thank her in person) may well have saved my life and had that not happened, NAPAC wouldn't exist.

CHAPTER FOURTEEN

SMILES ON CHILDREN'S FACES

Society has changed since 1986. One of the biggest changes to affect ChildLine has been the invention of the mobile phone. In the early days, children often rang from the only safe telephone they could find, where they could not be overheard: the scarlet public phone box on the corner of the street. And often our counsellors would hear children being interrupted by irate adults wanting to use the phone and banging on the glass. Now they can ring us from their own bedrooms, using a mobile phone hidden under the bedclothes.

One child whispered, 'I'm so tired of coming home from school and being locked in the shed.' Another rang from the back row of her class at school to tell us she had taken an overdose and we were able to get an ambulance to her in time. So the mobile has been liberating. And so of course has been the internet: our online counselling is helping many, many children. And texting actually saved Lucy's life.

I met Lucy when I was visiting one of our bases. She was a

charming teenager – tall, with a sweet face – and we giggled together over how many mince pies I was eating. She took me into a quiet office and told me her story. Recently, Lucy had been groomed over the internet by a man in his forties, who pretended to be much younger. He had flattered her, groomed her, persuaded her to meet him and abducted her. But very, very luckily, before she disappeared she had begun to be concerned about him and had started to text ChildLine.

The police were alerted when she disappeared: they feared for her life and asked for ChildLine's help to find her. So they came into our office, and as soon as she began to text ChildLine again – secretly, when the man left her momentarily – they were able to trace her whereabouts through her mobile phone. They found Lucy and the man she was with was arrested and charged with sexual grooming, molestation and drugs offences.

It took months for ChildLine to help Lucy come to terms with what had happened because she felt tremendously guilty. After all, she had agreed to meet him, she had allowed him to groom her via the internet. But eventually she saw that he was to blame, not her, and she forgave herself and ChildLine for saving her.

She wrote me a letter expressing her feelings now:

Dear Esther, I hope you remember me from the ChildLine base where you kept asking me to stop you eating all the mince pies? Well, I hope you don't mind, but I just wanted to write to you to thank you for letting me meet you.

I am so glad you made ChildLine, as I have two amazing counsellors, and God only knows where I would be if it wasn't for them. When I went missing, Debs from the Base kept texting me asking whether I was okay. Luckily, I managed to reply and the police traced me and found me. ChildLine is my best friend – because I can share secrets with them – and that's important with true friendship.

I am a big supporter of ChildLine and am trying my hardest to help fund you. I do promise I will try my hardest: you have helped me through so much, now it's my turn.

Please keep up all your good work. It works well and just think about all those smiles on children's faces after speaking to ChildLine, including mine.

Best wishes,

Lucy

Our statistics show that many, many children are using our new counselling online service when they would never have dared phone us. And our statistics tell another hopeful story: When ChildLine first opened its lines, sexual abuse was the biggest problem and well over half the children who were being sexually abused told us it had been going on for over a year (37 per cent), many of them for more than five years (20 per cent). Now only 4 per cent of the sexually abused children who contact us tell us that the abuse has lasted more than five years. A third ring us less than a year, often less than a month after it starts, (24 per cent), which has to be progress.

ChildLine itself has changed and expanded, and in 2005 we joined up with the NSPCC. We have more ChildLine bases (twelve around the UK) and more skilled, trained volunteer counsellors – well over 1,000 who donate their time to us every week. We are now a valued part of a far larger charity, which means we have more security, but we have not lost our special link with children, the strength of the ChildLine brand, and of course, thanks to BT, our iconic number: 0800 1111.

But for all the changes that have happened over the years, essentially ChildLine must always remain the same in order to fulfil our promise to children that we will always listen to them and tailor our service very precisely to their needs. We strive always to put children first. And it's worth it. The reward, as I hope this book reveals, is safer children, many dangerous criminals prevented from abusing children and in the end, a wonderful unanticipated result: that the children we save are inspired to save other children.

That is not the received opinion. There are professional experts who will tell you that abuse victims often become abusers in their turn. That has always seemed to me to be monstrously unfair. After all, there are millions of people who survive abuse and who may carry the scars in later life, but who would never harm a child.

The stories in this book carry a far more hopeful message. They demonstrate that the experience of abuse need not wreck lives, nor spiral down through the generations. Provided abused children are believed when they ask for help, if they are told that they are precious and that they deserve to be protected from harm, and above all, if they are reassured that the abuse and neglect are not their fault, they can survive the pain and may emerge strengthened and inspired to protect others from suffering.

On a dark winter's night I was travelling home on a crowded train from one of our ChildLine bases. I was tired. Next to me was a group of young women who were downing vodkas and loudly enjoying themselves, and their noisy laughter sawed its way through my exhausted brain.

Away in the corner of the carriage were a young mother and her daughter. The young woman was slender and pretty, her child was adorable, and I smiled at them both. They returned my smile. At the first stop they got up to leave, when suddenly the young mother turned and pushed a note into my hand. It read:

Hi.

Sorry. I didn't want to intrude on you, but I did want to let you know how highly I regard ChildLine.

Everything you have done for vulnerable children is fantastic.

I'm sure it's through your hard work that has made my job exist. I'm a family support worker in [*she named a northern city*]. I work with families that have disabled children. It's so sad to see the children that have become disabled through parental neglect or abuse. I didn't have a very rosy childhood, in my life I have faced poverty, abuse, sexual abuse, domestic violence... I could go on! I rang ChildLine when I was younger and they were a great source of comfort to me. I knew through them and through *That's Life!* I wanted to help other children and families.

I also had a massive crush on Adrian!

You are a very lovely lady. Wishing you peace and happiness.

And she and her daughter signed it, with kisses.

Suddenly the raucous laughter around me no longer seemed so harsh, the train seat felt more comfortable and the night didn't seem so dark.

I still treasure it, that letter from a stranger – its warmth continues to inspire me. Although she praised me, I know that her praise should really be for all the staff and volunteers who have day in, day out answered the phones, the emails and the letters, twenty-four hours a day, seven days a week, throughout the twenty-five years of ChildLine's existence.

Each week ChildLine receives letters, emails and phone calls thanking our counsellors. I'll quote one more, from Sarah who was terribly badly bullied at school. (Bullying is numerically one of the biggest problems children ring us about and, our counsellors tell me, prompts some of the most difficult calls.)

Sarah wrote:

I was getting bullied very badly two weeks ago and I was getting very upset. I wanted to kill myself. I wanted to kill my bully if I could not kill myself. I turned to jelly every time I

saw her and I was seeing myself as a nobody. I hated the way I was. I am fat and ugly and got spots and she kept taking that out on me. I hate it. I phoned ChildLine and I spoke to the most wonderfulist woman put on this earth. She asked me to be strong and some more things. If I only had her name I could thank her personerly. Thank you ChildLine. I hope I don't have any more problems with my bully. I can live with myself now and I feel good about myself now!
Thank you ChildLine
From
Sarah

How I wish we could stamp out the bullying that still exists, like a plague, in our schools and communities. I wish we could adapt our judicial system so that it can protect children more effectively. Our law courts often provide a travesty of justice for children. What is the point of the live cross-examination of a dyslexic fifteen-year-old, humiliating him in open court, but never discovering that the reason why he cannot answer the questions is that he cannot read? What is the point of denying abused children the counselling that could start to heal them and would make them better witnesses without 'tainting the evidence'?

What is the point, let's face it, of using an adversarial system which was originally designed for adults, but only confuses and bewilders children when every guilty paedophile who is set free condemns hundreds more children to pain? And yet the legal profession is still wedded to the current system. I met a very successful barrister at the criminal bar, who defends many alleged abusers. He told me: 'I don't care how great a monster my client is, or what it takes to break down a child, it's my job to do it, and that's what I will do.'

I believe those who run our institutions should become more vigilant. As the careers of the teachers at Crookham Court School and the Reverend Roy Cotton in the Church of England prove, organisations all too often protect themselves at the expense of children.

When I was in my twenties I regularly visited a children's home. Thirty years later I met one of the children who had been in care there, who told me that the man running the home had abused ten of the children. He was a violent bully. They were all terribly damaged by their experience but as adults, with great courage, they agreed to complain to the police and let their cases go forward. But so much time had gone by, and because there was a muddle in the council's records, the judge stopped the trial. So the man who had abused them never had to pay for his crimes against the children in his care. When I asked one of the boys why he had never told me what was happening in the home, at the time when I was visiting them every week, he said, 'Those times when you took us out and gave us egg and chips for tea were the only happy memories I have of my childhood. I didn't want to spoil them.' No organisation working with children is immune from being infiltrated by criminals with their own motives for getting close to children.

I visited that home twenty years before ChildLine was launched. I hope those children could have, would have, rung us today or contacted us online. For over the twenty-five years of ChildLine's existence, our records show that we have helped more than 2.5 million children. We have not been able to make their lives perfect – whose is? But we have been able to assure them that they matter, and that their safety and happiness are hugely important. Our first slogan was 'speak to someone who cares' and we do. That caring, that empathy, is central to ChildLine's work and always will be.

So, on behalf of all the people who have contributed their stories to this book, I want to thank those other millions. The unsung, hardworking heroes who have made our work possible, who have cared so deeply about the welfare of vulnerable children that they have chosen to support us financially and in many other ways. Without their support not one single child could have been answered.

There's the widow who could not afford a donation, but sent us her wedding ring; children like Damien, aged ten, who played his cornet in freezing winter streets to raise money for us; the event organisers, who created fund-raising auctions, balls and dinners; the politicians who understood how crucial our work is and helped us to expand; the companies who have sponsored us; the media who have made children aware of us; the teachers, the lawyers, the social workers, the parents who all make the protection of children their absolute priority – as little bullied Sarah put it so well, you are 'the most wonderfulist' people on earth.

On behalf of all the children ChildLine has helped over twenty-five years, thank you. And here's to the next twenty-five.